FREEWAY
RICK
ROSS

FREEWAY RICK ROSS

THE UNTOLD AUTOBIOGRAPHY

BY RICK ROSS 2·1·15
WITH CATHY SCOTT

DEDICATION

To my parents, my mother Annie Mae Ross, who selflessly raised my brother, sister, cousins, and me, but also raised the neighborhood, opening her house to all the homies. If not for that, we would have been out on the streets. While we don't always agree, she's been there for me when I've needed her; and to my late father, Sonny Leon Ross, from whom I inherited much of my determination. Even though I barely knew him, I have a lot of admiration and love for him. You both made me who I am today.

Contents

FOREWORD

A few years ago, I was conversing with one of the most distinguished members of the City of Refuge, the indubitable Congresswoman Maxine Waters. During our conversation that typically focused on the welfare of our community, she asked if I knew Rick Ross. I immediately responded I had no clue who Rick Ross was, and, of course, she was flabbergasted at my ignorance in not being aware of such a notorious character as Freeway Rick Ross.

I abashedly attributed my unfamiliarity with such an infamous person to the fact that I was not a native of Los Angeles. However, to my chagrin, the Congresswoman made it clear that Rick was known globally. I found that out later when he did an interview with South Africa's most-popular radio talk-show host, Thabo Touch.

My witlessness in not knowing who Freeway Rick Ross was seemed lucid in comparison to my obliviousness in knowing what a gangster looks like and how he comports himself. Meeting Freeway Rick caused me to rewrite my conceptualization of what gangster profiles entail. He looked like an unobtrusive, unintimidating specimen of a man. I was expecting a rough-and-tough mass of street-hardened protoplasm, not some reticent soft-spoken, small-statured man.

So now, only now, hanging with Rick has certified indelibly that there is an intellectual distinction between a gangster in a business environment and a businessman in a gangster environment. Rick puts it like this: "I approached drug dealing as a businessman, even though the government associated me with gangs like the Hoover Street Crips" (who were my neighbors for three years). His uncanny ability to separate the businessman from the gangster explains the reason for his inconspicuous dress and low-key demeanor. He had no desire to impress anyone with his physical appearance in the typical designer clothes and excessive bling-bling so common to the gangster, because any ostentatious display of ill-gotten wealth was bad for business. After all, he was a businessman in a gangster environment. The secret to his longevity was to remain in the shadows and not take to the stage with repeated encores.

His goal of "getting in the drug business and then going legit" is indicative of the mindset and entrepreneurial skills of any Corporate America magnate. His was a journey to escape poverty on the first bus leaving the station, but to Rick, he bartered away all of his legitimacy by selling drugs.

This *Untold Autobiography* is not only personal, but also historical in its implications. Rick chronicles the times by highlighting the social climate that made crack cocaine so desirable, and he points out that at the time, the "cops in the area didn't know what crack was; they didn't associate the small white rocks they saw on homies as illegal drugs." All he knew was that people wanted it.

There is no question that with all his success and years of avoiding detection, along with the inordinate behavior of the government in Rick's case, he still is repentant and quite remorseful. I would not regard his exceptional life, expressed in this well-written autobiography, as a braggadocious attempt to extol the virtues of using God-given gifts to amass ill-gotten gains. In contradistinction, this work portrays the heart of a man who is seeking the opportunity, in whatever form, to right the wrongs he has done to his community.

Godspeed to you, Freeway Rick Ross.

—Bishop Noel Jones, City of Refuge Church

PREFACE

The San Diego skyline was the vista from my cell on the maximum-security floor of the federal high-rise where I was housed. Inmates called it the Million-Dollar View. Looking out at the skyscrapers across San Diego Bay offered me time to reminisce. And reflect.

I ran from poverty, turning to drug dealing to get a head start as an entrepreneur. That was always the goal: Get into the drug business and then go legit.

As a young kid in grade school, I wanted to be a Crip, but my mom wouldn't have it. I never became a gangbanger, though I got close.

At Dorsey High School, playing tennis on the varsity team was my ticket out of the 'hood. It saved my life, even though my dream of a tennis career took a major shot when Coach discovered I couldn't read or write. I wasn't going to college after all, and I wasn't going to be the next Arthur Ashe either, so there was no point in staying in school. But tennis matches took me out of South Central after school and kept me from gangbanging.

It was at that crossroads, when my sports scholarship fell through, that I put down the tennis racquet and hit the streets. I kept a low profile with my street cred. Though I never flashed gang colors, I always had key relationships with people who did.

One day, I sat on my porch, dead broke, trying to work out ways in my head to earn cash when a kid from the 'hood called me. It was Mike McLoren.

"I got a deal for you," he said.

I went to Mike's house and he pulled out a small plastic bag with white powder in it.

"It's the new thang, man," he said as he waved the baggie in front of me. "I can sell this for fifty dollars."

The powder was cocaine. The real shit. Coke was right in front of me, just like the character Youngblood Priest in the movie *Super Fly*. My homie, who'd left South Central Los Angeles to attend college, explained how he'd been selling powder cocaine to white students at San Jose State to make extra money. I barely heard the words "students or "San Jose," or even "cocaine." I was totally focused on "extra money." I wanted in on the game.

It was 1979 and I was 19 when I was introduced to the drug that would forever change my life. Powder cocaine appeared as a bright, shining star of opportunity. I bought my first baggie from Mike and doubled my money. I had no doubt it would make me rich in a way that up to that point I'd only imagined.

My instinct on breaking into the drug trade was right on point: I was a millionaire by my 23rd birthday, in the late '80s. "Rick Ross" became a household name throughout the black ghettos of South Central L.A. and reached halfway across the country. A bunch of homies worked for me, and they had even more dealers selling for them. We cooked like a hundred kilos every night. We didn't call it crack. We called it Ready Rock. We maintained houses where buyers drove up to a window to be served, just like at McDonald's. I had money-counting houses, cook houses, rock houses, apartment buildings, a Laundromat, and an auto-body shop. I had everything I needed: money, cars, women, and thriving businesses. As time progressed, I was making millions every day. By 1985, executives from major record labels chased me around Los Angeles trying to get me to invest in their artists. I was the *man*.

I approached drug dealing as a businessman, even though the government associated me with gangs, like the Hoover Crips. The feds said no one could have sold drugs and made that kind of cash without being a gangster, so I must have been one. They had it backwards and thought the game was tied to gang violence. It was always about business, never about gangs.

Crack was not in the 'hood before the '80s, so in the '70s as kids, none of us knew the side effects that could and would occur amid the crack epidemic that would sweep over black neighborhoods across the land. Even the cops in the area didn't know what crack was; they didn't associate the small white rocks they saw on homies with illegal drugs. All we knew was people wanted it; back then, it was a party drug, recreational. Movie stars were using crack on sets. Crack was considered the ultimate upper. And it was all about supply and demand. I was a young entrepreneur making a good living and building a business. I wasn't thinking about the consequences. I was about making money.

Something else I didn't know: On top of being a drug lord, my supplier was also a paid informant for the U.S. federal government.

Most people to this day are unaware of what really went down in South Central with crack cocaine. My raw materials came from Oscar Danilo Blandón Reyes, a Nicaraguan national who, unbeknownst to me at the time, had ties to the CIA and sent his proceeds to fund the Contra rebels. I was the first black drug dealer in South Central Los Angeles to forge a direct tie with a Central American drug lord. I knew him only as Danilo, but he was a trusted member of my inner circle. He supplied me with cocaine at bargain-basement prices that I converted to crack and sold wholesale.

The U.S. government didn't sell the drugs, of course, but they did supply the dealer, turning a blind eye to the operation and allowing massive shipments of coke into the U.S. until it became public and they needed a scapegoat—namely, me. The government wanted to put a face on the failed War on Drugs, and Rick Ross became the image of the kingpin behind it all.

The DEA eventually hired Danilo as a federal undercover informant with the goal of taking me down. He set me up in a reverse sting operation orchestrated by the feds. By my 37th birthday, I was in the pen serving a life sentence without the possibility of parole—a sentence that rarely gets reversed. While inside, I kept thinking, "What can I do to better myself?" The one nagging thing that always came back to me was to learn to read. Prison, as odd as it sounds, was a second chance. I couldn't change the past, but I could educate kids on making the right choices. My goal was to get out and help my community, to try and prevent kids from making the same mistakes I made. I couldn't do that without knowing how to read and write.

My self-education began by visiting the prison law library every day. I read more than 300 books. Each day I read the *Wall Street Journal*, *Time* magazine, or *Forbes*. Most nights I fell asleep with a book on my chest or next to my pillow. It paid off: While behind bars, I went from being illiterate to super-literate. Information and knowledge, I learned, are powerful. And that's what I tell kids today as I speak to them across the country, from high schools in the ghettos of California, to Brown University in Rhode Island.

My name is Ricky Donnell Ross. People know me as Freeway Rick. This is my story.

CHAPTER 1
LOCKED UP FOR LIFE

"Twenty years to life without the possibility of parole."

I stood behind the defense table, next to my criminal defense attorney, where decades of verdicts and sentences had been rendered. I glanced at the federal seal on the wall above the judge's head. I still hoped the judge would be fair. I expected a harsh sentence, but not this. Not life. When the judge pounded the gavel on the hardwood block on his desk, it felt like a hammer coming down on my head, a nail in my coffin. At 36 years old, I was being sent down with no possibility of getting out. I was going to die behind bars.

It was November 1996 and nearly a year after a government sting operation had sent me to jail. In the courtroom gallery to watch the judge hand down my sentence were a few of the same federal agents and sheriff's deputies who, for years, had pursued me.

While the sentencing hearing was still underway, I knew that the court couldn't legally restrike me. I hadn't committed three separate offenses for the same thing, so the three-strikes law did not apply. My lawyer, for whatever reason, didn't agree. So there I stood, stoic, taking the life sentence, helpless to change it.

As I was led away in shackles by U.S. marshals at my side, my eyes locked briefly with my mom's. She broke down, and all I could hear were her cries.

My jailers processed the conviction and entered me into the federal prison system as inmate number 05550-045. It was official; I was destined to die in prison.

That helpless feeling of having no control over my own life didn't last long. I knew I had to get busy and fight for my freedom, even if it meant being forced to do it from behind prison walls. I was determined to find a way. I was up to the challenge.

———◆◆◆———

The challenge I faced was the matter of getting the United States Ninth Circuit Court of Appeals to agree with me that I was over-charged, in state and federal court, and over-sentenced. Until then, I was stuck in a federal holding prison in downtown San Diego. I looked out from my ninth-floor cell and thought about where I had been, where I had come from.

As I settled in to do my time, I had many opportunities to look back and reflect on the path that led me to a federal pen. I stood on the ninth floor of the Metropolitan Correction Center, where I was housed, overlooking San Diego Bay. I had made it to the top of the dope game, regularly earning six figures, with plans already moving forward to get out clean with assets and legitimate business enterprises in place. Then it all came toppling down. Now, I was serving hard time. Standing there, behind bars, I felt far removed from my past.

I never would have imagined, as a young boy living in the rolling hills of East Texas, the turns my life would take. It had started simple enough. But one event in my childhood stood out from all the rest. And I've never forgotten it.

CHAPTER 2

BRUTHAS AND BULLETS

I covered my ears with my hands, trying to drown out my aunt's cries. I squeezed my eyes tight, attempting with all my might to erase the bloody scene in front of me. Yet, I could still see Uncle George's eyes, fixated and staring up at the ceiling. I could still hear Aunt Bobbi Jo's sobs.

It was 1966 and I was six years old. That was the night I lost my innocence.

Uncle George, my mother's brother, became like a father to me. He took me to a drive-in theater. We went racing in his '63 Buick. Sometimes he took me to work with him on the trash truck he drove for the city of Los Angeles; though noisy and always smelling of garbage, it was exciting. He drove me around and, from his garbage truck, I saw the world—from the downtown Los Angeles skyline to the Watts Towers. I grew to love Uncle George. He became my hero.

Those first three years living with Uncle George and Aunt Bobbie Jo, when my mom and I lived with them until she made enough money to support us, were some of the best times of my childhood. But there were also bad times, because Uncle George was a drinker with a temper.

My Uncle George was in the habit of stopping at a local bar on his way home from work. One evening, he arrived home drunk and accused Bobbi Jo of seeing other men. The more Bobbi Jo denied it, the angrier Uncle George became.

"Don't lie to me, bitch!" he screamed. "You think I'm a play thing, huh? Yeah, that's what it is. You think I'm playing with your ass, huh?"

Then he quickly reached across the kitchen counter, grabbed a steak knife, and stabbed Aunt Bobbi Jo. The tip of the blade went through her shirt and into her left breast as if both were butter. Bobbi Jo screamed and tried to fight her way out of his grip. He only pinned her down harder, bending her nearly in half with the sheer force of his weight. Again, the knife came down, this time cutting open her shoulder.

My mother screamed at him to let her go, but he wouldn't listen.

By then, Mama carried a small-caliber pistol with her. I think it was a .38. I don't remember seeing her pull the gun and point it at my uncle, but he must have seen it in her hand, because he stopped dead in his tracks and backed away.

"George, I don't know what the fuck your problem is, but you got to leave here! Now!" Mama hollered at him.

"Why you gettin' in our business, woman? This here ain't got nothing' to do with you!"

"Fuck that! You done lost your mind if you think I am goin' to stand here and let you kill that girl. Just go, George."

"Okay. I'll leave," he shouted as he turned and looked at my aunt, "but it's not over, Bobbi Jo. I'll be back." Then he stormed through the living room and out the front door.

Mama went to Bobbi Jo. She sat at the table trying to hold her shoulder and chest at the same time. Blood covered the front of her shirt. There was blood on the sink and on the floor. I stood just outside the doorway, tears of fear running down my face. I had never before seen that much blood.

"Girl, we got to get you to a hospital," Mama told Bobbi Jo.

"Annie Mae, why did he have to do this to me?" Bobbi Jo said in a trembling voice. "Don't that man know I love him too much to mess around on him? What am I going to do, girl? What can I do?" She started to cry.

"You goin' to get your ignorant ass outta here, that's what you gonna do." Then Mama called to me, "C'mon! Let's go, Ricky!"

Mama took Bobbi Jo by the arm and helped her to her feet. I ran behind them out the back door.

It was dark and cold outside and I stayed as close to Mama as I could. We went across the backyard, into an alley, which led to a 1950s' three-story apartment building. We ran through the gate and up the back stairs, and out of the darkness. Bobbie Jo trailed a lot of blood during our short get-away. Her breathing sounded funny, as if she had a cold.

"C'mon, baby." Mama encouraged her. "We almost there."

We walked up the stairs to the apartment of Mama's friend, Jimmy D. Mama pounded on the door. From inside, an apprehensive voice asked, "Who there?"

"It's me, Annie Mae. Open the door, Jimmy D."

"That you?"

"Yeah, dammit, it's me. Open the door!"

A nervous Jimmy D swung the door open and we all poured into his small one-room apartment. It reeked of stale cigarettes and flat beer.

Jimmy D, slightly built with a large afro, saw the blood that covered Bobbi Jo's shirt and almost went into convulsions, he was shaking so bad.

"Good God Almighty! What happened to you, Bobbi Jo?"

"That jealous husband of hers happened to her, is what. C'mon, help me stop the bleeding," Mama told him.

5

"What he did to her?"

"He cut her. Would you please get some rags or something so we can stop the bleeding, Jimmy?"

"Yeah, yeah. Wait here," he said, disappearing into the bedroom.

I sat on the couch watching everything that was going on. Thinking back on it now, I realize how easy it is for kids to accept as normal the things that grownups do. No matter how exciting or how horrible, we as children see them as normal, because at a young age what the adults around us do is all we know.

Mama and Jimmy D spent 10 minutes locating and bandaging the wounds on Bobbi Jo's chest and shoulder. Uncle George had stabbed her three times, leaving wide-open wounds that needed stitches. We hadn't been there 15 minutes before Uncle George showed up.

Bam! Bam! Bam!

"Open the door, Jimmy," George hollered as he pounded on the door. "I know they in there!"

"Oh, God! Oh, God! Please, Jesus!" Bobbi Jo moaned.

"C'mon. Quick. Over here," Mama whispered to Bobbi Jo and me.

Jimmy D helped Bobbi Jo as Mama grabbed my hand firmly and took me out onto a small terrace through the living-room window. Jimmy D pulled down a yellowing window shade and closed the even dirtier curtains across the shade, hiding us from view.

We could hear Uncle George yelling through the front door.

"Jimmy, if you don't open this door, I'm a kick they ass and yours too for playin' with me, nigga! Now open this fuckin' door."

Jimmy opened the door while Uncle George must have leaned against it, because the door slammed into the wall as if someone had slammed into it. Mama and I were as quiet as church mice out on the terrace. I thought Bobbi Jo had stopped breathing, she was so still.

We heard George close the front door and pound his feet across the apartment floor, opening and closing a closet door in the living room. He cursed and threatened Jimmy D.

Jimmy D begged him to calm down. "George, you know damn well if they was here, I would've told you. C'mon. Don't break my stuff, man."

"Shut up!" George yelled. "I'm leavin', but if I find out that you had them up here, I'll put a stump and mud hole in yo' ass, Jimmy D."

We heard the front door slam behind him as Uncle George left, but we didn't budge. Bobbi Jo started moaning. Below us, a single beer can rolled on the concrete alley. Suddenly, the curtains opened and the window shade came up. Jimmy D looked like he'd seen a ghost.

"Y'all gotta leave here, Bobbi Jo," he said. "I don't know what he thinks you've done, but he mad as hell. You can't stay here."

"Bobbi Jo hasn't done nothin', Jimmy. George need to quit drinking is what he need," Mama explained. "Furthermore, he needs his black ass kicked!"

"Well, nobody doin' no ass-kicking 'round here. Y'all got to go!" Jimmy D said.

"You know we don't have a car, Jimmy. Could you go down to the phone booth and call a cab?"

"Yeah, but go on out to the downstairs and wait for the cab."

Jimmy D walked us out of the apartment and down to the first floor to the apartment lobby, where he used the phone to call the cab company. Outside the glass doors, the street was quiet. We waited nearly a half-hour before the taxi showed up. By that point, I was no longer frightened. I was more tired and cold than scared. Bobbi Jo was still terrified, and Mama was still mad as hell.

"Where y'all going tonight, ma'am?" the driver asked, seeming not to notice Bobbi Jo, the blood, and her injuries.

"Watts," Mama answered.

When we arrived a short time later at Charles Harper's, Mama's boyfriend's house, Charles about went through the roof.

"What the hell happened?"

"George actin' up again," Mama said.

"Where is he?" Charles asked as he helped Bobbi Jo walk into the kitchen and sit down at the table.

"I don't know, Charles. He was just over at Jimmy D's house acting a fool. We had to hide out on the balcony to keep him from us."

"Well, he better not bring his ass around here," said Charles, who lived in a garage apartment behind his mother's house. He walked to the window at the front of the garage and looked out.

"Somebody's gonna have to do something about him. This is crazy."

"Yeah, I know," Mama said. "But first we got to get this girl to a hospital, Charles. He cut her up bad. I know she need stitches."

Charles walked into the kitchen and pulled back the front of Bobbi Jo's shirt.

We could all see through the gaping wound to the fat layer under her skin. It hit me then just how bad it really was. My chest felt like someone had punched me. I started to cry again.

"Don't worry, baby, everything is going to be all right," Mama said, putting her arm around me. I turned and looked up into her strong face and tried to smile, but tears streamed down my face.

That was when Uncle George kicked in the door. I just about jumped out of my skin.

Uncle George stormed into the apartment like a raging bull. Charles stood in the kitchen doorway trying to block Uncle George from walking in. But he was noticeably smaller than George; he probably weighed 20 or 30 pounds less.

"George, there's no fighting in my house," Charles said sternly.

"Outta my way, nigga," George responded. "Bobbi Jo! Get yo' ass over here. Now!"

Bobbi Jo got up from the chair. I couldn't believe it when she started to go to him. I cried even harder. Mama stepped between Bobbi Jo and George.

"No, girl, stay out of this," Bobbi Jo told Mama.

"You stay outta my business, bitch!" Uncle George hollered at Mama. "Get over here, Bobbi Jo! Don't make me tell you again!"

The next few moments are a kind of fog. All I remember is after Uncle George slammed Charles into the wall next to the kitchen door, Mama pushed Bobbi Jo and me back, away from them.

"Please, Jesus. Please, Jesus. Pleeaase, Jesus!" Bobbi Jo sobbed.

Then I heard a thunderous sound.

BOOM!

Uncle George stopped in his tracks, looked down at his chest, and fell like dead weight into the kitchen doorway.

Mama had shot her brother George dead. Then she went to jail.

Nothing would ever be the same again after that day. Nothing.

———◆◆◆———

The police came, then an ambulance. I became hysterical when the cops handcuffed Mama and walked her out the door, putting her in the backseat of a patrol car. I didn't know if I'd ever see her again.

Afterward, Charles walked me to his mother's house in front of his converted-garage apartment. As I cried myself to sleep that night, the booming sound of gunfire played over and over, like a broken record in my head.

Bobbi Jo was released from the hospital the next day, but I stayed with Charles's mother and she took care of me. It felt like a long time before I saw Mama again, but it was probably only a week or two before she was released, after investigators determined she'd killed Uncle George in self-defense with a single gunshot wound to his chest.

Soon after Mama was released, we moved out of Bobbi Jo's and into an eight-unit apartment building on West Cordova Street. It wasn't a house, but it was perfect for the two of us.

A couple years later, we moved to a small, white, three-bedroom home in South Central L.A. surrounded by freeways, from the 110 to the 405, and the 10 to the 105. My mom and Auntie Bobbi Jo had a dream to buy a house together. They saved their money and combined it. Just after we all moved in, my auntie died. Her children—my cousins—stayed with us and my mom raised them too. So, now my auntie's portion of the monthly mortgage payment was no longer there, and it left a burden on my mom. She struggled, working two jobs and raising two families, but she got by.

The first kid I met on the street was Ollie Newell. I was in the fourth grade and Ol' was in the second. We became the best of friends and, ultimately, we'd become business partners in an enterprise neither of us could have predicted.

The house was very close to the 110, or the Harbor Freeway, near the corner of 87th Place and Flower Street. The 110 was the reason that, years later, my homies called me by the nickname Freeway Rick. The 110 runs through the geographical line of division in L.A. between the haves and have-nots. Later, to widen the 110, they took my mom's house at 430 West 87th Place through eminent domain. It was the same year I went to prison.

Mom and I rarely talked about Uncle George or his death. Years later, however, she did say how much she cared about him. "I loved my brother. He and I were so close," even though he had what she called "spells." The year before he died, Uncle George had such a severe argument with my mom, punching her and in the process permanently knocking out one of her eyes. She has a glass eye. George hid out in Texas for a year after that attack before returning home to California, where he lived until the day of the shooting.

Ironically, Uncle George had bought Mama a gun a couple years earlier to keep her safe while living as a single woman with her children in the tough L.A. 'hood in South Central. It was with that same gun he'd purchased for her that she fatally wounded her brother.

"I shot one time and it hit him," she said.

Mom and I, on our own now, settled into life on 87th Place.

CHAPTER 3

JOURNEY TO THE CITY OF ANGELS

I am a descendant of slaves. My mom often talked about her great-grandfather, Mike Britton, working as a slave for a Texas farmer, and her great-grandmother picking crops in the fields beside him. After slavery was abolished, he became a sharecropper. They were a hard-working, strong family. Mike Britton's son and my great-grandfather went on to retire from the railroad.

The first three years of my life were spent in Arp, Texas, a rural, partially wooded town near Tyler in Smith County, with about 800 people living there. It was just my big brother David and me, living on the outskirts of town with our mom, Annie Mae Ross. I didn't know where my father was. And it didn't matter to me at the time. Soon enough, though, I would learn his whereabouts.

The town was made up of mostly small farmers owning 10 to 100 acres each. I later found out that my father, Sonny Ross, a former Army cook, worked as a sharecropper on one of those farms. He also was a pig farmer.

State Highway 135 ran through our section of town. The International-Great Northern Railroad was built in 1872 with the Arp community one of the stops on the line. School records show that in 1903 the town, called Strawberry at the time for its crops, had both a white and a black school. By the time we lived there, the schools had nearly all integrated.

Our house was a small two-bedroom cracker box my mother purchased for $1,600. The front windows faced the highway. It had a small living room, a tiny but adequate kitchen, and one bathroom. The house wasn't much to look at—we were poor—but it was home, and it didn't matter to us. My brother David and I were happy there.

We lived on the outskirts of town in an area that was more woods and weeds than road or neighborhood. The constant heat and humidity seemed as much a part of Arp as the people who populated the small settlement. It made the rich, fertile land that surrounded the houses a virtual garden for every kind of wild-growing weed, thorn, and bramble bushes that existed there. The job of keeping the grass-choking weeds in our small front yard under control was an unending task that my brother David, because he was seven years older, had been delegated to do, along with watering it each morning.

Next door to our house was an unkempt vacant lot overrun with brown grass and tall weeds with small thorns we called "stickers." The lot separated our home from an ancient, wood-framed gas station that had two old, rusted pumps in the front that were hardly ever used. It was probably because the broken-down building that also served as the neighborhood convenience store sat so far off the road running through our part of town that drivers couldn't see it.

An older white woman, known to local kids as Opal, owned and single-handedly ran the town gas station and store. Opal was decent toward everybody, always smiling when people came into her store and saying something nice. I remember many days of riding my tricycle, pulling a big red wagon, back and forth to Opal's store, and my dog Pooch bouncing eagerly along by my side. I drank the sodas and ate the free cookies she seemed to have an endless supply of. I can't imagine how she made a living with her seemingly rundown business, but she always managed to give away free food.

A little farther down the road lived my mother's best friend Doris. On weekdays while David was in school and when the weather was nice, Mom and I'd walk to Doris's little shack of a house. Sometimes we stayed all day. Doris had a son, Keith, who was also one of the only children my age available for miles around for me to play with. Besides my brother, Keith was my best friend.

At home, I remember a worn-out couch David and I regularly curled up on to watch cartoons on Saturday mornings. That couch wrapped itself around us like an old overcoat. A wood-burning fireplace in the living room warmed us during cold Texas winters. We didn't have much, but what we did have was comfortable, always clean, and, to my three-year-old mind, it seemed more than enough. Mom made our lives as pleasant as she could, given her limited resources.

Though we were dirt poor, Mom, who worked as a maid cleaning other people's houses, made sure we were well-fed, had clean clothes, and the house was spotless. Mother was strict on cleanliness. On those Saturday mornings that my brother and I snuck into the living room to watch cartoons, our mother always caught us, because our laughter woke her up. She playfully scolded us about being up so early watching TV without first doing our chores, namely, cleaning our room and David watering the yard.

Because of the long distance between houses in the section of town we lived in, which was more country than city, very few people visited our house. The only people we saw were inside the cars speeding by on the highway. My mother had a boyfriend, but neither David nor I liked him much. Whenever he came over, we avoided him. When he wasn't there, it was just the three of us—Mom, David, and me. Our father had left us not long after I turned three.

The isolation living in a rural area of town gave our little family plenty of time to be together. When my mother wasn't at work, or David wasn't in school, the three of us were inseparable. Whenever my mother wasn't at home, David and I had the best time playing together inside and outdoors.

David and I were more than typical brothers; we were best friends. I not only looked up to him, but I loved him. Living so far out in the country, David and I were often left alone when Mom went into town to work. We did almost everything together, and David was there if I needed him.

Once, after David and I walked into our bedroom and discovered a 3-foot gopher snake coiled up on the floor, he saved me—at least I thought he did. We didn't know that the snake was harmless. To us, the snake looked vicious. At first, it didn't move. It just sat there with its small dark eyes staring at us. David wasn't afraid of anything. He ran out of the bedroom, into the kitchen, and grabbed a large, thick-handled broom. When he returned to our bedroom, I hadn't moved from my original spot. Without hesitating, David charged the snake. The snake avoided his attempts to push and poke at him with the broom. While David was doing that, I dodged the snake's jerking and whipping movements. David finally forced the frightened and seemingly angry snake out of the bedroom and eventually out of the house. After that day, I thought David was the bravest and coolest brother a boy could have.

Our little house was also home to rats. Big ones. David set up rat traps, equipped with small copper bars that had to be manually flipped back. He spread them throughout the house. Whenever we found a rat caught in one of his traps, I stood far enough away to be safe in case it wasn't dead and decided to jump out at me. I marveled at how my big brother picked up the traps, rats and all, and took them outside.

My big brother was my buddy and my hero, which made what happened next all the more devastating.

Before the close of the year 1963, David and I would be separated and would not see each another again for eight long years. It was a gut-wrenching event in our young lives.

The separation happened one day after school. At just 3-1/2 years old, I was too young to attend school legally, but I'd been allowed by the school to go with David a few times, probably because my mother didn't want me home alone while she worked because I had been involved in what luckily turned out to be a minor automobile accident. I bumped my head hard enough to require stitches and I was still wearing the bandage.

I remember the school desk chair being too tall for me to sit down in and I had to climb into it. David's teacher would get upset during lessons when some of the girls in the class babied me. I was always small for my age so the girls coddled me, which irritated the teacher.

On that day, when school ended, David's teacher, with a big sigh of relief, dismissed class for the day. I didn't know it would be the last time.

We ran all the way home, skipping, jumping, and laughing. Seconds after David and I burst through the front door of our house, still laughing and talking in loud voices, my mother stopped us in the living room with a sharp verbal command.

"Go to your room and pack your clothes and toys. Grab Pooch. We're moving to California."

Our dog Pooch followed us everywhere we went, except for when David went to school.

I had no idea where or what California was, but moving wasn't the biggest shock. It was the news that came next, that David would be staying in Texas with our father, who lived, I learned for the first time, not far from us. With our mom's declaration that David wasn't coming with us, I became hysterical. I cried and cried when Mama told me we would be traveling by bus and I had to leave all of my toys, my dog, and my tricycle in Arp with David at our father's house. Everything I loved was being left behind in Arp, Texas. Mom and me took nothing with us except a small basket of fried chicken, potato salad, and a few clothes in a laundry bag. Life without David was unthinkable. I broke down and cried until there were no tears left to shed.

Back in the '60s, Texas was considered a racist state, because blacks were still having to say "yes, sir" and "no, sir" to white folks. California offered Southern blacks more opportunities, and Mom wanted to give us the best shot at a good life. The only opportunity she had in Arp was limited, and that was cleaning houses.

She wanted more for herself and her kids. And if that meant temporarily separating David and me, then that's the way it was going to be.

At the time, Mom didn't know how long the separation would be. She told me, "It won't be long, Ricky, before David comes out to California to live with us." As it turned out, it would be a very long time.

We walked David and his things, and our dog Pooch, to our father's house. It was the first time I recalled seeing my father. I didn't remember him before that time. Before I knew what was happening, my mother and I were at the Greyhound Bus Station in a downtown section of Arp waiting to board a bus that would take us to our new home in the city of Compton, California, in southern Los Angeles, better known as South Central L.A.

It was afternoon when we arrived at Aunt Luretha and Uncle Johnny Wilson's house. They had five children of varying ages—Ted, Bennett, Evita, Rene, and Yvette. My cousins were still in school when we got in. When they got home, I met them for the first time. That was the big benefit of moving to California; I had cousins I didn't know existed. They became my friends.

I don't remember much about our stay with Aunt Luretha and her family, other than it was a short period—a few months at the most. Mom and I slept on the sofa in the small living room.

Eventually Mom got part-time jobs doing janitorial and lawn-service work, what she called "maintenance." At some point, in between jobs, we went on welfare.

While she looked for work, Mom sometimes took me with her. I think that's when she learned that by leaving Texas she couldn't necessarily escape racism; despite the California sunshine, palm trees, and positive image, our skin was still black. One of my earliest memories was during our first weeks in Cali when my mom took me with her to fill out job applications. It was a "whites only" restaurant and we had to enter the business from the back alley because blacks weren't allowed to walk through the front entrance.

Once she landed a full-time job and her work hours increased, I spent much of my time alone while my cousins were in school. Being left alone was a new experience for me. But during the short time we lived with Aunt Luretha and Uncle Johnny, it wasn't too bad.

In no time at all, Mom and I packed up our few belongings once again. We left Aunt Luretha's house and moved in with my mother's brother, Uncle George Mauldin, and his wife, Aunt Bobbi Jo. Mom and I had our own bedroom, which was much better than a living room and a couch. Uncle George and Aunt Bobbi Jo had two younger children, George Junior (we called him Tootie) and Kenny, who became like brothers rather than cousins.

From the first moment we moved in with Uncle George and Aunt Bobbi Jo, life for me became a never-ending episode of fun, games, and happiness that I had previously experienced back in Arp, Texas, with David. It was like I'd always known my cousins. The sadness at losing David was soon replaced with happiness in having young cousins to play with.

We got into all the mischief making that three young boys could muster. Kenny, Tootie, and I jumped on the bed, had water fights, and wrestled. We were scolded thoroughly for it, but we didn't care. It was all good fun. Because I was the oldest of the three, it felt like I had gradually taken on the role as leader of our little trio. Whenever my mother or aunt blamed me for the trouble Tootie or Kenny got into, which was never anything serious, it validated my leadership.

Up to that point, life at Aunt Bobbi Jo and Uncle George's was wonderful. I was having such a good time as the days and months turned into years, I just about forgot Arp, Texas, and my life with David. I didn't know it then, but the good times at the Mauldins' house were about to abruptly end. Losing Uncle George the way I did is something that's stayed with me my entire life.

CHAPTER 4
GROWING UP IN THE 'HOOD

It was a typical California day—warm, with a slight breeze blowing. And nothing out of the ordinary happened at St. Lawrence of Brindisi Parish Catholic School, where we went through our usual daily activities. That is, until the noon recess period.

There was no way those of us in the schoolyard that afternoon could have predicted that an event about to occur would have a major impact on my life. It all went down during a game of marbles.

St. Lawrence Catholic School opened in Watts in 1924. It was just two blocks from where the Watts race riots erupted a couple of years earlier in August 1965 with six days of upheaval. While other buildings were burned to the ground, St. Lawrence remained untouched. My mom was able to enroll me there, instead of public school. She wanted me to get a good education and thought the nuns who staffed the school could do the best job.

Shooting marbles was the most popular pastime for the boys of St. Lawrence, including me. I thought it was the most fascinating game ever invented.

I collected hundreds of marbles of all different types, shapes, sizes, and colors. There were the dark, mysterious, solid-colored pearlies and the lighter, multicolored catseyes. There were the huge, rugged boulders and the tiny usually solid-colored peewees.

I had what I thought was a huge collection—400 in all—kept in every place imaginable, from old coffee cans to shoe boxes and all that my pants pockets could hold.

We shot marbles all day, every day. We played during morning recess, noon recess, and before we left for home at the end of the day. All the kids knew that when we played, it was for keeps—at least that was how it was supposed to be. We called it "keepsies."

Even though we could buy a bag of mixed-color marbles for a quarter, it was rare to find the greatly prized pearlie or aggie in a store-bought bag. They had to be won, but they weren't always given over easily, even if won fair and square; fights could break out. This day would be no different.

Lunch ended with our daily ritual of Dennis, Larry "Bird" Jonson, Freddie, and I putting our lunch pails away and heading as fast as our little legs could carry us to the section of the schoolyard next to the monkey bars, where the blacktop ended, to play the second game of the day.

Our spot was large and covered with fine sand. We smoothed away the top layer of sand and then Dennis drew the pot. It was nice and big, about three feet wide. When I saw that big pot, I smiled. By the size of the circle, we knew that the pearlies, aggies, and bumblebees were going into the pot. The larger the circle, the harder it was to knock out the marbles from the circle—that is, unless you were good. And I was good.

We didn't use steelies, the small ball-bearing marbles found inside spray-paint cans, because they could damage glass marbles. No boulders were allowed either. A single boulder could knock out three to four marbles from the pot with one shot. Everyone feared them.

No one knew where Dennis got his marbles from, but he always had some of the best and prettiest. On that day, I could hardly wait to see what he'd put in the pot.

"What y'all gon' put up against this?" Dennis asked loud enough to get the attention of everyone on the yard. I'd already dropped the three marbles we'd agreed on into the pot and stood, staring at Dennis, waiting to see what he was going to do.

Dennis was older by two years, bigger than the rest of us, and was in the habit of showing off whenever there was a crowd around. When he was sure he had everyone's attention, he reached into the front pocket of his short pants—everyone at St. Lawrence Catholic School wore the customary Navy-blue shorts, white shirt, and plaid vest sweater. We all thought we were about to see one of Dennis's beauties, but he just stood there, staring at everyone. Suddenly, he broke out laughing, like his little joke was on us. "Yeah, Dennis," I said, "C'mon. Whatever you put up won't be yours for long anyway. You can't even shoot."

It was true. Dennis couldn't shoot. He was a sore loser, to boot.

"*You* can't shoot!" Dennis spat back at me as he walked to the circle. "I can outshoot yo' little peewee ass any day!"

Dennis dropped his three marbles into the pot, and my mouth fell open.

"He's got a bumblebee!" somebody exclaimed.

"Where'd you get it, Dennis?" Freddie gasped, staring wide-eyed at one of the most sought-after marbles of that time, now gracing the center of the pot.

I couldn't believe it. A bumblebee. Its bright-yellow and dark-black swirls made it stand out like no other marble in the pot. I stared down at it.

"Let's lag!" Bird shouted. "We don't have much time left."

Standing just behind the circle, Freddie, Bird and Dennis, and I began to lag for shooting positions.

"I'm up," said Dennis.

Dennis always tossed first.

"Shit!" Dennis swore again. His marble hadn't come anywhere near the line.

Freddie laughed. "You can't even lag, and you're always talking," Freddie said as he tossed his favorite marble, a deep black pearlie. "Beat that!" he challenged the rest of us, running over to stand proudly by his toss.

Freddie's marble had landed only inches from the line. It would be difficult to beat.

It was Bird's turn to throw.

"Ha! Ha! Ha! Man, you skinny," Dennis yelled at Bird.

"Man, you don't know what you're talkin' about," Bird shot back. Bird didn't weigh as much as Dennis, but he was just as tall and he could fight and wasn't afraid of anything or anyone.

Bird tossed his marble, which hit a soft spot in the dirt and stuck about six inches from the line. "Ah, man," he said. "You made me mess up my throw. Man!"

Now it was my turn.

I preferred going last and usually hung back deliberately, to better observe those I had to beat. Dennis stared at me as if to say, *You better not win the lag or I'm gonna beat your little ass.* He knew that if I won the lag and shot first, his chances of even getting a good shot were slim and his bumblebee would be mine.

I bent a little at the waist, swung my arm backward just enough to give my marble the push-roll. It was a beautiful catseye with gray, brown, and yellow swirls. It fit my small fingers just right. I tossed it.

It made a high arc and hung there for what seemed forever. When it hit the dirt, it made the drag-slide-roll I'd practiced for so long, rolling past all the other marbles as if it had a mind of its own and knew exactly where to go. I sucked in my breath as it neared the line and showed no sign of slowing. I thought maybe I'd tossed it too hard; if it crossed the line, it meant automatic last place.

Instead, my catseye rolled up the small crest in the dirt where Bird made the line. It tottered for just a moment, causing me to rise up with my fist balled. Then it slid down at the line and stopped.

I was first and Dennis' bumblebee was as good as mine, and everyone—including Dennis—knew it.

I smiled at Dennis and stepped forward to pick up my catseye.

But Dennis had something else in mind. For a moment, he just stood there, stunned, staring at the pot. Then suddenly, he bent down, scooped up all the marbles in one hand, and bolted through the crowd, pushing some of the kids to the side and knocking down some of the girls.

"Hey, man!" Bird shouted.

"Whatcha doin', Dennis?" Freddie cried, then to the rest of us, "He's got our marbles!"

In a flash, without thinking, I went after Dennis.

I was smaller, but faster, and I quickly caught up with him. I jumped onto his back with one arm around his neck. Dennis twisted, spun, and grabbed at my hands, trying to dislodge me. Unknowingly, as I struggled to hold on as tightly as possible, I was choking the life out of him.

The kids cheered us on as if we were fighting for the boxing championship of the world. Rolling in the dirt, I held on, still choking Dennis.

"Give . . . me . . . my . . . marbles!" I uttered between clenched teeth, squeezing his neck tighter.

We tussled and rolled and I bit Dennis on the back of his head.

"A-R-G-H-H! A-R-G-H-H!" Dennis tried to scream.

I bit him again, and I held on, terrified of letting go. My heart pounded inside my chest, and buzzing filled my ears. Then, without realizing how it happened, I felt myself being lifted off the ground, into the air, and my arms removed from around Dennis' neck.

I looked down and saw Dennis lying in the dirt with his hands clutching his throat and his mouth wide open, and I instantly recalled Uncle George with his jaw hanging slack and his eyes staring blankly up at the ceiling. I thought Dennis was dead, and I started crying, kicking, and screaming, and I couldn't see.

That was my last day at St. Lawrence.

———◦◆◦———

I'd already been involved in a few fights, and, around the same time, for reasons unknown to me, I'd developed a major spelling and writing problem. Both issues, school officials told my mom, made me no longer a good fit for St. Lawrence.

The look of hurt in my mother's eyes when she came to pick me up from school that day has stayed with me. I could hear the disappointment in my mother's voice and see it in the way she looked down at me as we left St. Lawrence for the last time, immediately after I was expelled. My mother's dream of my Catholic school education was gone. Upon learning that I wouldn't be returning to St. Lawrence, I was initially confused. I didn't understand what my mother meant when I overheard her say to Aunt Bobbi Jo over the phone that she'd have to find another school for me to attend. I had no concept of the differences between public and Catholic schools.

When it finally was explained, I felt like jumping for joy. Deep down, I was bursting with elation. No more uniforms. No more praying three times a day. No more rigid rules.

I was born into a religious Baptist family and I was baptized into that tradition. Not being Catholic was the reason the sisters didn't allow me to participate in communion with other kids. I felt left out, sitting alone on a bench outside of the chapel, wondering what I'd done wrong, and longing for it to end quickly. I no longer had to suffer through that, and I was glad.

For my mother, my expulsion meant something altogether different. I didn't understand exactly why at the time, but I could see it in my mother's eyes, the sad expression on her face, and the slowness in her voice. It hurt her to have me expelled after working so hard to get me into Catholic school in the first place. It was important to her on so many levels.

My mom and I were part of the black migration that began in the 1940s after World War II from rural Southern states to the West Coast seeking jobs and better lives, only to find ourselves excluded from the suburbs and restricted to blighted communities in East or South Central Los Angeles, which included Watts and Compton. The earliest settlement of the black population, in an area 6.5 miles wide and 18 miles long, was South Central, which once housed hordes of blue-collar workers. By the mid 1960s when we arrived from Texas, educational and economic opportunities in the minority community were substantially restricted. So getting me into a Catholic school instead of attending public schools meant, to my mom, that we'd bypassed those restrictions.

But it was not to be. And that was what she was so sad about. Mom never shouted at me for fighting with a classmate over a few marbles. She didn't seem angry. Even though St. Lawrence and the events that day began to fade from my memory, I still slouched around while listening to my mother talk on the phone to Bobbi Jo about it. I was sad because my mom was sad.

My mother was all I had, besides Aunt Bobbi Jo, who treated me like her own son, and my little sister, Angie Richardson. She was born when I was seven and was expected to attend St. Lawrence too. Now, that hung in the balance. I felt my mother's hurt, which all started because I'd fought with Dennis James.

As I look back on it, I realize it was then, at St. Lawrence Catholic School, that I first became dispirited. I was punished for doing what I thought was the right thing, defending fellow classmates and myself. I also felt I was looked at as an idiot for not being able to perform up to expected educational standards.

I was beginning not to care about school work.

My lack of confidence affected my decision-making. I was only nine years old, but I still remember how it felt.

———◆———

Soon after I was expelled, my mother enrolled me at Manchester Elementary School, on the corner of Manchester Avenue between Hoover and Figueroa avenues. My cousins attended the same school.

Manchester was a brave new world compared to St. Lawrence. I reveled in the newfound freedom, away from the strict rules of Catholic school.

Each morning my cousins, Kenny and Tootie, and I raced to school. Some days, we had a ritual. We left by the back gate of my house, sprinted east up Flower, then west on 89th, and continued all the way to Figueroa Avenue, where we took a left to Three G's candy store. After loading up on Lemon Heads, Red Hots, Boston Baked Beans, and wine candies—what today are called Jolly Ranchers— we bolted across Figueroa, then straight up 89th, and cut through Manchester Park to where the western boundary ended on Hoover Street. That took us to the back of the school auditorium. I didn't know it then, but we were entering the home turf of the notorious 92nd Street Hoover Crips set, formed around the area of Manchester Park.

My Aunt Luretha's daughters Rene, Yvette, and Evita, who also attended Manchester Elementary, and Tootie and I were at an age too carefree and young to realize that we were in the middle of gang territory.

At Manchester Elementary, reciting the Pledge of Allegiance was the only required ritual performed during the school day; there was no getting down on our knees to pray. School had now become a place that I looked forward to going each day. Though I continued wrestling with an ever-worsening writing and spelling problem and my new teachers agonized over methods to correct what they assumed was a learning disability, I thought public school was wonderful. My mother seemed content with me as she built a life for us in California. My remaining two years at the elementary level were uneventful, when it came to my classmates. I completed the fifth and sixth grades without getting involved in a serious fight.

When it came to teachers, however, it was entirely different. I acted out in class. Not being able to read and write were big handicaps. Earlier, when I was four and five years old, my mom had tried to teach me how to read and to learn my ABCs. Reading was the furthest thing from my mind, and I didn't know the devastating effect it would have on me for the rest of my life. I'd already started relying on my physical abilities rather than my mental aptitude. My mother started calling me a leader about that time.

But going to school and not knowing how to read was no fun. In elementary school, people tried to help, but I guess I wore their resistance down with numbers, because that was one thing I was good at; at five, I knew all my times tables by heart.

My mother even hired a couple of tutors for me. One was a girl named Taylor who was kind of cute. I enjoyed going over to her house. She did get some work out of me; even then, I was a sucker for the pretty ladies. But the spelling, reading, and writing stuff, I just didn't get. Even to this day, it's still tough for me, but I force myself to write.

In school, I learned a few tricks, by acting out, to avoid having to read. It got so bad that the school recommended I get psychological help, like going to a psychiatrist. I remember one time going to see a fat man in an office on Century and 74th Street. He was a county evaluator, and he asked me all kinds of questions about why I acted up in school. An example of me acting up was when a teacher opened a book to read in class, and when my turn came, I made fun of the teacher to get out of reading because I was too embarrassed to try. I did that over and over even at the expense of going to the principal's office to get swatted.

While still at Manchester Elementary, an event happened on the way to school one morning with my cousins Kenny, Tootie, and two friends, Maurice and Terry, that, once again, disrupted my life to where I became saddened, frightened, and as insecure as I'd been after my mother was arrested for killing Uncle George. All of the confusion, fear, and uncertainty I experienced that night came crashing down on me like a tidal wave.

That morning, we took the long way around on our way to school.

The city of Los Angeles had built a swimming pool at Manchester Park, and even though we'd seen swimming pools before, we were excited to have one in our own neighborhood, only a 10-minute walk from our homes. As we ran through the park gate and onto the gravel-covered parking lot, we noticed a crowd of people surrounding the fence that circled the pool. People pushed and pointed. Everybody seemed excited about whatever was going on at the pool. I couldn't imagine what it could be.

With the inquisitiveness of young boys, we boldly shoved through the crowd to the fence and peered through.

Floating on the surface of the water was a bloated body, the skin marbled and purple.

In that instant, I was again brought back to Charles Harper's converted garage, running around in circles, screaming, my mother trying to contain me as Uncle George lay dead on the floor in the kitchen doorway.

That dreaded thunderous sound—*"BOOM! BOOM! BOOM!"*— once again played in and with my head.

I turned and struggled to get away from the fence. My stomach heaved like I was about to puke while the booming pounded in my head.

Then we were all back together and on our way to school. "Man, that was nasty! Did you see his dick?" Terry said.

"Wasn't nobody lookin' at his dick but you, faggot!" Kenny replied.

"I wasn't lookin' at his dick!" Terry insisted.

"What you talking 'bout dicks for, then?" Maurice asked.

"Fuck y'all, man," Terry said.

Then I spoke up, saying, "Y'all shut up!"

I was still struggling to free myself of the image of my uncle looking up at the ceiling and his dead eyes wide open.

31

The memories of that terrible night had returned to haunt my thoughts. Even when I slept, I couldn't escape the vision of death and the ensuing sadness when my mother was taken away. Seeing the floater in the pool threw me back to that frightened six-year-old boy, and I felt alone.

For a long time after that day at the pool, I feared that my mother would leave me. I couldn't think clearly. All I could hear was thunder.

———— ⬦ ————

The school year ended and the summer of 1972 began. We looked forward to the sun and freedom from school with the enthusiasm of wild birds finally released from lives in captivity.

Also that summer, my brother David finally moved to California from our dad's home in Texas to live with Mom and me. I was glad to have not only my big brother back, but my best friend too. I finally had someone to talk to again and play with at home.

With my brother home, I slowly started to lose the sense of insecurity I'd developed when our mom moved me away from David. A lot had happened in the 7-1/2 years I lived in California without him. I felt safe in the knowledge that David would protect me.

Summer was a time for the beach, with the California coastline less than a half-hour away by car and not much longer on bicycles, and I was grateful to have David back to share in the fun. The beaches we frequented were Playa del Rey, Santa Monica, and Venice.

My buddies, cousins, brother, and I frequented these crowded stretches of sand and turf, unless one of our parents said "no." Even then, we snuck out of the neighborhood. The shores of the Pacific Ocean were like a second home to the kids in the 'hood.

We also hung out at the neighborhood parks, where we swam or played football on the grass or baseball on a dirt lot. Los Angeles was full of parks—Manchester, Will Rogers, Athens, Helen Keller, and Centennial—and, if we weren't at the beach, we were at a park, sunup to sundown.

That summer of 1971 was also when I began to discover my athletic ability. With my growing confidence and strong drive to excel, I put my efforts into learning how to play football with the same devotion and enthusiasm I'd focused on becoming an expert at shooting marbles. That summer was filled with good times.

That fall after school started, David played varsity football for Fremont High in the Watts area.

When David wasn't practicing football or attending school, we played catch in the street. I got good at intercepting the ball. It wasn't long before I stood out when neighborhood boys my age played with us. A vacant lot at the end of the block made for an excellent football field.

We cursed, fought, and threatened one another as we played, even though we were all friends before and after the games; on the field, it was competitive. When we weren't playing football on the block, we competed at Manchester Park against kids from other blocks, where we continued cursing, shouting, name-calling, and "talking shit." We tore our clothes sliding in the dirt and were bruised and banged up by the time the sun went down and we could no longer see the ball and our mothers began calling out for us to go home.

At the end of the games—beat, bruised, and sore—we'd head home, complaining all the while, if our block lost, about the mistakes someone else made, and the cursing and name-calling started all over again. If we won, the swearing was accompanied by laughter and talking shit about whoever made the best touchdown or the greatest catch. It was all about football and it was great fun.

Two guys from those games, Allie, nicknamed "Killer," and Derek "Dee" Brown, became my friends. They lived on 89th between Broadway and Grand, but they played football with the team from our block. Then there was Terry Bowman, the very first friend I made after we moved to the house on 87th Place. We first met in the alley behind his house while I was on my way to Burger Dan's, a small hamburger joint down the street that was owned by Miss Betsy. We hung out there, played pinball, and chased Miss Betsy's cats. Miss Betsy was white, hated it when we chased her cats, and yelled at us for it. But she'd pay us small sums of money to do odd jobs around the hamburger stand for her. Betsy was the last white person to move away from our block.

Once spring training ended at Fremont High, my brother started scrimmaging with the varsity football team in preparation for the upcoming football season and the beginning of the new school year.

Meantime, I'd been promoted from Manchester Elementary in June '71, along with friends my age in the neighborhood, and we began making our own preparations for the upcoming transition to junior high school. Bret Harte Junior High was where most of us would be attending. I was not only nervous, I was terrified.

Sure, there was always a sense of excitement and anxiety associated with going to a new school for the first time. But in this case, moving up from elementary to junior high, while representing growing up and becoming mature, also meant attending a school with an infamous reputation, and I dreaded the day I would walk onto the grounds of Bret Harte.

During walks home from the football games at Manchester, Bret Harte became the number-one topic of conversation. Or while lying on the warm deck of Manchester Park's new swimming pool, someone always brought up the subject of advancing to the seventh, eighth, and ninth grades.

While my mother bought school clothes for me, she concerned herself with the cost, the right fit, and how fast I'd outgrow them.

Me? I worried about Bret Harte and the reasons it had earned the title as the "toughest" school in Los Angeles; it was home to one of the largest and most vicious adolescent gangs that ever combed the streets of Southern California. They were called the 92nd Street Crips.

If there was a point in my early life that had to be marked as the true beginning of my adolescence, it was that September of 1971.

Although I'd never become a genuine member of the notorious Crips street gang—as in taking a vow of membership—by association, I'd become just as much a member as any one of the most devout originals.

I was more than an ordinary homie throwing ghetto slang; I became someone altogether different from the person I'd once been. I never ran the streets with gangbangers, but I lived among them.

I was 13 years old, and I felt it was my destiny to become a Crip.

CHAPTER 5
GANGSTERS, GUNS, AND HOMIES

My first day at junior high, at 92nd and South Hoover streets in the heart of Watts, I was certain I was about to learn first-hand why Bret Harte was one of the most feared junior highs within the Los Angeles Unified School District. I was, however, pleasantly surprised with a boring, uneventful day—that is, until the final bell rang at 3:30.

Along with hundreds of other incoming freshmen and returning students, I spent a good part of the day filling out forms associated with registering and choosing classes, plus becoming familiar with the school grounds. I could write my name and address on the forms, because I'd memorized them. That was the extent of my writing ability back then.

Homeroom was first period. Although I didn't initially know any kids in homeroom, I became fast friends with Frank Jones, also one of the founders of the 107th Street Crips who earned the revered title of one of the most feared kids at Bret Harte. Frank, known by his gang moniker of Moomoo, was as large as a bull and just as tough; he was known for bench-pressing 290 pounds. I thought Moomoo was the coolest dude. I also became friends with Darrel Ranier, also with the 107th Street Crips, plus Anthony Edgar and Jeff Hill, two of the few boys in homeroom who weren't gangbangers but were rugged enough to hold their own. Anthony would become one of the best football players ever at Bret Harte (now called Bret Harte Preparatory Middle School).

My homeroom teacher, Mr. Vick, was cool and everybody liked him. He spoke our language, using the same slang and expressions.

After homeroom that first day, I went to the next three classes and tried to memorize the directions to each one. Bret Harte wasn't that large, but finding my way around its stairways and halls took some doing.

Lunch was similar to the midday break at Manchester Elementary, with some kids standing, some sitting either alone or in groups, eating, and talking. Many students ate in the school's large cafeteria, while others sat outside on park benches.

Still a little nervous about being on campus, I didn't eat much that day. I stood around looking at girls and tried to find kids I knew. Lunch ended and the afternoon dragged on with more classes and talking, sitting, signing forms, and getting assigned textbooks.

The bell rang, signaling the end of sixth period and the close of the school day. As students moved out into the hallway to head to their lockers, I thought my first day of junior high was just another ordinary day and all the stories I'd heard seemed terribly exaggerated. I even ran into one of my neighborhood homeboys and told him so. I spoke too soon.

After putting my books in my locker and walking out of the building, I headed toward the north gate, looked up, and nearly pissed my pants.

At least a hundred boys, most wearing 92nd Street Crips colors, were gathered inside and outside the north-gate entrance, as well as on the sidewalk that surrounded the rear of the schoolyard, with no teachers in sight. The crowd sealed the street just outside the gate, closing it off. For me to get through, they'd have to move out of the way. I couldn't imagine that happening.

They stood watching me as I approached.

I've always been small, reaching no more than five-foot-five inches tall and maybe 145 pounds at the most. I was even smaller in junior high. Maybe it was because I was conscious of my own small stature, but as I approached the group of Crips, I was too afraid to turn around or stop, and I didn't know what else to do but keep walking.

They all looked so big.

They also looked tough and mean, wearing their Levis, Wallabees, and blue bandannas either tied around their heads as doo rags or hanging from their rear pants' pockets.

I was scared. I thought if I turned around to walk the other way, they'd chase me. I blindly kept walking, frightened almost into a daze.

Still, I knew instinctively that if I showed fear, I'd never be able to hold up my head in school again, and it was just the first day.

As I walked closer to the group, my heart racing, I noticed someone I knew. Leon Washington was from the 'hood and attended Manchester Elementary with me. He went by the gang name "Baby Bam." But in school, I knew him as Leon. He also watched me, while at the same time talking with one of the gangbangers. As I slowly walked forward, I did my best to appear casual.

I stopped in front of them, grateful that I knew someone.

"Hey, man, what's happenin'?" I said, looking at Leon.

"Wassup, cuzz?" Leon asked.

"Nothin' much, nothin' much," I said as I gave him a shit-eating grin.

The short exchange ended, and I breathed easier. I noticed out of the corner of my eye that the guys standing around the yard looking on were trying to figure out how I knew Baby Bam.

I felt even more emboldened when Leon walked away from the crowd with me and we headed home. I felt brave walking down 92nd Street. Later, I felt protected whenever I saw someone having their money or leather coat stolen by gangbangers, a common occurrence when a non-gangster got caught on Crip turf. Because I knew Bam, I felt protected from that ever happening to me—on the street, anyway. It separated me from the kids who walked as many as three blocks out of their way to and from school to avoid contact with the Crips, some of whom by age 12 and 13 had already been to juvenile hall for robbery, assault, and even armed assaults. I felt good, confident even, as if I were one of them. I felt proud.

During the seventh grade at Bret Harte Junior High, I fared no better academically than I had throughout grade school as I continued having trouble spelling. No matter how hard I tried to understand simple ABCs or how much time a teacher devoted to helping me, I couldn't grasp any of it. I disliked science, English, and history classes and only made a real effort in plastics shop and physical education. I did fairly well in math, though. I never had a problem with numbers. It was a skill that would come in handy in my later endeavors.

When the time came for me to advance to eighth grade, junior high followed in the footsteps of elementary school and passed me without question. I imagine some of my teachers felt sorry for me and, by moving me along, believed they were doing me a favor. By that time, I was 12 years old and it didn't matter—at least to me. As long as there was a gym to play basketball in, a field to play football and baseball on, and my friends to hang out with, I was satisfied. I didn't realize how difficult I was making it for myself, with each passing year, by heading toward adulthood as illiterate.

Still, appearances and what people thought of me were important. While at Bret Harte, I wanted a pair of Converse All-Star sneakers, just like all the other kids. We called them "Stars" or "Chuck Taylors." Every boy wanted a pair. I was no different.

On Christmas day in the eighth grade, my mother surprised me by making my wish come true. As I opened the box, my excitement turned to horror. The Chuck Taylors she bought me were bright red! I tried to explain to her why it was the worst color that Converse ever made and that no one wore them. No one! Not to mention, they were the same red that represented the Bloods street gang, which could have made me a target of Crips members.

I was devastated, but my mother refused to exchange the red sneakers for another color. She thought I was being difficult and ungrateful. I had to wear them, because I needed them for PE class.

I became the laughing stock of my homeroom and the school in general as I earned the nickname "Little Red Shoes" and "Dragon." My dream tennis shoes had become my worst nightmare. Man, I wanted so badly for that pair of shoes to wear out.

<hr />

In January 1972, I became more involved with the Crips, coming just short of joining up. The majority of my friends, outside of those who lived on my block, were already gangbangers. I slowly drifted away from home to the streets. Without realizing it, I was becoming just as hardened and uncaring as a lot of the gangbangers I used to fear.

But an incident in eighth grade caused me to do an about-face and reevaluate what could happen because of my growing relationship with 92nd Street Crips members.

Many gangbangers at Bret Harte were from different sets within the Crips. The gang members I associated with were from the 92nd Street clique.

The early '70s —1970, 1971, and 1972—signaled the beginning of what would become one of the most turbulent eras in South Central Los Angeles history as it related to gang evolution, the increase of violent gang-on-gang activity, and the reign of terror and violence on the affected neighborhoods.

A number of other black adolescent gangs emerged from the greatly underdeveloped, stagnated, angry ghettos of South Central, and many became just as notorious as the LA.-based Crips. None, however, experienced the widespread fame, the size in the number of members, or the longevity of the Crips.

The gang called the Swans was a small but violent group of 40 to 100 young black males who lived in and dominated the predominantly black 'hoods ranging from Florence to Manchester avenues on the northern and southern boundaries and Central Avenue to Avalon Boulevard on the eastern and western boundaries.

On the eastside of Los Angeles between Central and Compton avenues, at the east-west boundaries, and Imperial Highway and 108th Street, on the north-south sides, the Nickerson Garden Bloods held the occupants of the housing projects by the same name virtually hostage, in abject terror.

The Denver Lane Bloods was a black youth gang primarily centered around Denver Street on the Westside. The Van Ness Park Boys, also a black youth gang but led by a 5-foot-6 black teen named Donald Ray, controlled the West Los Angeles area in and around Van Ness Park, located just north of 54th Street and west of Van Ness Boulevard.

Bret Harte Junior High was not exempt from gangs.

By mid-1973, my school had become almost completely dominated by both the 92nd Street and 107th Street Crip gangs. Though a small number of Denver Lane Bloods continued attending, most Denver Lane gangbangers had either been driven out by rival gang members or graduated. For those students who weren't Crips, Bret Harte was a dangerous school; for those students who were Bloods, it could be deadly.

I'll never forget the one incident that made me stop and take a serious look at myself. It was the first time in my young life that I began to search my soul over the direction in which my life was surely headed.

After classes ended one day, my homies Jeff, Moomoo, and I walked down the main hallway to our lockers. Coming to my locker first, I stopped and dialed the combination of my lock.

I put my books away, locked my locker, turned around, and found myself staring down the barrel of a .38-caliber pistol. I froze in terror.

I couldn't move or speak. Sleepy, a member of the Denver Lanes gang, held the gun inches from my forehead and I looked at his eyes pierced at me in anger, as if he were going to shoot me any minute. All I could see were his eyes, because he wore a deep-red kerchief, or bandana, that covered his mouth and lower face.

Moomoo and Jeff were nowhere to be seen. They'd both taken off when they saw Sleepy and another gangbanger approaching us.

For what seemed an eternity, we stood, no one moving, no one saying a word. Sleepy held the gun at my head and I stared breathlessly forward. Everything at that moment became frighteningly clear, all the way down to the bullets inside the cylinder of the gun.

Finally, and unexpectedly, Sleepy and his homie simply turned and walked away. It was over as suddenly as it had started.

All the way home, I nervously scanned the streets that I had to walk down, first in front and then behind me. My head never stopped turning. I walked as quickly as I could without breaking into a run. I breathed a sigh of relief when 87th Place finally came into view.

It wasn't until I was once again in the safety of my own home that the full impact of what had just happened hit me with the force of a jackhammer. It was strange, because even though I knew I was scared to death, during those few moments, I seemed to have gone into a kind of daze, where everything around me disappeared, and the barrel of the gun, the copper-colored rounds, and Sleepy's leering face were all I could see or think of. All sound stopped. It was as if I knew exactly what was taking place, yet, at the same time, I was helpless to change it. I didn't understand how it came to be that I was standing in my school hallway with a gun at my face.

Once in the safety of my own house, I made a conscious effort to keep from trembling. But then, right on cue, the thunder came. First, it pounded home the vision of a dead, bloated body floating in Manchester Park's swimming pool. Then, Uncle George's face appeared to me, his mouth and eyes wide open, staring at the ceiling.

It made me never want to carry or even own a gun.

At that moment, I decided never to join a gang.

Indeed, I drifted away from most contact with gang members. I couldn't forget how closely I'd come, within just the twitch of a trigger finger, to getting shot in the head—for no reason other than being in the wrong place at the wrong time, in the school hallway.

I saw how dangerous gangs could be, and I wanted nothing to do with them.

CHAPTER 6
THE NEXT ARTHUR ASHE

Around the time I became disenchanted with gangs, I started playing tennis. The timing was perfect.

My major interests before tennis centered on sports that I was too small to be good at—namely, football, basketball, and baseball.

Besides being threatened at gunpoint, some credit for my turning away from running on the streets of South Central as a full-fledged gangster, which no doubt would've ended in an early death or lengthy prison term, was my introduction to tennis by an instructor we called Doc. I might never have played had I not been open to an alternative sport.

I met Coach Richard Williams one weekend after 20 of us convened at Manchester Park to turn one of its four tennis courts into a roller rink. We emulated the Los Angeles Thunderbird roller-skating team, grab-assing in and out of the court's net, trying to tear it down. That was when Doc showed up with racquets and a large basket of tennis balls.

No one in the group had met Coach Williams before, although we'd seen him around Manchester. As it turned out, he was the one who introduced tennis to the park.

At first, we horsed around by throwing the balls at each other. Then Doc offered a dollar to anyone who could hit the ball over the net into a box he'd put there. Like a pack of wild animals, or just the young boys we were—the same homies who'd later become known as the "Freeway Boys"—we rushed to get ahead, yelling and declaring first position. Doc explained the object of the game and we tried to hit the ball.

It wasn't easy. The first balls sailed over the net and past the box, landing some 50 feet beyond the fence, which became the focus of our efforts. We hit ball after ball over the fence with forced grunts and wild laughter until we got bored and quit, much to Doc's visible displeasure.

By the time the day ended, we'd turned the racquets into hockey sticks and the balls into pucks as we played our own variation of tennis.

From what I could tell, tennis wasn't a sport played by tough young black boys. It wasn't physical like football. I looked at it as a game played by girls and rich white people.

Coach Williams introduced us to Doc, who held a position with the parks and recreation department and coached tennis at Manchester. My good buddies Larry, Tony, Robert, and Terry, however, not only started practicing with Doc, but they began receiving gifts of shoes, tennis suits, racquets, and wristbands. In no time, Robert was ranked number 14 in the state and Larry number 20 in their age groups. *The state of California*, I thought. I was impressed, so I signed on to play too under the guidance of Doc.

I worked hard at tennis, which I no longer considered just for girls, and slowly improved.

Robert, a 10th grader attending the magnet school Dorsey High, recommended I talk to Larry Smith, his tennis coach. If Robert, who was ranked statewide, thought I was a decent enough player, then maybe, just maybe, I'd finally found a sport I could excel at where size didn't matter. After school one day, I took Robert's advice and talked to Coach Smith.

Dorsey High was far west of Compton, in the posh West Los Angeles community just east of La Cienega and north of Martin Luther King Jr. Boulevard. The school was attached to Rancho La Cienega Park, made famous because at the time, rising black sports figures and film stars frequented it. Even though I wasn't familiar with Los Angeles that far west and had to catch two different city buses to get there, I was excited as I approached the gate to the park's tennis courts. Because Dorsey didn't have courts, the team used Rancho park's facilities for practice.

I quickly located Mr. Smith. We talked about the game, and just like that, he invited me to practice after school with the high-school team. I was elated! Here I was, not even out of junior high and shortly after finding a sport I could excel in, offered an opportunity to practice with a bona fide tennis team. I couldn't believe my luck. To make it even sweeter, another friend, as well as Robert, was already on the team.

The fact that Robert had spoken to Mr. Smith about my ability, before my meeting Coach, had to help. Still, the meeting with Coach Smith had gone well. Even so, it wasn't yet a done deal. I had three issues to address before I could accept the invitation to practice with the team.

The first was the bus fare. Supported by my mother's meager income, we were still relatively poor, although our house was much improved compared to our old home. The small allowances David and I got were for clothing, food, and school lunches. I was determined to practice with Dorsey's team three times per week, which was all my small allowance could accommodate.

The second issue was where I lived, which was in the district for Washington High, not Dorsey. It was suggested I use an address other than my home when the time came for me to enroll in high school.

An aunt lived in Dorsey's district and I knew it wouldn't be an issue with her for me to use her address as my place of residence. A few of my friends used addresses of relatives or friends to take advantage of Dorsey's better educational facilities, including, I was told, a superior teaching staff.

The third issue was the most difficult, not to mention distressing. Soon after my meeting with Mr. Smith, the reality hit me that I was failing horribly in all my academic classes. I did well only in shop and gym classes; they were my favorites, so I put a real effort into them. To make it onto the high school team, I had to get passing grades. While I sweated it out, my teachers continued to pass me.

While still in junior high, I began practicing with Dorsey High's tennis team whenever I could. I played well enough so that by the end of the 1974 school year, I believed my chances of becoming another great black tennis player, maybe as successful as Arthur Ashe, were good. I tried to convince myself that I didn't need an education or good grades to achieve that goal.

Because I'd passed my classes and had report cards to prove it, my mother rarely questioned me about school. She worked hard all day and often fell asleep watching TV after fixing dinner for my brother, sister, and me. She assumed I was doing well.

In June 1974, though I couldn't make sense of the written word, I was promoted from Bret Harte Junior High School.

It was surprising, since while at Bret Harte, my acting up in class had gotten so bad that I went to the principal's office on a regular basis. I was on the verge of suspension and knew my mother would kill me. See, my moms used to whip me with telephone cords, ironing cords, and belts. I thought she enjoyed leaving welts on us kids. I got hip to her game and wore two pair of pants so the whipping wouldn't leave welts. Even with all the trouble I caused in school, I still got along well with the kids. The teachers kept passing me along, from grade to grade, even though I wasn't doing the classroom work. How embarrassed I would have been had I flunked out of any of those grades.

I now had a junior-high diploma, though I'd done little to earn it. Three years of junior high and six years of elementary school, with a myriad of teachers, and I was still illiterate. Yet, all that mattered to me was that I played a better-than-average tennis game.

For me, Bret Harte Junior High hadn't lived up to its reputation as one of the toughest schools in L.A., other than a few initial scrapes after I first enrolled. To me, it was no more threatening than elementary school. While at Bret Harte Junior High, I'd gotten a pass—in other words, they left me alone—from the 92nd Hoover Street Crips.

Although the gang problem continued to rage increasingly throughout the city of Los Angeles, including in my neighborhood, my fear of them turned into nothing more than a passing thought. It was difficult to completely escape the growing gang problem in L.A., where not one neighborhood was immune from infestation. I had very few gang-affiliated friendships and I had no trouble avoiding the dangerous areas. It had become something I heard about on the news or when friends talked about it, rather than something I experienced. I wasn't part of it, and that's what mattered to me.

I was 14 years old with a diploma in my hand, on my way to a good high school, a possible tennis career, and a bright future—or so I thought.

CHAPTER 7
MEAL TICKETS

In September 1974, Robert, Larry, Tony, Terry, and I sat on a city bus headed to Dorsey High School, all attending at the behest of Coach Larry Smith and all using addresses of friends and relatives who lived in the district.

The first day of classes ended and the four of us hurried to our lockers, stashed our books and notebooks, then sprinted to the gym to change into our tennis clothes. It was our first official team practice of the school year.

Thanks to Doc, who continued working with me at Manchester Park when I wasn't practicing with Dorsey's team, I now had new tennis clothes and the best-quality gear, which he paid for. Having worked out with the team for months before school began, I already held the 10th position. To play on the varsity squad, though, I'd have to be in the ninth spot or lower, and the competition was tough. To earn the position, I needed to move up to varsity, and I knew it wouldn't be easy. My new friends and fellow players—Moss Cart, Louis Lane, Tony Wingo, Reggie Stanton, and Reggie Bass—were all excellent players.

That first practice was fierce as we battled for position on the team. It was exhilarating. On the bus ride home, we talked of nothing but who beat who, who was the better player, each other's faults and good points. Each of us, according to our own high opinions of ourselves, was well on his way to becoming the number-one ranked player in the league, and we'd yet to play even one league game. We were filled with the innocence and optimism of youth.

Classes at Dorsey High seemed identical to courses I'd taken at Bret Harte, with the exception of driver's education and wood shop. My lack of effort in academic classes remained unchanged.

Throughout 1975 and the 10th grade, my ability to grasp the rudiments of simple reading and writing slid to a new low, while my aptitude for tennis grew by leaps and bounds. Along with continuing instruction from Doc, I practiced as much as three hours a day with the school team and on my own. I was driven, as if all my unfulfilled desires were finally being fulfilled through tennis. It was like magic; I felt as if I'd been playing all my life. The game was a visible representation of an ability I'd always know I had. Tennis proved it.

I made no time for schoolwork, homework, parties, or even girls. Tennis was the focus of all my energies, consuming my free time. It became my life.

During the 10th grade at Dorsey, I played well enough to get as far as junior varsity, a step just below varsity, yet above B-level players. I became a dominant force on the JV squad and was soon allowed to play singles matches with the varsity team. With it, I developed a credible reputation with some of the team's top players. And Coach Richard Williams took an interest in me, spending time giving me tips.

High-school classes went a lot smoother for me with each year. I still cracked a joke from time to time, to try and get out of doing class work. Mostly I learned how to go through textbooks, recognize key words, and find the answers in the back. I copied the letters and words, even though I couldn't read everything they said. When I wasn't able to copy from the back of a book, I cheated off of students' papers by copying their words. At Dorsey, they ultimately put me in special education, and everyone in the class was embarrassed to be seen walking to and from the Special Ed building. We hurried in and out of that classroom hoping no one would notice. My tennis coach helped by nudging me along, not realizing it was actually setting me back. He talked to the teachers and told them the school needed me on the tennis team. The coach said, "Just give him a passing grade," and they did. I didn't cause any trouble for my teachers. I went to class, sat down, put my head on the desk, and fell asleep.

Though barely literate, I completed a driver's education class and got my license. Robert got his license too and, when his parents bought him a car, our bus rides to school ended. All of the money I would have used for bus fare, I began saving. For the very first time in my life, I had extra cash. I quickly discovered a lucrative way to invest my savings: meal tickets.

To qualify for meal tickets—vouchers paid for by the county that subsidized hot lunches prepared by the school cafeteria—your family had to live below the poverty level. At Bret Harte, it was considered a disgrace to use the "welfare tickets"—which they were called back then—and embarrassing if you were one of the poor unfortunates who had to out of necessity. Most students who attended Dorsey came from middle- or upper-middle-class families and didn't qualify the meal-ticket subsidy. So it seemed odd to me that students who were well-off financially desperately desired meal tickets, in part because the meals were better—with more variety and larger portions—than the standard cafeteria fare, plus it was considered cool to game the system. Whatever the reason, the tickets were a hot commodity, and I had access to them.

All I had to do was purchase tickets from Bret Harte underprivileged students. They were more than happy to get money for something they were ashamed to use, then I'd sell the tickets to those who could afford them, and I made a profit.

For the first time in my life, I was making money through a private enterprise.

Although my mom took good care of us—which now included my brother and three cousins, left behind when my Aunt Bobbi Jo passed away while I was in junior high—she had house payments and regular bills on top of feeding five children. There was very little money left over. Now, however, with my financial venture in full swing, I was rolling in pocket change. I'd never before experienced the feeling of financial independence and the happiness those few added nickels, dimes, and quarters afforded me. After buying all the sodas, pastries, and candy I could eat, I still had money left over to stash away. It was a good feeling.

At the end of 10th grade, our varsity squad was seeded number three in the city of Los Angeles and we were headed for the playoffs.

In the first round, we defeated Van Nuys High, a school in the top four. In a hard-fought game, Terry, our number-one varsity player, defeated Vance Van Patton, Van Nuys High's best player. Terry, to everyone's surprise, became an overnight star when local TV stations covered the game, with footage airing every hour, repeatedly, the following night. I remember being happy for Terry, watching him beam during interviews as if he'd just won a million dollars. I also remember feeling envious. At the same time, Terry was considered our best player and he deserved the media attention for getting the varsity squad through one of the toughest seasons they'd ever played.

Next came Birmingham High and once again, Terry saved Dorsey by defeating David Robinson, Birmingham's top player, in another tough game.

Although the varsity team had done exceptionally well in the first two rounds, they were soundly defeated in the third round of play by Palisades High, a game that marked the end of the season.

Junior varsity hadn't done as well and didn't make the playoffs, but we shared in the success of the varsity squad. Because I'd never before played organized sports, other than in neighborhood vacant lots, I didn't know how to take the defeat. I was crushed, but even more determined to return the next year and earn a position on the varsity squad to help the team take the championship.

Just as it had been in junior high and grade school, the teachers passed me on to the 11th grade without so much as a whisper of concern about my obvious lack of academic skills. I was surprised, since Dorsey was such a better school. Still, with each passing year, I felt more hopeless, even lost. It was no easy feat to get through the harder classes without knowing how to read and write.

No one seemed to care.

———————◆◆◆———————

The summer of 1976 was one to remember.

The areas surrounding Rancho Park in Westside Los Angeles, where I practiced with the team, were high-end, with the Wilshire District and Westwood, View Park, Baldwin Hills, and Beverly Hills all within a few minutes' drive. Even as far east as Main Street were mostly middle- to lower-middle-class-income neighborhoods where the homes, streets, parks, and surrounding neighborhoods represented one of Los Angeles's better mix of a well-kept, decent community that was safe.

During the early to late '70s, before black youth gangs infiltrated the Westside, making it dangerous and all but unlivable, many rising black stars from all walks of entertainment and sports frequented Rancho Park. With its immaculately manicured grass and greenery, the park covered an area on the outskirts of the Crenshaw District at least five square miles and provided its users, in both equipment and facilities, a wide range of physical-fitness and health-related choices. With its indoor, Olympic-size, heated, swimming pool, green tennis courts, and miles of all-weather grass, the Grade-A Rancho Park drew a continuous string of black celebrities.

Jim Kelly, a rising martial-arts movie star, who also had a dojo—a small martial arts studio—on Crenshaw Boulevard, was a frequent visitor to the famous park. Tennis legend Arthur Ashe also worked out there. Bill Cosby, a TV and film star by then, was known to use Rancho's tennis courts. But it was Kelly, the young black Kempo Karate expert, who Larry and I met at Rancho.

Often, Jim went to the park to jog or play tennis. One day he noticed Larry and me practicing tennis. He introduced himself, said he was impressed with our abilities, and asked if we'd like to hit a few balls with him.

Larry and I knew exactly who he was before he introduced himself. What teenager during the early 1970s martial-arts craze didn't know the name Jim Kelly from his movies? We were excited just to meet him, let alone play tennis with him. With a grin that spread all over my face, I shouted, probably too loudly, "Sure!"

From that day on, I knew tennis was for me. If someone like Jim Kelly played, then it was the right thing to do.

To our delight, after a few practice sessions, Kelly began commenting on how much better players Larry and I were compared to other partners he'd practiced with and how much he enjoyed playing with us. We soon became friends.

I vividly remember when Jim got his first Porsche 911. It was black on black, and it was fast.

One day, he gave Larry and me a ride home from the park, so we crammed inside the small car. I'd never been in a Porsche before; it was thrilling as he drove fast. I was out of breath with excitement, but a little worried all the way home; I just knew the police were going to stop us for speeding. They never did. I was brimming over with glee the remainder of that day. I kept thinking, *Man, what a car.* No one on my block who saw us that day even knew what kind of car it was. They're never seen one before. And they couldn't believe it was Jim Kelly driving.

After that day, Larry and I were considered cool. All told, my first year of high school, I'd been associated with a team that came close to winning the city championship and I'd met a real-life movie star and karate expert who drove a Porsche. Life was wonderful and it had all come about because of the game of tennis.

————◆————

During my junior year, once again the varsity team made it to the playoffs. Although we failed to win the championship in a repeat of the previous year, we managed to deliver a crushing defeat to Hollywood High, whose team at that time was mostly white and considered one of the best. Our team, not expected to do well against them, scored a 7-0 victory, dispelling the tournament and media hype over the Los Angeles School District's prima-donna team.

During the playoffs that year, I met Norman Tillman, one of the few black guys who at the time played for Hollywood High. Everybody thought Hollywood High would not only beat Dorsey but any other team, with little effort. When we destroyed Hollywood, with Norm on their team, we found it oddly funny that Norman appeared to share in our victory excitement with just as much verbal enthusiasm as the rest of our team.

By the end of the school year, Norman and I were friends. I later learned that not only did he live in South Central, but his brother was a Hoover Crip and a member of one of the most recently organized factions of the Crip gang.

Norman told me, "Dorsey whooped us." So he went to Coach Smith and told him, "I wanna go to your school." For his senior year, Norman transferred schools and played for Dorsey instead of Hollywood High.

During my senior year at Dorsey, I finally made the singles varsity team. Things were going well until disaster struck during playoffs when we were soundly beaten by Birmingham High, a white high school in a wealthy suburb of the L.A. Valley just off the coast. I couldn't wrap my head around how we'd just lost to a team we'd beaten earlier in the year. To make matters worse, it happened in the first round of play, before my match came around.

I was devastated.

I no longer wanted to go to school. It was close to the end of senior year and I was determined not to continue. But I didn't stop attending, even though I wanted to, and I didn't tell my mother about it.

The final decision came soon after my conversation with a Long Beach State University tennis coach, who'd invited me to his campus to talk after he saw me play a match earlier in the season with a guy who was ranked number three citywide.

The conversation moved along fine until I shared with him the secret I'd kept from so many people.

"Son, what do you think you'd like to major in?" Coach asked me.

"I don't know."

"Well, what do you like to study? What are you good at?"

"I'm good at math," I answered, before I dropped the bombshell. "But I can't really read or write. It's been a problem for a while."

I'll never forget how strangely the coach looked at me. It was as if I suddenly smelled badly.

Coach was quiet for a few seconds, then he said, "There is no way you can attend Long Beach State."

From his words and his burrowed forehead and squinted eyes, my illiteracy seemed like the most distasteful thing he'd ever heard.

I felt terrible, like a loser. Tennis had offered me a promising future and with Coach's few words, it was over, and with it, my dream of being a pro tennis player.

To make matters worse, my illiteracy spread like wildfire and all at Dorsey High soon knew what I'd told Coach. Kids who didn't even go to Dorsey had heard it.

The final blow was when Richard Williams embarrassed me, although not intentionally, to the point of tears welling up in my eyes when he handed me a newspaper on the tennis court and pointed out an article he wanted me to read. I couldn't do it, of course, and it was in front of a group of classmates, so I felt humiliated.

At that very moment, school was over for me. Just before the end of my senior year and not long before graduation, I dropped out of high school.

CHAPTER 8
PARTY SUMMER

It was the summer of 1978, I was 18 and a high-school dropout. I didn't tell my mother right away. When I finally came clean, she didn't take the news well. To her, I was a bum—no school, no job, no prospects for the future.

I couldn't understand where I'd gone wrong. I'd been hitting balls at Rancho with Lawrence "Cornbread" King, a tennis star ranked number two in the U.S. for the National Parks. He was a fellow dropout, because he, too, hadn't done well in school, yet he went on to become a successful player; all that reinforced my belief that I could do the same. If someone as talented as Lawrence King had asked me to volley balls with him, I was sure I had some talent and was on my way. It turned out to be the opposite and I slipped into a depression.

I soon fell back into hanging out with my homies Ollie Newell, Wayne, Bruce Dog, and my cousin Tootie, who spent the majority of their time smoking weed, drinking beer, and low-riding. They each drove '66 Chevys that were lifted, custom-painted with big hubs, the works. I still practiced tennis, occasionally hitting balls at the courts.

Norman Tillman came back around that summer to invite me to work out again at the park. He hadn't seen me for a while and wondered if I'd stopped playing.

"I haven't stopped playing completely," I told him. "I'll work out with you."

For a short while, we practiced together. Norman's free time was divided between intramural games, practicing tennis with me, and going out with his girlfriend. As for me, I still hadn't developed any real interest in girls.

Then the summer got crazy. My mother announced that she was going to Texas and asked if my cousins or I wanted to go along. She said we'd be gone for about two months. No one wanted to go. We didn't want to leave L.A. We knew it would be fun to have the house all to ourselves. She was okay with it. She packed her bags, made sure the refrigerator was stocked, gave my cousins and me some money, and left for Texas.

As soon as she walked out the door, it was party time! We had the entire house to ourselves, all the food in the refrigerator we wanted, and nothing but free time on our hands. The only things missing were girls and beer.

Girls? No problem. My cousins and friends knew plenty of girls who would love to attend a house party.

Beer? Different story. We were underage. But we knew how to get it. And though we could put our money together and buy enough beer for a few parties, no one wanted to spend their cash on beer for other people to drink. So, we used our own system to get it.

At Thrifty, a combination appliance, drug, and grocery store on the corner of 87th and Broadway, they sold everything from bread and Pepto-Bismol, to TVs and fishing tackle.

Whenever one of us wanted something free, we put 10 to 15 guys together and piled into the store all at once. One guy broke away from the group and slunk around, wandering from aisle to aisle pretending to be watching the camera, like he was casing the place. While the manager kept watch on him, the rest of us grabbed cases of beer, bottles of wine, and bags of potato chips and ran out the door. We usually laughed so hard, it was difficult to run. We got so good at it that we moved to the Safeway store at the corner of Manchester and Hoover and experimented with our new system.

This one was as simple as it got. One homie grabbed a shopping cart, put an open, empty grocery bag inside, and walked through the store filling the bag. Aisle by aisle, he loaded up with meat, bread, cereal, milk doughnuts, and chips. Then he picked up the bag and walked out the door as if he'd paid for the groceries. No one noticed. It was as if this tall, skinny, black teenager were a ghost, pushing a shopping cart through the store and loading up a bag—the oldest trick in the book. It was so successful, we expanded to other supermarkets in the neighborhood. No one ever got caught.

For two months, we partied and raided the markets like we had a license to do whatever we wanted. Sometimes after all-night parties, people were so exhausted from dancing, drunk from drinking beer and wine, and zoned out from smoking marijuana that they'd crash in the garage or outside behind the house. That was where the party started up again the next day. Occasionally, someone might drift home. Otherwise, they stayed the whole summer.

Even though I'd dropped out of school and had no plans for the future, with the homies, it didn't matter. I was somebody. My homeboys would have done anything for me, and I would have done the same for them.

Then, my mother came home from Texas and the summer of 1978 ended.

Mom was on me hard. Everyone else—my homeboy Ollie and my cousins Tootie and Kevin—were getting ready to go back to school. Not me. I had nothing going on—until I heard about a community college that offered adult-education vocational classes.

When he learned that I'd dropped out of high school, Mr. Dan Foster, an auto-upholstery instructor I met while playing tennis at Rancho Park, recommended that I learn a skill. He suggested attending the college where he taught auto upholstering.

After thinking about it, especially since Mr. Foster said I could be paid for going, I decided to check it out. Because low-riding was growing in popularity and, with it, customized auto interiors, I thought auto upholstery might be a good skill to learn.

I applied for and received a grant from the Education Equal Opportunity Group and in September 1979, I enrolled at Los Angeles Trade Technical College.

Trade Tech was a medium-size junior college located on the outskirts of downtown Los Angeles, between Figueroa and Flower avenues just south of Washington Boulevard. It was a well-known, long-established, two-year college attended by a wide range of students of different ethnic backgrounds. It offered a variety of trade and university-prep classes.

Norman Tillman had also enrolled at Trade Tech, and I learned that Lawrence "Cornbread" King had gone to the school as well. Best of all, Trade Tech had an excellent tennis team. Eventually, Norman and I started playing together again and we both made the squad.

Rather than take up auto upholstery, I instead decided, for no particular reason, to take bookbinding classes. Soon, I was chipping away at a trade I hadn't even known existed.

Trade Tech was much more exciting than junior high and high school. Besides playing tennis and competing with a much more advanced and better all-around group of players, I couldn't get over the freedom of movement a college campus offered.

In addition, an almost palpable joy came from the students, like they thoroughly enjoyed school. Excited laughter filled the hallways; friendly students offered help when classmates needed it. Maybe it was their desire to learn, especially since they were there by choice. Whatever it was, it produced in me a warmth I'd never before associated with school. I began to like attending classes and developed a genuine interest in learning. I took one course a semester and played tennis on the school's courts.

It didn't matter to my mother what classes I took; she was just happy I was in school again. I was, indeed, in school, and this time it was at the college level. And I still could barely read or write.

A few months into the school year, I met a girl named Marco. It was the first time I'd had a real interest in the opposite sex, mostly because I'd always been self-conscious about the way I looked. Despite trying to convince myself that it didn't matter, I had a feeling my height did matter. Or maybe, I thought, I was even ugly.

Marco played on the girls' tennis team and I hung around in a semi-secluded area, close enough to see every detail of her, yet far enough away that I couldn't be detected. She had short hair, cocoa-brown skin, an athletic body, and a friendly personality. I wanted to run to her whenever I saw her and tell her of the strong feelings I had for her. I was mesmerized by her and unable—almost fearful, even— to act on my feelings. My insecurities about my appearance and inexperience in talking to girls prevented me from saying anything more than casual, meaningless phrases friends say in passing.

Soon, though, I got a little further with her. We started practicing together and had fun. Sometimes she gave me a ride home after school, because she lived in South Central too. My eyes were set on Marco.

I was the only one among my friends and family who didn't have a girlfriend. My brother had one; my cousins had them. I wanted at least to be able to say I had a steady girl. That would make me look cool—or so I thought at the time.

To my utter disappointment, I learned from one of my friends that the girl of my dreams was a lesbian.

That ended my first love affair, albeit one-sided, and, about the same time, the school year.

— • ◆ • —

The second year at Trade Tech was a repeat of the first. Once tennis season ended, I stopped going to classes and drifted back to hanging around in the 'hood with my homeboys, doing absolutely nothing. My college experience ended as abruptly as it had started.

With the summer of 1980 in full swing, I found a brand-new love: hanging out at carhops.

Carhops were get-togethers—at a park, a hamburger stand, or a large parking lot—with low-riders who partied through the night. There were low-riders from Los Angeles, Compton, Pasadena, and the San Fernando Valley with cars of all makes, but predominantly Chevys, Fords, Buicks, and trucks. Some had lifts, others didn't, but they were all decked out, including with women: tall women, short women, beautiful women, and not-so-beautiful women. Some were loud; others were quiet. Some had long hair; some had short hair. Many wore short skirts whether their thighs were thick, skinny, long or short, dark or light. Low-riding and women went hand in hand, both equally exciting, beautiful, and freaky. Along with flaunting cars came a never-ending flow of drugs, hard alcohol, beer, and what I imagined to be sex.

Carhops were the thing to do, and they soon became my thing.

Before my introduction to carhops, girls didn't seem interested in me and I was too shy to reach out to them. If the male juices had been dormant up to then, with so many wonderful, sexy, scantily clad girls gathered in one place, my luck was about to change. Young women were now irresistible and within reach.

I forgot all about playing tennis or attending school. All I wanted was a girl of my own. Other than one who wore short skirts and lovely perfume, it didn't matter what she looked like. Man, I didn't care. I just had to have a girlfriend.

CHAPTER 9
'66 CHEVY CONVERTIBLE

To say I was inexperienced when it came to women was an understatement. Truth was, I had *no* experience.

After hanging out at carhops and Church's Chicken, I came to realize that to get a girl—the type who kicked it with low-riders at the carhops, anyway—I needed a car. That was the ticket.

At carhops, I saw some of the finest women with the ugliest niggas. When I spied a beautiful girl with a tight-rounded butt, creamy complexion, and thick thighs hanging out with a dirty, big, hulk-looking guy, I wondered how in the world that could have happened. It didn't take long to figure out why: It was his car.

For a while, my insecurities about my physical appearance were forgotten and I'd say to myself, *If someone that ugly, trampy, or stupid can get a girl, then so can I.* Once I realized it had nothing to do with me as a person, I focused on acquiring my ticket.

The automobiles at carhops were seductive. The pretty paint sparkled like diamonds whenever they were under electric lights. The low-riders' favorite songs pumped out through pricey stereo systems while they sat in the comfortable interiors, upholstered in luxurious custom-fit mohair, velvet, and velour. The excitement of 2,000 pounds of metal and gold—and chrome-laced rims on rubber tires bouncing as high as three feet at the touch of a switch—was alluring, not to mention the view of the moon through the sunroof. Now that I'd learned the secret to getting women—at least I believed

I had—I was determined to land one. The only problem was, I didn't have a dime to my name.

That didn't stop me from getting a car. I soon located a wrecked '66 convertible Chevy at a Long Beach junkyard. The car didn't have an engine or transmission and it had a big dent in the quarter panel on one side.

With $100 I earned helping pimps on Figueroa by watching the backs of their hookers while they turned tricks at sleazy motels, I bought the junker and talked the yard into towing it to my house. My mother couldn't believe I paid a hundred dollars for a worthless heap of metal. She told me I needed my head examined for being so stupid, and that I had to keep it on the side street so she wouldn't be embarrassed by it. It didn't matter to me. I was sure, with hard work and some cash, I could fix it up and get me a girl.

When I began putting new life back into the shell of my '66 convertible, I knew nothing about cars. I had the help of my friend Ollie, who worked at Downtown LA Motors. In addition, the same young blacks who'd grown up in the 'hood and used to be gangbangers and car thieves were now auto mechanics, electricians, and auto-body workers; some ran chop shops full of stolen car parts. In no time at all, my shell of a car had an excellent running engine, a partial dashboard, a red front, and one black and one blue door. It looked like a car that had been stolen, stripped, and left on the street to rot, but it was slowly coming to life. Better yet, I'd become knowledgeable in auto mechanics, not only doing much of the repairs on my own car, but also helping others while they worked on theirs. Best of all, my future as a low-riding ladies' man was about to begin.

When I got my '66 to the point of being drivable, it was time to get it juiced.

Getting a car juiced, lifted, and hopping was an exciting part of low-riding. When the opportunity came to get my own car lifted, I wanted the works. But hydraulics—or lifts as they were commonly called—was an altogether different science than auto repair. Attaching cylinders shared with hydraulic fluid to the A-arms of an automobile's front axle, cutting out, and reinforcing the frame in the rear, and setting up pressure pumps required an expert, and I wasn't even close to being one.

The man for the job, Athen Nelson, was not only the foremost expert in hydraulic-lift installation, but also the guy to see if you needed a quick laugh.

Athen was a chronic drunk, and both his makeshift auto shop at 64th and Central and the old '57 Chevy sitting in front were ramshackle—visible proof of the man's love for the bottle. For $25 and a case of beer, Athen would cut you out, construct, and weld your gates inside the trunk, then install the cylinders and batteries, all in one day. He could cut out as many as three cars a day—if he stayed sober. If he didn't, he was also known for the destruction he'd cause with the same expert efficiency.

Despite his eccentricities, Athen Nelson was a decent guy—short, skinny, black as night, 120 pounds soaking wet, and gut-busting funny. Everyone I knew who had anything to do with low-riding hung out at his house.

During 1981, the year of my introduction to low-riding and women, Athen and I spent a lot of time together.

One day while Ollie and I were at Athen's, an incident broke out that once again took me back to my days at Bret Harte Junior High and memories of my worst experiences with gangs.

Ollie and I were at Athen's kickin' it with him as he worked. Ollie had been working at Downtown LA Motors for some time, making good money. He'd spent $400 for a set of sparkling rims.

Both Ollie's and my cars were parked at Athen's house. Also at Athen's that day were my cousin Evita's boyfriend Donnie Young, a member of the Imperial Court, or PJ Crips, and a handful of other friends from around the 'hood, plus Jake Clayton, a member of the 62nd Street crew, which was a new gang formed from older and former Crips members.

Jake was responsible for coming up with my nickname "Freeway Rick," a takeoff on the name "Junkyard Freeway Boys" that he'd given to Ollie, Wayne, me, and the other guys who lived in my neighborhood near the Harbor Freeway. He was a car and parts thief who was looking to take Ollie's car away from him.

One minute everyone was standing around on the driveway talking shit and listening to Athen crack on one of the guys. The next thing we knew, Jake was pointing a gun at Ollie.

"Nigga, I'm taking that fucking car!"

Ollie and the rest of us in the driveway stood shocked, looking at Jake like he was crazy and about to shoot us all. It was like we were total strangers to Jake and he was holding us up. Everybody froze. I was afraid to move, unsure if Jake was serious.

"Whatcha doin', Jake?" Ollie asked. "Man, you actin' crazy. Whatcha mean you takin' ma car? Why you got yo gun on me?"

"That's right, muthafucka! I'm takin' yo fuckin' car. Gi' me da fuckin' keys, fool." And he reached out his other hand in an attempt to grab Ollie.

Before Jake could grab him, Donnie was all over Jake.

Everybody in the driveway, except me, dove for cover as Jake and Donnie wrestled over the gun. I stood paralyzed, unable to do anything, except hope the gun wouldn't go off and accidentally kill me.

Benches turned over and tools clanged to the ground as the two struggled. After what seemed like an eternity—in reality, it couldn't have been longer than 15 seconds—Donnie beat the shit out of Jake. The gun ripped out of Jake's hand and slid three feet away.

With the gun now out of Jake's hand and no one in danger of being shot, the guys rushed Donnie and Jake, breaking them apart.

Then Donnie yelled, "If you ever pull a gun on Ollie again, I'll kill you. You want a rim, get one from somebody else, nigga!"

Athen also screamed at Jake: "You trippin', nigga! Don't pull no gun on nobody in ma place again. Get the fuck outta here!"

"I was just playin'," Jake said, offering a lame apology.

After everyone calmed down, Jake left without saying a word.

I remember thinking, *Goddamn, I coulda been killed, and that crazy muthafucka was just playin'? Playin' with a loaded gun. Anyone in the room could have died just like that, over nothin'.*

It reminded me of that day at Bret Harte Junior High School when Sleepy from the Denver Lanes pulled a gun on me. Even though I wasn't directly involved—just in the wrong place at the wrong time—it scared me to death, because it happened so quickly, before I had a chance to get out of there. I couldn't even say how it all began. Sleepy had smiled as if he were just playing that day too, simply putting the gun back to his waist band and walking away, like it was no big thing. It was another close call.

Not long after, we were at Athen's shop kickin' it in the driveway when Donnie spotted Jake Clayton cruising by. Donnie, who was still jacked up over Jake holding a gun on Ollie, pulled his pistol and opened fire on Jake's car.

It was dumb luck that Donnie didn't hit Jake or an innocent bystander, because the police arrested *me* for it. I was the leader of the Freeway Boys, they said, so the cops attached my name to the shooting and arrested me for assault with a deadly weapon, even though I had nothing to do with it. I was in jail 72 hours, they released me without charging me, and then they arrested me again a while later for the same thing, saying they had new evidence. The district attorney eventually dropped it from a felony to a misdemeanor charge. At the preliminary hearing, Jake Clayton, who was named as the victim, didn't show up, plus I wasn't the shooter, and everybody knew it, so the D.A. dropped the case and I beat the charge.

Whenever I saw Jake on the street, I wondered whether he was serious about stealing Ollie's rim that day or if he was just playin' that day.

With my car coming along, I looked forward to the carhops at Church's Chicken with the same enthusiasm I'd once held for tennis. Besides hanging out on the street with my homeboys, the carhops pretty much represented the full extent of my social life.

My mother was still all over me, constantly encouraging me to find positive activities to get involved in. Because of the not-always-legal nature of Athen's shop, I hadn't told her about my time at his garage. She was under the impression that when I stopped attending Trade Tech, I hadn't developed skills that would lead to a job. She was right. While I wanted to earn money, I didn't have the skills to go out and find a decent job.

Still, I no longer thought of Cornbread, Jim Kelly, Arthur Ashe, and tennis. I no longer worried that I could barely read or write. My new fascination—carhops—was what occupied my time.

With nowhere to go, no one special to go with, and no money for gas to get there, I wound up at Church's Chicken on Vermont and Century at least three times a week for a carhop. Most of the time Ollie, Wayne, Bill, and I went together. We parked our cars around the corner; they were still an embarrassment compared to the elaborately painted, expensively customized, and sophisticatedly equipped show cars at the carhops.

The guys at the carhops included "White Boy Eric," a light-skinned black with a '64 Chevy Impala, which was the cleanest. White Boy Eric became my idol. He was what we called a "jumper," a guy who competed at carhops in interior design, paint jobs, and hopping contests with low-riders from other areas of the city.

Then there were the Parker Boys, a group of brothers whose customized cars were the favorites to challenge White Boy Eric.

The girls, who were crazy over the cars, served as judges at the competitions.

One event that was popular but was also dangerous was "flashing." While hauling down the street, the driver dumped the lift switch, lowering the car to the ground, so that it scraped a piece of angle iron welded to the underside of the car. The scrape bar caused a rooster tail of red, white, blue, and orange sparks to shoot out high into the air. Sometimes the sparks ignited the exhaust from the car's tailpipe, causing flames and making it look like the car was on fire. The kids would holler and yell for more stunts.

While watching the flashing and hopping, we talked shit, drank 40-ounce bottles of Schlitz malt-liquor beer, and smoked weed with radios blasting from the cars in the parking lot. Barring fights and shootings between rival car clubs or gangs, the carhops lasted into the night until local cops showed up. It was usually the Los Angeles County Sheriff's Department, which oversaw South Central, who'd surround Church's Chicken, ordering everyone to disburse. That didn't usually happen until the early morning hours, around 2:30 or 3 o'clock. The hundreds of rowdy low-riders and spectators would leave Church's in a caravan and head to another popular spot. The caravans, at times stretching as far as a mile from the lead car to the last, were as thrilling to be a part of as the carhops themselves. After lowering the rear ends to within inches of the ground and raising the front ends, that's when rear ends bounced. Rolling down the boulevard, the chrome—and gold-plated rims and spokes looked like the Mardi Gras of cars.

A favorite spot to move the carhops to after leaving Church's was the Burger King just off the corner of Crenshaw and Jefferson. It was a block outside the Los Angeles County Sheriff's Department's jurisdiction and within the Los Angeles Police Department's territory. Even though the majority of young blacks I associated considered the LAPD as prejudiced toward blacks—low-riders, in particular—the LAPD was better than the Sheriff's Department, which had a well-publicized history of beating and sometimes killing blacks within their patrol area.

And so it went. Ollie and I hung out more and more at the carhops. My '66 had a long ways to go before it qualified as a low-rider. And a girlfriend seemed just as far out of reach. Soon, though, that would change.

About this time, I started going to church with my mother. I don't know why. Perhaps it was born from inner turmoil. Or I felt guilty for having turned to a life of crime. Or maybe it was the anxiety of being charged with auto theft and not knowing if I was going to jail or not, even though the case was ultimately dismissed for lack of evidence. Whatever the reason, I wanted to do the right thing. I was determined to try, so I turned to the church.

My mother's church of choice was a converted neighborhood market at the corner of 92nd and Western on Los Angeles's Westside. It was a small brick building painted white with the name "Thompson Memorial" stenciled in black above an unevenly drawn cross. The church, I felt, was in sorry shape even for an underfunded place of worship.

But that little makeshift church was also where I met Sharon. Talking to her alone at church was difficult, because people were always around, but I pursued her anyway. Sharon became my passion.

To my surprise, we hit it off. I'd almost given up on girls being interested in me, let alone one like Sharon, this beautiful young girl who looked to be straight out of a fairy tale. We not only talked at every available opportunity, but I started sneaking over to her house when her mother was at work.

Sharon lived on 47th Street. I hopped on my 10-speed bicycle and made it to her front door in 15 minutes, tops. Each evening, from around four until nine, just before Sharon's mother got home, we spent hours together, hugging, kissing, and groping. I was convinced that luck had finally come my way. Sharon, the young woman of my dreams, was my girlfriend.

I started picking up cash by working in a chop shop, because of my homie Dirty Benny. The nickname barely scratched the surface of how unkempt he was. Not only was Dirty Benny's raggedy clothing always soiled and stinking, but also even his black skin appeared to be covered with a layer of grease and dust.

Dirty Benny, nevertheless, was more than the caricature of a greaser. He was the best car thief in the city and the best at using an acetylene torch to chop cars in his shop.

One day, TQ, another homeboy, called and asked me to go to Benny's shop.

When I got there, TQ asked if I'd like to make $50.

I didn't have a job and was desperate for some cash. I wanted to restore my car, so I was more than willing to do just about anything that was required, just as long as it wasn't too crazy.

"Yeah, I'll work for fifty dollars," I told TQ. "What do I have to do?"

"Drive a stolen car to Benny's shop."

I thought, *Why not? I need the money.* "I'll do it," I told TQ.

That was that. I was enlisted into participating in an auto theft, and I was ecstatic. All I had to do was drive. *Man!* I said to myself, *This is your lucky day.* I was in, and I was lovin' it.

Aspirations to become the Arthur Ashe of my own generation, to play professional tennis, were forever dashed in exchange for the opportunity to make $50 and become a car thief.

That same night, I found myself in a Westside Los Angeles neighborhood at about 2 in the morning playing lookout while Dirty Benny used a snatch bar to break into the Seville so TQ could use the front end for parts.

Within minutes, I was driving down the street in a stolen Seville. I admit, I was a little nervous. It was as if all eyes were on me as I drove the car down the street. I kept looking around expecting any second to see the police coming for me with their sirens blaring, lights flashing, and guns drawn, just like on TV shows. It didn't happen. After I'd driven the car several blocks, I settled down and concentrated on getting to Benny's chop shop on Hooper. In no time at all, I turned into Benny's driveway. The garage door slammed behind me, sealing off noise from the street and locking out anyone from going in.

I was elated. My introduction to auto theft went without a hitch. It had taken no more than 10 minutes to locate the car, start it, and drive off. It was the easiest $50 I ever made, and certainly the quickest.

No sooner had I gotten out of the car than Benny, dressed for the job in his standard dirty grease-monkey jumpsuit, put on his welder's hood, fired up his torch, and got to work cutting off the front end of the Caddy.

In less than 45 minutes, and much to my amazement, the front end of the car sat on the concrete floor next to what had once been a top-of-the-line luxury car. It was almost surreal, observing this black man, covered in grease with just the whites of his eyes showing, quickly and expertly dismantle the body of a Cadillac.

While I watched Benny eviscerate the once-elegantly crafted machine, I was entranced by the process and hypnotized by his surgeon-like aptitude. Pulling that off was a serious offense. And I knew that what I'd done was a crime. But having money in my pocket made it easier for me to overlook that important detail.

Later that morning, at home, I told my homies about the theft and showed them the $50 I'd earned. Both Ollie "Big Loc" Newell and my cousin Tootie—who I referred to as my brother—said it was cool.

That made me feel better, and I soon forgot my earlier apprehension and feelings of guilt. I was now a bona fide car thief, and there was no looking back.

The next night, Dirty Benny, his homie Jumping Jake, and I were back at it.

Some guy from Bakersfield had paid Dirty Benny $300 per stolen car, and Benny asked if I wanted to help—with the promise of $100 per car as my pay.

For two months, Benny, Jumping Jake, and I stole just about every make of luxury, sedan, compact, and sports cars ever manufactured. The anonymous buyers phoned in their orders to Benny, then together or individually, the members of our trio located the car and planned a night—the majority of thefts were made during the early morning hours, when most working people were asleep. We drove the cars to Benny's, where they were either parted out or delivered whole, depending on how or what the buyer wanted. It was a simple yet efficient system. I made good money and learned more about dismantling cars than I could have learned in any school.

Not long after that, Dirty Benny was busted for theft—GTA, or grand theft auto, to be exact—and his previous parole was revoked. He was sent back to prison.

Without knowing whether he had relatives and no word from Benny himself about what to do with his shop, I simply moved in and took over. I enlisted a number of my homeboys and began teaching them exactly what I had been taught just months earlier. It was not long before I had a fresh crew of eager young car thieves and cut-up men. We grew with the absence of Dirty Benny, and, under my management, we abandoned Dirty Benny's place and I opened the first chop shop of my own.

My place was an old garage on 66th and Vermont; I paid $500 a month in rent. As for the equipment we needed, I used Dirty Benny's tools, as he wouldn't be needing them for a while. I heard out on the street that he'd gotten one year for grand-theft auto added to the time he was sure to get for violating parole, which had not been determined yet. I didn't think he'd mind.

The shop flourished and I was once again making good money. My '66 Chevy was looking good. I still didn't have a girlfriend, but that was all right too; I kept busy.

Everything ran smoothly for six months until one night, as two guys in the crew stripped a '79 Pontiac Grand Prix, the heart-stopping sound of a police helicopter hovering overhead brought us to attention. Instantaneously, our movements were instinctive, automatic. In a flash, I ran to the front of the shop and peered through the window, afraid of what I knew I would see, yet too afraid not to look. I froze. Police were swarming the place. I could see them grab Donnie, my cousin Evita's boyfriend, who'd pulled his car up to the shop a couple minutes before the police pounced on him.

Breaking from my temporary stupor, I spun around.

"We gotta get outta here," I yelled.

With the police already inside the yard at the front of the shop, we needed to be quick. The homies dropped their tools and broke for the back door. I was sure they'd make a quick getaway.

I sprinted for a side door leading out of the shop yard and into the neighborhood.

As I left, I heard the noise officers made as they tore through the shop yard, knocking car parts to the ground and cursing loudly as they stumbled over debris. Under the threat of jail and feeling confident my two homeboys had made it out, I ran as hard as I could, thinking I was increasing the distance between my freedom and the Los Angeles County Jail.

I headed down the center of the street, ducking behind parked cars, dodging through front yards, and jumping small hedges. Then, the very words I feared rang out over the police radio: "There he goes!"

Those three words conjured a new burst of speed from me. The cool night air washed over my perspiring body. I heard the sound of my own footsteps, my own labored breathing, loud and exaggeratedly clear. I chanced a look behind me.

Police were everywhere.

I turned back, feeling like a caged mouse with no escape. I ran and ran and ran, not paying attention to where I was headed. The police helicopter was directly above me, tracking my every step while unrelenting police officers chased me on foot. Finally, after what felt like an eternity, but was probably not more than 10 minutes, I was too exhausted to take another step. I collapsed face down on the damp lawn of someone's yard and lay completely still, waiting for police to grab me.

One of the officers caught up and stopped just to one side of me, raised his foot and planted it on the back of my neck. More cops arrived. I was cuffed and then tossed into the back seat of a black-and-white squad car.

I sat inside the car as the cops, now a group of five or six, stood talking 10 feet away. Eventually, one of the officers came over to the car, got in, turned on the ignition, pulled onto the street, and drove right past my shop.

We continued down Vermont, and the cop turned the corner onto 65th Street. Just as I wondered where he was taking me, he stopped at a large group standing in the street as a number of other officers and units gathered around an old black woman. One officer talked to her as he wrote on a notepad. The cop stepped out of the car and left me cuffed in the backseat. After a little while, an officer and the woman walked up to the back passenger door.

The officer pointed his flashlight through the window at my face. "Is this one of the guys?" he asked the woman.

The old woman stared down at me for a few moments, studying my face. She paused, turned back to the officer, and said, "No, that's not him."

By then, I figured my two homies working on the car with me had gotten away. The cop who'd earlier had his foot on my neck walked back to the rear passenger door, leaned down, stuck his head in the window, and started questioning me.

"Why were you running?" he asked.

I didn't answer.

Then, over the radio, I heard a voice say, "He came out of that shop."

My heart sank. It had to be the helicopter pilot talking. Before that, I honestly thought they'd let me go. Now, they'd surely check it out, and that would be the end for me. *I am on my way to jail for sure now,* I thought. All I could think of was the next stop, the Seventy-seventh Division Police Station.

That's exactly what happened. Within an hour, I was handcuffed to a bench inside the station and grilled. As hard as I'd prayed for a different outcome, the questions all had to do with the activities going on at my shop.

"What were you doing at the shop?" one big redneck cop, whose shirt looked like it was three sizes too small for him, kept asking.

"Nothin'," I repeated. I didn't tell him I was the owner of the business.

After about a half-hour of this, the officer left me handcuffed to the bench, where I remained for what felt like hours. I couldn't see a clock. I was tired and uncomfortable, and I lost all track of time.

When the officer finally returned, he and another uniformed officer had my homeboys Donnie and Ollie, plus "San Jose Mike" McLoren, my co-partner in my chop shop, with them. I was most surprised to see Ollie.

To the four of us, the cop said, "I know that you guys were stripping cars in that garage. It's a chop shop and you are all going to be charged with grand theft auto."

None of us said a word. While he fired questions at us, another cop walked in and whispered something to him. The cop questioning then turned to the uniformed officer with him and said, "Book 'em."

We were ushered, silently, through a heavy metal door and into a small, gate-topped holding tank. No sooner were we in the holding tank than we were removed individually, me first, and walked to the booking area. We were photographed, fingerprinted, and transferred to a permanent cell.

When Mike was brought back to the holding cell after booking, he looked close to tears. After the officer slammed the door, locking Mike inside with me, Mike started pointing fingers.

"It's all your fault," he told me.

Even though Mike, who'd been outside the shop when they grabbed him, hadn't stolen cars earlier that night, he'd gone on runs with us before, plus he was my partner in the ownership of the shop.

We both knew his role in the business. To me, he was just as culpable. But I didn't say anything to him about that. I just sat silently, listening to his rant. He was feeling sorry for himself, which was understandable.

Donnie was brought into the cell next. As soon as the door locked behind him, he laughed like he'd just heard a good joke. Then I remembered he'd driven up to the shop minutes before the police arrived, so his fingerprints more than likely wouldn't be found anywhere inside the stolen Grand Prix. Therefore, he was confident he couldn't be convicted of participating in the theft. To my surprise, the next to be arrested was Ollie, my homie since junior-high school.

Ollie got busted after he'd fallen asleep inside the trailer we kept on the property, so the crew had a place to crash when they didn't want to drive home after a long night's work. The cops found Ollie sleeping in the trailer and took him into custody. He was officially named a partner in the car-theft ring.

Once our booking paperwork was completed, we were offered a pay phone to make collect calls. I called a bail bondsman we all knew. Mike and I made bail a couple hours later and were back on the street. Then Ollie was out not long after.

Donnie, however, convinced that the police had no case against him or us, chose to remain in custody until the preliminary hearing rather than waste money on bail, believing his case would likely be tossed before it ever reached court. I felt, for no particular reason I could explain, that my chances would be better back on the street. I was determined to take advantage of even the slightest edge. With possible prison sentences pending, we all decided it would be unwise to go anywhere near the shop, as it was more than likely being watched. We didn't want to add to whatever the police believed they already had on us.

True to his prediction, the felony case against Donnie was quickly dropped, and Ollie's was dropped too. But Mike and I were arraigned for felony grand theft auto and operating an illegal auto chop shop.

Our public defender had each of us plead "not guilty." Then the wait began for our preliminary hearing, which would decide whether the case against us would be carried over to trial.

The lawyer gave us no indication of the extent of evidence the prosecutor had against us. He thought we could beat the case based on illegal search and seizure, but we knew that if the court felt that the evidence was strong enough to bind the case over to Superior Court, we were in deep shit.

On the day of the preliminary hearing, as Mike and I sat next to our attorney at a large wooden table, awaiting our fate, the judge, citing illegal search and seizure, said, "Case dismissed," and dropped his gavel on his desk. It was just as the attorney had hoped based on the motion he'd filed with the court, because the police had gone back to my shop the night of our arrests to search the place, but they didn't have a search warrant to legally do that, so the case was tossed.

Just like that, it was over. San Jose Mike and I breathed big sighs of relief as we walked out of the courtroom.

At the same time, the arrests meant that my days of running a chop shop had come to an abrupt end. But that was okay. It was too close of a call for me to want to continue.

We shut down the chop shop for good.

I was free, but completely broke. I went downtown and signed up for general relief, which paid $75 a month. I didn't have an education, my aspirations to be a professional tennis player had dwindled to non-existent, and my future was uncertain. I was determined to do what I quickly came to consider "the right thing."

It was around this time that I was formally introduced to another way of making money. Big money. And it was about to change my life.

CHAPTER 10
WHITE POWDER AND POWER

My homie Mike McLoren, a one-time partner with me in the operation of my chop shop, was back in town from college. He called and asked me over to his house, off of Adams and 22nd Avenue. It was a nice one-story home with a back house, where Mike stayed when he was in town. Marvin Gaye had a house around the corner.

Mike was home during what I thought was a break at San Jose State to visit his parents. When we got together for the first time, during the course of our conversation, we got onto the subject of making money, which led to the game of selling drugs.

Mike, nicknamed "San Jose Mike," told me how he painted cars to help pay college tuition. The money he earned, however, didn't stretch far enough to cover his school expenses. So, he turned to selling powder cocaine to university classmates.

I'd only heard about people snorting cocaine and had no idea what the so-called "drug of the wealthy" even looked like. From the stories I'd heard since I was a kid, and from watching movies like *Super Fly*, I understood cocaine to be used mostly by movie stars, musicians, and black pimps. I'd also heard that some women used it as an aphrodisiac.

Before my conversation with Mike about cocaine, its money value, and how to acquire cash by becoming a dealer, I had no idea that so much could be possible with so little—all held in a small Baggie.

"Fifty dollars and you're in," Mike said.

"That's all?"

I was stunned. I had to know more. I fired a dozen questions at him.

That day, after that one conversation, my fate was sealed. Little did I imagine the role I was about to play in a government scandal involving that white powder.

Then Ollie dropped by. He walked over to where we were sitting, on the couch at Mike's house. Mike had a mirror and he put it on the coffee table.

He poured a small pile of the fine, rock-like, yellowish powder onto the mirror. The yellow substance appeared to be dense, hard, and with very few crumbs surrounding two or three large, irregular rock-like balls.

We didn't speak. Mike had a single-edged razor and a plain white paper straw.

Ollie and I looked on as Mike used the razor to gingerly, yet expertly, chop up one of the rocks into a fine, yellowish powder. The strange, heavy, and medicinal smell of the stuff filled the garage. Mike continued to reduce the dust as he chopped it into even finer particles. I wondered what he was going to do with it once he was finished.

Mike pulverized another small rock, then used the razor to divide the pile into smaller flattened hills of six equal portions. From that, he stretched them into six lines of powder.

Mike was intent as he worked, as if it were a ritual. Once he finished, he turned to Ollie and said, "Watch me. Pay attention." Then he demonstrated a nose full of powder.

Mike bent forward over the powder lines on the mirror and, with one end of a straw held in a nostril, he loudly snorted one of the lines into his nose so quickly it was almost funny. But we didn't laugh. Then he snorted a second line and sat back, squeezing his nostril with his thumb and index finger to keep the powder from falling out. All the while, he sniffed like he was trying to keep his nose from running, just like I'd seen in the movies.

Finally, he sat back against the sofa and said, "Ahh, man! This is some good shit,"

Sniff, sniff.

Then, "Ahh, yeah. This is good shit."

Ollie and I watched, somewhat dumbfounded. It was almost as if we couldn't believe our eyes.

Mike turned to Ollie and gestured with his hand for Ollie to try a line.

Ollie, even though he seemed apprehensive, copied Mike by snorting not one, but two lines, of the powder. Ollie grimaced as he snorted it, but he didn't say anything.

Then it was my turn.

Ollie and most of my homeboys smoked cigarettes and pot and drank beer. Even though they tried to get me to join in, I never had the desire. But on this day, my curiosity got the best of me, plus I didn't want to be the odd man out and appear square. So, that day I lost my long-held record of staying clean.

I dove in with the enthusiasm of any sucker who believed he'd finally stumbled upon that one big break.

To my disappointment, I felt nothing.

After hearing about the so-called rich-man's drug of choice and watching movies with Hollywood gangsters shooting it out and killing each other over the expensive powder, I felt I knew from personal experience what it was all about.

Absolutely nothing.

That was okay. I planned to never snort it again.

Before we left Mike's, he gave me a going-away gift: a gram of cocaine worth $50 to $100. It was wrapped in a white plastic-like piece of paper shaped into the form of a small envelope.

From that moment on, Ollie and I were driven to learn as much as possible so we could tap into the river of money that Mike described.

I put the bag of remaining cocaine in my pant's pocket and Ollie and I jumped into Ollie's raggedy '64 Chevy with its wrecked driver's-side door and headed west on Manchester Avenue to my ex-tennis instructor Dan Foster's house. I thought Mr. Foster, a middle-aged man, might like to know about the cocaine game; he seemed well-informed about a variety of subjects.

We arrived at Mr. Foster's house in the affluent West Los Angeles neighborhood of Baldwin Hills and found him in his back yard removing a seat from a small boat. Ollie and I helped him. As we worked, we got into a deep discussion about the true purpose of our visit.

To my amazement, Mr. Foster told us how, earlier in his life, he had sold cocaine for a living. I'd taken for granted, being young at the time, that a man in his 50s wouldn't know the first thing about street drugs. But this was Mr. Foster. He shared that he'd done so well dealing drugs that he'd used his profits to travel the world in style.

Here we were, trying to come up with ways to make a measly $500 and Mr. Foster told us he'd made $200,000. We couldn't imagine what that kind of cash looked like. I thought, *Man, this is so unbelievable, it can't be true.* We were awestruck. My teacher was the cokeman. That seemed upside down.

We went inside his house, which was conservatively, yet expensively, furnished. Ollie and I'd been to Mr. Foster's house before. He ushered us into the large living room, then said, "I'll be right back." He left the room and returned with sodas. He sat down and went into a detailed explanation of the ins and outs and pros and cons of the cocaine business. He included the dangers involved, as well as the enormous fortunes to be had. He warned us that we could go to prison if we were caught selling the stuff and that drug dealers can be killed during robbery attempts. He also talked about the women, the houses, the cars, and the hundreds of thousands—even millions—of dollars to be made. He even said we could buy from him if we had the money. But when he told us the large quantities he sold, it was way above what we could manage or pay for.

My desire to learn more about the small mound of powder Mike had introduced us to turned into an all-day adventure.

When we arrived at my house, it was dark. My mother wasn't home, but my cousin Kenny and his friends "Group" and "Cruz Dog" were in the garage watching TV. My brother David, my cousins Tootie and Kenny, and I had converted my mother's garage into a comfortable—and private—bedroom. It was like the neighborhood clubhouse where we hung out and spent much of our time.

Ollie and I were anxious to see if our homies would be keen on the idea of selling cocaine with us. As soon as we walked through the door, Ollie locked it behind us. I reached into my pant's pocket and produced the packet of cocaine.

They crowded around me to see.

"What you got there, Ricky?" Kenny asked. Neither he nor his homies had the faintest idea what it was—though these guys always bragged that they were in the circle of homies who knew what was going on, that they were players and down hustlers with street smarts. Real cool dudes. But not one of them knew what was in the plastic bag.

"Cocaine," I answered.

Cruz Dog looked at me and laughed. "You stupid motherfuckers just got beat!" he said. "Ain't cocaine supposed to be white? This is yellow."

What? I wasn't sure about it myself, since I didn't know how to tell, but I wasn't willing to let an implication that I'd been conned by a friend go unchallenged.

Figuring they were more clueless than I was, I quickly shot back. "You don't even know cocaine when you see it. This is the real deal, straight off the boat." I didn't want to hear what Cruz had to say. I wanted to believe that Mike wouldn't have tricked me. I put the baggie back in my pocket, turned, and burst out the door, with Ollie trailing behind, and made a beeline for his car.

"Get in," I told Ollie.

"Where we goin'?" he asked.

"To find out if this is real from someone who knows, someone who can verify that it is."

Heading west on 87th toward Figueroa Avenue, we stopped at Irene's Liquor Store to pick up something to snack on. Just inside the door, I saw an old friend, Barney, a shermhead known around the neighborhood who was hooked on PCP so bad, it caused him to tremble.

I didn't have a problem showing the powder to Barney inside the liquor store. That store was like an open market for marijuana and PCP sales.

I pulled the baggie out of my pocket and showed it to Barney. He opened the bag, dipped a finger in, then put it on his tongue.

"That's cocaine," Barney said after a couple of seconds as pointed at the bag. "It's real."

"I knew it!" I exclaimed.

The next day, I eagerly contacted friends and quickly sold lines from my first gram of cocaine. Just like that, I was a drug dealer. I was in the game.

I was excited about the drug and Mr. Foster's eye-opening stories of women, luxury cars, and cash.

But now I needed more cocaine. It would cost Ollie and me $300 to buy cocaine from Mike to peddle on the street. To get it, we were about to do a fool thing, but we didn't dwell on how wrong it was.

In the middle of the night, we spotted a Buick parked behind a locked gate at Bret Harte Junior High. The car probably belonged to a night janitor.

It was the wheels we wanted, not the car. They were eight-wires with Vogue yellow tires and whitewalls. All the pimps had them on their cars.

We checked out the area to make sure it was clear before we went to work. When we were certain no one was watching, we hopped out of our car, bounded across the street, and ran to the parking-lot gate like two desperate junkies about to score a fix.

I climbed the 12-foot gate and dropped onto the blacktop. Ollie was next. Once on the other side, we wasted no time making our way through the parking lot to the Buick. It was my job to find the Buick's alarm and disconnect it. I located it just inside the left front wheel well and rendered it inoperable within seconds.

"Got it," I whispered loudly to Ollie.

Ollie then went to work on the door while I stood lookout. For whatever reason, Ollie couldn't get the door open and I took over.

I locked the vise grips tightly around the lock cylinder of the driver's door. The cylinder popped out of the door panel, I opened the door with a screwdriver, and we were in.

To pull the ignition, I twisted the screw on the end of a dent puller into the butterfly lock, slammed the heavy slide backwards on the bar, and ripped it out.

Ollie handed me a three-eighths ratchet-wrench socket that fit snugly on the ignition bolt. I turned the ignition to the "on" position. Nothing happened.

When the Buick didn't start a second time, we knew there had to be a kill switch somewhere. So we searched for it.

A kill switch is a back-up on-off toggle the car owner has placed in an inconspicuous spot to prevent knowledgeable car thieves like us from getting past an alarm but not necessarily a kill switch. We searched, but neither of us could find the switch.

That wasn't about to stop us. I just had to have those wheels.

"We need a tow truck," I told Ollie.

We hopped the fence, got back in our car, and drove around town looking for a tow truck to heist. Los Angeles was loaded with them. We were about an hour into our search when we found one parked in a yard on Vernon Avenue.

We snatched it. I drove back to the Buick, hooked it up, and towed the Buick to the location where we'd planned to remove the wheels and leave the car behind. Once we had the wheels, we found a spot on a side street for the tow truck and left it there.

I believed that Buick was going to make me rich, because it put us one step closer to getting more cocaine to sell for cash.

We weren't worried about getting caught. Police only fingerprinted cars if they nabbed thieves in the act of auto theft or if the car was used in a violent crime, like a homicide. We never wore gloves, knowing that the cops wouldn't lift fingerprints.

We quickly sold all four wheels for $300. We could have gotten $500, but all we needed was $300 to buy more coke from San Jose Mike.

I was hooked on the idea of what cocaine could do for me.

CHAPTER 11
SHOOTOUT ON 81ST STREET

Word spread fast in the 'hood and I made good connections in the game. It was typical business networking, except the product wasn't exactly of the Chamber of Commerce variety. One of the new contacts I'd made through networking was Pip, my cousin Evita Wilson's boyfriend. Pip was a drug dealer like me, with his little brother, Keith. Both were Hoover Street Crips who sold PCP, the street name for phencyclidine (chemical name phenylcyclohexylpiperidine), also known as angel dust, a potent animal tranquilizer. It was yet another 1980s' drug used throughout the black ghettos that eventually reached epidemic proportions. Pip and Keith were experts in dealing PCP.

Ollie Newell and I moved in with Evita. This was a convenient and strategic move. It allowed us to hook up with Pip and Keith and receive their instruction about the drug industry. Plus, Evita lived near the hub of drug sales on 81st Street.

From 1980 through '83, 81st Street between Vermont and Hoover avenues was a smorgasbord of illegal substances and drug dealers. All anyone in search of PCP, cocaine, or marijuana had to do was drive down the street and choose whatever product they wanted from the various dealers who lined both sides of the street waiting to make sales. Buyers never had to leave their cars.

About that time, Norman Tillman joined my crew fresh out of the Marine Corp after three years of service. He played intramural basketball, broke his ankle, and could no longer play. He didn't see any job prospects, other than selling some marijuana—nothing big—on the street. His mom told him, "Call Rick." I put him to work. Within six months, Norman was a millionaire. He spent most of it, including buying a Rolls Royce, and he gave a million to a man in the film industry. Norman was supposed to get 25 percent of the distribution earnings off the movie, but it didn't do well and he lost the money.

It was crazy wild, but it was also dangerous to drive down 81st during that era. Any car on that street was approached, whether or not the intention of the occupants was to score. The minute a new or different car was seen turning the corner onto 81st, it was instant service. Street dealers approached a slow-moving car, holding in their hands whatever they were selling. They were quick, slick, fast-talking, and ready to spit out a well-rehearsed sales pitch at 90 miles a minute. Customers varied from well-dressed to raggedy, ranging from wearing head rags to expensive jewelry. Some were incredibly young, others noticeably older. It didn't matter who they were or where they came from. They were buying customers.

Eighty-first Street was a sight to see. Dealers and customers alike were always on edge, with everyone packing, carrying cash, and on the lookout for cops, rip-offs, and snitches. All this went on day and night, and just the next street over from Evita's house. The year we lived with Evita was memorable not only for marking the early days of my drug-dealing career and for the wild scene on 81st, but also because this was when my sales really took off, as I soon came to know the major players operating in the area.

It was a laid-back time. Ollie and I spent our days lying around listening to the radio, partying non-stop, and dining on hamburgers and fries, all the while making unbelievable amounts of money. Back when Ollie and I lived in my mom's garage, we had to shut down our operation whenever she was home or be discreet enough so she wouldn't catch on. At Evita's house, it was the opposite. She knew what we were all doing—Pip and Keith selling PCP, Ollie and me pushing cocaine, with the cops the only outside fear.

Ollie and I soon became astute in the world of PCP by hanging out with Pip and Keith on 81st, to watch them at work. The sale of PCP by a substantial number of black youth, both male and female who called themselves Hoover Crips, had already skyrocketed by the time Ollie and I moved in with Evita. In fact, the popularity and availability of PCP may very well have originated with the Hoover Crips' turf in the area of 81st through 83rd between Hoover and Vermont. By 1983, PCP was out of hand in the 'hood.

Tony Stacey, Evita's previous boyfriend and the father of her two daughters, had been one of the leaders of the Hoover Street Crips, which thrived on gangbanging youth selling the debilitating PCP. Even after Tony went to prison to serve out a life sentence, Tony's power in the Crips was not curbed by his absence from the streets.

Customers new and old looking to acquire a stick for PCP's deadening high needed only to walk or drive down 81st. During that period, most everyone who lived on that section of 81st, from Hoover to Vermont, was either using or selling PCP. Pip and Keith were major players in the spread of angel dust on the street, supplying a seemingly unending string of men and women, young and old, at $15 for a half-stick and $30 for a whole. The drug was contained in a small, clear, glass jar—a container available from the many liquor stores that peppered the community. Cigarettes were used to make a half or whole stick. Usually, when a sale was made, the dealer dipped a Sherman cigarette, half or whole depending on what the customer wanted, into the strong, distinctive, chemically smelling liquid.

In other parts of South Central Los Angeles and farther east, the drug was commonly doled out wherever a natural form of cover existed, such as an alleyway, abandoned building, or a house, which formed a blanket of security between the dealer and police.

Back on 81st Street, however, fear barely existed. For street peddlers, all caution of being seen by the cop was thrown to the wind. It was an open market. Young blacks stood openly on sidewalks and even in the street to hawk their product to passersby as if it were the most legal thing they'd ever done. It was like they were hiding in plain sight. I thought it odd that drug deals were transacted out in the open, while the cops were practically non-existent. I thought, *How could they not know?*

The Hoover Crips were also headquartered on 81st. To be honest, I was somewhat intimidated. Even though I went to school with a lot of those homeboys, I still didn't know what to expect from them. The group mentality changes and empowers people. In our neighborhood, friends often fought friends they grew up with. Shooting and even killing each other wasn't unheard of if a beef broke out. Many kids were forced to grow up and become street-smart fast, because it was so violent in the 'hood. We lost the better part of our youth in the 'hood.

South Central didn't have low-income projects; the closest were the apartment buildings that lined the streets, each representing a set of the Crips.

I'd been away from the streets for a few years playing tennis and competing. Once I got back into the flow, I had to work on playing it cool. By no means was I afraid to mix it up with somebody if I had to. Winning and losing was a matter of perspective. However, in South Central, if you got into it with the wrong person, it wasn't a fair fight; you had a better chance at winning the lottery.

Still, the 'hood made the perfect spot to launch my drug enterprise, though operating there had to be done with the right mix of attitude. I had to play my cards just right, because gangsters could take advantage of the weak. At the same time, if I got too strong, I'd be the one to take down, because homies could get street famous taking after a rising star, like the guy who killed Billy the Kid in an ambush when the Kid dropped his guard.

I had a few things going for me. First, Evita was my cousin and she was connected to Crips leader Tony Stacey and Crips gangbangers Pip and Keith. A little connected street cred never hurt. Plus, she was well-respected in her own right by the Hoover Crips. She was a "Hoover Crippelette"—the female equivalent of a Crip member. Evita was a straight gangster.

Second, having Ollie as my partner didn't hurt. Ollie, whose Crip moniker was "Killer," had no problem using a gun. Homies knew and respected him as a 94 Hoover.

And third, I had a reputation of my own, for having put down the tennis racquet in exchange for the drug game. While dealing on Crips turf, I carried a gun, despite the bad experiences as a kid when I was exposed to guns. Now, it made all the sense in the world to carry. My experiences taught me the street credo that it was "better to be caught with a gun than without."

For all these reasons, as we got to work in the game, we started slowly.

We never held too much money on us at one time, because that would have made us easy targets for homeboys who stayed on the business people. Believe me, there were plenty of them.

One was nicknamed "Ballhead" and the other "Underdog." I worried the most about Ballhead. He was only 17, a youngster, but he was mean. I hadn't met him before I arrived at 81st Street. I learned fast. I saw him jack plenty of PCP customers on the street. He had no problem putting a pistol or a sawed-off shotgun in somebody's face for $15, $10, even $5. I pictured him doing the same to me, putting me in a tough spot. I'd known Underdog since grade school. Since then, he'd spent time in juvenile hall, which hardened him.

On top of that, not only the regular dealers, but even the O.G. Crips, were hooking them up with sherm sticks and beer, which served two purposes. First, it kept them at bay, and second, it put Ballhead and Underdog in a position to pay back the favors. It was simply a cost of doing business, no different than a street tax.

My best protection, however, was that nobody had a clue I was making money, at least not on 81st Street. A few of the homies who sold PCP were starting to suspect that I was doing well in the game, although nobody knew for sure, because I handled business transactions as privately as I could. My customers didn't want other homeboys to know when they copped, because then they might have to share. So, it was done in secret. For instance, one homie might walk by me and say, "Meet me in the back of the building." Business kept growing, until my cocaine sales began to dominate PCP. The money made on 81st, before vice got hip, was big. The funny thing was that when cops did start to come around, they were looking for PCP, not cocaine. We were ahead of the power curve. And it was relatively easy to beat them.

Cops spent their time doing standard pat downs, looking for bottles filled with half-ounce and full-ounce liquid PCP. They also looked for sherm sticks. Another thing the cops did was smell homies' hands. If a homie had been dipping PCP, the cops could easily detect a chemical odor.

For my part, I could stand on the block all day long and not worry about getting caught. I only carried a few rocks in my pocket at a time, which I could easily put in my mouth. Besides, vice cops had so many people lined up for pat downs, they rushed and missed rocks.

The cops didn't like searching us any more than we liked being searched. This was a Crips spot, so gangbangers just hung around, not selling drugs, getting high, or getting drunk, which put the cops on edge.

At one point, I had to sell PCP. Ollie and I found ourselves a little short of funds, so from time to time we'd go out at night to put down a car lick. By then, our homie Keith had become a partner and mentor. He'd tried his hand at selling cocaine, but it didn't work out, because he smoked away his entire product. He had no problem, though, successfully selling PCP to keep himself going.

One night, I felt confident enough to leave my drugs and cash with Keith while Ollie and I went to work to find a car we could make money off of. We rode around the Valley for at least four hours but never found an easy lick.

I walked back into the house disgusted that we'd wasted our time, and saw Keith, Pip, Evita, and Rene sitting at the kitchen table. They were sprung. The apartment had no furniture in the living room, only a table in the kitchen, which was where they sat. They were higher than kites. I was in no mood for bad news, but as soon as we walked into the house, I immediately sensed something was wrong.

"Hey, Keith, gimme the money and my package," I told him.

He asked me to go outside with him to talk about it. Ollie followed me down the stairs.

Outside, Keith handed me $125, but he owed me $1,400, or some portion of that and the rest in cocaine. He claimed he put the rest of the half-ounce out on credit.

I grabbed him by his neck, pushed him up against the wall, and said, "Man, where's my money at? I ain't playin' no games."

101

Keith and I were about the same height. He wore a perm that was in desperate need of a touch-up. He also had a distinct odor, probably from not taking a bath for several days. I'd never paid attention before, but now that he was directly in front of me, I couldn't help noticing it.

Keith put his hands in his pants pockets and turned them inside out to show us that they were empty.

"I love you, man," Keith pleaded. "I ain't gonna beat you outta nothin'! I swear. I smoked a little bit, but that was it."

That was my first lesson not to leave a package with a smoker.

I thought about it for a moment and realized I still needed him. He knew more about the drug business and had more experience than I could have gotten on my own. I needed to keep him and his knowledge close to me.

Even so, when he started to say that he'd work off the debt, I stopped him. I didn't have any product left for him to work off his debt with.

Ollie and I huddled up. We were back to being broke and at square one. We only had $125, and an eight-track (or three grams) would cost $375. More than likely, an eight-track would be about half-cut, which meant it would only be 50-percent pure. From that, we could make around $1,100 if we didn't take any shorts. We agreed to get a good night's sleep, then start over fresh in the morning.

The next day, as soon as we got up, I already had a plan: to dip my way back into the drug business. By dip, I mean selling PCP with Keith as the runner. That would take some of the stress off of us, as Keith was a slick talker and already had clientele in place. We took $100 of our last $125 to Waterman Tone, the top supplier for PCP in the 'hood. I'd met Tone before; he sometimes hung out on the block. He had the gold necklaces and rings, cars, crib, and ladies—all the accouterments we were after. He knew I sold cocaine, but he didn't see a future in it. In fact, just about everybody thought the same thing. So, Tone didn't feel at all threatened by my presence. He was almost patronizing in the way he welcomed us, as if he'd been expecting us to call on him. Now that I look back on it, I know why. He figured he was finally selling to someone who wasn't getting high or gangbanging.

What he didn't know was that my plans didn't include working for him. There was no way I could compete with him for PCP sales. Luckily, I didn't want or need to. I'd already figured out how we could make money. With a half-ounce of PCP, we could make $600. Then we could get ourselves an eight-track and be back in the cocaine game.

We bought the half-ounce, went to the store, and bought a pack off of a shermhead. Except for Keith, who was still asleep, we were on our way.

I'd never touched PCP in my life and had no plans to. I'd seen plenty of people smoking and selling it, but only vaguely knew how it was dipped into a bottle. I knew a lot of the customers, so I rolled right along, almost from the start. My PCP moved fast. Then Keith finally showed up from his long nap.

Keith explained that I was dipping the cigarettes way too deep, which was why everybody was coming back so fast for more. He demonstrated how to dip the tip of the cigarette into the liquid, just barely, then suck on the cigarette to bring up the PCP.

What he failed to mention was, "Don't inhale."

I unintentionally inhaled a cigarette and my world turned upside down, twirling and twisting. I dropped down to one knee and that was the end of the day for me. Ollie, Keith, and I went back to the crib. I chilled—vowing to forever stay away from PCP—and they went to work. One experience with it was plenty for me; I no longer wanted anything to do with the stuff. After recovering from the episode and scraping together enough money to get back into the coke game, it was on again.

In the process, I learned a valuable lesson the hard way: Never give anyone my whole sack. If I let someone hold onto my sack, I had to be prepared to lose it.

After we got our eight-track, our business took off, at least that was how I saw it at the time. I was making anywhere from $300 to $400 a day, and I was happy. Little did I know, I could make far more.

Still, at that point, it was good enough for me. Every so often, I could afford to take all the Freeway Boys out for pizza at Dr. Munchies. The pizza there was greasy and delicious. Before the business picked up, everybody chipped in to buy pizza. Nobody ever got full and we all walked out wanting more pizza. Now, when we left, everybody was stuffed. Even so, the homies still couldn't see the potential, the big picture, and weren't on the level with what Ollie and I were doing.

Once, we ran into a situation where we couldn't get drugs from either Mr. Foster or Mike. Ollie had an old girlfriend whose mom, Doris, operated a smoke house. We went to talk to Doris, to check out her operation and see if we could buy product from her.

Man, was that a good idea.

When we got to her house, the place was in total shambles. It looked like it hadn't been cleaned in months. What the house did have was plenty of people, maybe 15 or 20, inside snorting coke. She was super thin, appearing like a skeleton tightly wrapped in skin. I remembered Doris from a few years back when she was heavier. It looked like her hair hadn't been brushed in weeks.

"Can you hook us up with an eight-track?" I asked her.

"No problem," she said.

Bingo. We were back in business.

All I had to do was give her $50. She asked us to sit down while she went to the back of the house. She returned with the eight-track and some extra she'd purchased for herself from her profit.

Then she cooked up her piece and politely offered each of us a hit. I declined.

Ollie went ahead and took a hit. Then he turned, looked at me, and said, "This is all right. Take a hit."

I didn't snort. The most I'd ever gotten high on, besides my introduction to two lines of cocaine with Mike and Ollie during my introduction to the powder, was maybe a sip of beer. It wasn't my thing. On this occasion, I gave in and tried it.

After leaving her house, I felt guilty. I'd learned from all the players, from the car thieves to the pimps, to never use. If you get strung out, you smoke up, snort, or shoot all your profits and then you become just another junkie. Also, you never know when it's been laced with something else. After that day, I promised myself that no matter who asked me to do it, I wasn't going to.

That wasn't true for my partner, Ollie. Each time we went to houses to buy and sell product, Ollie was offered free hits. I couldn't see a difference in his actions. At first, it seemed harmless enough. But then, I started noticing the changes and pulled him aside, warning him about his developing habit.

Then, Keith came to me. He was jealous and whining like a little kid.

"Man, I run for you guys all day, and Ollie's over there smokin' and trickin' with them hoes. And he won't gi' me none."

It caught me off guard. I knew Ollie and I had to have a serious talk, and it had to be immediately.

I put my working face on, walked downstairs, and ducked through a hole in the fence we'd cut in case we had to run out in a hurry. The police weren't quite as nimble as we were, and we knew how to disappear into backyards and between streets. As Keith and I made our way back to 81st Street, everybody wanted to talk to me. I was becoming the "Man." But with a quick glance at my face, they stepped back. They could tell something serious was on my mind.

I walked into the apartment Ollie was in. The air was filled with cocaine. Ollie was in the back bedroom. When I walked in, a girl jumped up and started putting her clothes back on. Ollie knew something was wrong.

I said, "C'mon. We gotta holler."

Keith followed us to Evita's house, where I talked to Ollie about his smoking. At first, he denied it, but then changed his mind and tried to convince me that he wasn't hooked.

I made it clear and to the point. "If you ever hit again, we'll be dividing our money right then. It'll be over."

Ollie was angry. He knew Keith had ratted him out. He grabbed Keith.

I stepped in and broke them up. I gave Keith a fifty and sent him on his way. I told Ollie that we could still work together. Though I had my doubts about him, I wanted to give him a second chance, especially since we were ready to buy our first half-ounce. We'd saved $1,400—something I'd never dreamed I could do.

While I was rolling, I ran into Richard Phillips, a friend from my car-stealing days. He became known as "Richie Rick" and "Tellin' Rich."

I explained to Richard that I was moving up. He had a friend he said would give us a half-ounce for $1,400 and it would be the bomb. I felt comfortable with Richard. He helped teach me how to steal cars. I've always had a soft spot for people who helped me.

We drove to 104th and Buntline and pulled in front of a blue house where Will, Richard's contact, lived. Will appeared to be well off. At least three Cadillacs with Zeniths sat parked in the fenced-in driveway. At the time, Zenith wheels went for about $3,000 a set. To top it off, a Mercedes-Benz 450SEL 6.9 also sat in the driveway. *These people are well off,* I thought as I looked through the gate.

Richard asked me to give him the money so he could go in and cop. I never liked giving anybody my money. I immediately thought of the episode with Keith. But I knew Richard. We went way back. At one time, we were homies and he even stayed with me for a couple weeks in my mom's garage. He was a skilled car thief who taught me a lot. He was the adventurous type. He stole motorcycles for us— anything we wanted, as long as money was involved. He'd actually lost a high-speed chase with a helicopter and ended up in the L.A. County jail and in court, but he beat the charges and was released. I liked hanging out with him back then. He also liked to be the boss— which, when we stole cars, didn't matter. But I soon learned that he had the same attitude when it came to cocaine.

I didn't know if he smoked cocaine or not, but I was sure he knew what Ollie would do to him if he tried to beat us. Besides, we were right there, sitting outside the house in our car. We gave him the money and he went inside.

It seemed like it took an eternity for him to come out, but he finally did. When he approached us, he had a big goofy smile on his face. Richard had always been a bit of a clown. I turned to Ollie and said, "Look at this fool."

Ollie took it all in. He said, "He'd better have our shit right." We were riding in a '68 Chevy, a theft recovery, I'd bought from the police impound yard for a hundred bucks. The front seat was a mismatch, and the sides had been smashed in. Also, the ignition was ripped out, so I had to touch two wires together to start it. All that aside, it ran like it was brand new.

Richard climbed into the back seat. As I stuck the two wires together and started the car, I asked Richard, "Where's my shit?"

He was all smiles as he put me in a headlock. "Who the man?" he asked in a playful manner, which was to say, "I told you I'd take care of you."

This made me feel good. Things must have gone right. But he still hadn't passed me my bag. We needed a spot to stop and check it out.

Richard said his girl stayed down the street. We pulled up and she happened to be in the front yard. *This girl looks familiar*, I thought. Come to find out, it was Penny from elementary school. My cousin Tootie used to be in love with her. She let us into her house to check out the goods, for a small fee. Ollie and I were cocaine-rich, so we agreed.

Once inside the house, Rich pulled out our sack. It was a lot of powder, but when we started to rock it up, it didn't come back right. When I complained, Richard got a silly look on his face, until he saw the seriousness in our expressions. So he explained that his source, a guy named Will, owed him some drugs and he had given him the package. From that package, he said he'd make things right with us. He pulled out another baggie from his other pant leg. It looked like this was also our stuff. He dipped us two or three grams from his bag, but it still didn't make me happy. I figured he was giving me back my own dope, which he'd cut inside the house. And who knew what he cut it with?

I told him exactly that, after he gave us the grams, that we didn't want it.

"Gimme my money back," I said.

"Hang on," Richard responded.

He got on the phone and made what sounded like a fake phone call. He hung up and said Will had just left, but we could return later that night to swap it out. I was skeptical, but had little choice but to play along.

We continued talking with Penny, catching up, and then we were off, leaving Richard behind at her house. That night at 11, when he was supposed to meet up with us, Richard didn't answer his pager. Ollie and I went out looking for him.

We went by Main Street Mafias, one of Richard's hangouts, then back to Penny's place—everywhere we thought he might be. No one had seen him. Ollie carried his pistol and we both were steaming mad.

At around 1:30, we pulled up to Manchester Park. Stephan and Fast Eddie were there. These were big dudes. Stephan, known on the street as "Big Petey" and "Shiesty Petey," and Eddie, nicknamed "Fast Eddie," looked like they'd just gotten out of the pen.

We told them the story about Richard beating us out of our money and the house with the Caddies and Benz in the driveway. Each one of those cars had an easy two or three grand worth of accessories. Stephan and Eddie were happy to assist, knowing there would be a come-up in exchange for helping us out, so they asked for time to run home and grab their gats.

Ollie and I were still angry as we waited for Eddie and Stephan. When they got back, we left the park and rolled to 104th in the '64 Chevy. Even though it was stock, it had a big trunk, perfect for carrying stolen goods.

This wasn't any ordinary car theft. It was the kind where guns were pointed at the front door of a house and if anybody came out, they got it. It was one thing to steal cars. It was another to steal from gangsters with plenty of firepower. The kind of cars those guys drove often got carjacked at stoplights, at gunpoint, and in broad daylight. Not just anybody drove cars like those into South Central. It was doubly dangerous being in the Lennox neighborhood in South Bay.

The sheriff's deputies who patrolled the area didn't play. They were hard-ass. In addition, homies retaliated for stealing their cars. I'd heard all kinds of stories about it.

As we rolled, all these things, and more, went through my head. They may not have been the guys who fucked me over; I knew it was Richard. But they sure knew about it when it went down. They had the money to pay me back.

We pulled onto 105th at 2:30 in the middle of the night to nothing but dead silence. We got lucky when we saw that the house had an alley behind it. We parked and then walked from different ends of the alley, two-by-two. Everybody was packin' but me.

The plan was for me to disarm the Caddy's alarm and, afterward, start the car. I'd done it many times before. This, though, was probably the most dangerous mission I'd ever been on. I knew it at the time. I could tell by the house, the cars, and the surroundings.

I jumped the fence, knowing that my boys would be looking over the top with handguns, ready for action. I slid under the front driver's-side wheel well of the first Caddy. The alarm was right there where I thought it would be. I took my cutters out and carefully clipped the wires. I ran back to the fence and exchanged the snips for a pair of vise grips and a Gizmo. The car was too close to the house to use a snatch bar, which made a lot of noise as the slide smacked the hammer. The sound would give us away. The Gizmo, a locksmith's tool that helps pull out the ignition of a car, took more time, but it didn't make a sound.

With ease, I used the vise grips to forcibly turn the door lock. Instantly, I was in the car, slipping the Gizmo into place. The ignition and locking mechanism came out without a hitch. So far, so good.

I used an extension to unlock the steering wheel, but not enough to start the engine. I signaled the fellas that the car was ready. Using bolt cutters, they popped the lock on the gate, and then came in to help me push the car into the alley.

As soon as we were in the alley, I fired it up and we rolled. We weren't outta there Scott free yet, because at 3 in the morning, the deputies pulled over everything that moved, especially young black men in a luxury car.

I'd arranged with my boy on the Westside to use his garage to stash the car for $200. We didn't want the car to pop up in our 'hood. It was a simple job. Nothing major: wheels, grill, bumper kit, and radio. We had the car stripped in less than an hour.

While we sat in the garage kickin' it, I looked at the moon roof and figured I could get probably $400 for it too. I took my guy's air chisel and made a convertible out of the car. Then I drove the Caddy about 10 blocks from the garage and parked it with its engine still running.

We went back, collected our goods, and headed home to South Central. The next day, we returned to the Westside to sell it all. We didn't want anyone on our side of town to know what had just gone down.

We ran into Fat Dopie, who had a Cadillac club. He and his homies bought everything they could get off of Cadillacs. Even though Zeniths were in high demand, Dopie must have sensed we were trying to unload them fast, because he bargained hard.

We agreed to $1,400, which was cheap, especially since these had Vogue tires on them. Even though the tires were somewhat worn, it was no problem for us: $1,400 was a fair price. We still had the roof, the bumper kit, and the radio to sell. The prices on those were standard.

Dopie got on his Motorola phone and went to work putting out the word about what we were selling. Before we knew it, guys surrounded us and threw money at us.

On our way home, we picked up Fast Eddie and Shiesty Pete, because it was time to split up the cash. They weren't going to get much. Their roles were minor, standing guard and pushing the car out of the yard. The four of us went to my mom's house. After we split up the money, they asked, "When are you going to re-up?" about getting more dope.

As Ollie and I walked out of the garage, suddenly, all hell broke loose! A barrage of bullets zinged past us. We looked up and saw three guys with fully automatic Uzis and Mac-10s blasting away.

As fate would have it, my mom's Cadillac was parked out front and it served as cover. It was the only thing that saved us from certain bloodshed and possible death.

I dove behind a brick wall and crawled to my next-door neighbor's yard. The shots continued as I moved away as fast as I could and as flat to the ground as I could get. I didn't know if they were chasing me or not. What I did know was Richard had snitched me out. Once in the yard next door, I got up, ran to the end of the street, and saw one of my homies who'd walked outside when he heard the commotion.

"You a'ight?" he asked.

"Yeah, I'm okay."

Sirens sounded out everywhere and we trudged back. Police had my house surrounded, and a helicopter buzzed overhead. Even before we got there, cops were ordering us down on the ground a few houses from my mom's house. Then they started firing questions at us.

In the meantime, we could see just to the end of the tunnel under the freeway, where the shooters came through to ambush us. We couldn't see what was going on at the other end of the tunnel, but we learned that the snitch Richard was also one of the gunmen.

When the cops let us go, my heart was still pounding against my chest as I headed back to my house, where police were questioning my mother in the front yard, with everyone surrounding her car.

It was riddled with bullets. My mom loved that Cadillac. She saw me and said, "C'mere, Ricky."

I walked up to her. "You okay? What's going on?" she asked.

I told her I didn't know and explained that we were standing around when the shooting broke out. Then the police explained how it went down.

They separated Ollie, Shiesty, and Petey and questioned them.

A cop walked up to me and said, "A detective needs to speak to you."

"Sure."

From the start of the questioning, I knew they suspected the whole mess was drug-related, but all of us kept quiet and said we hadn't the slightest idea what the shooting was all about.

It took a couple of days for the whole mess to die down.

Ollie, Donnie, and my cousin Evita's boyfriend were pissed. They kept saying, "We have to retaliate!"

But I knew those guys were too strong for us and they had way too much firepower. If they shot up the neighborhood over a car, imagine what they'd do if we tried to hit one of them.

By this time, the cops had officially labeled me as the leader of the Freeway Boys.

I told the guys that we needed to lay low for a while to see what more, if anything, developed. In the meantime, we needed to get up our money and firearms.

We were on high alert.

I told everybody, "No more casual outings. In fact, no one should go out alone, for any reason. No prostitutes. No partying. We need to keep it strictly business for now."

It ended up being a benefit. The 81st Street spot became a safe place for me. I was starting to be treated like a star in the 'hood. Everybody knew me. I did what I could to watch my homies' backs, and they did the same for me. Nobody dared to do anything to me while I was on 81st.

A few days after the shooting at my mom's house, I actually started to felt safe again, especially with Ollie armed and at my side.

Around that time, I ran into Moomoo. He and I'd gone to Bret Harte in the seventh grade. We worked the streets together early on in the game. Moomoo's reputation was near legendary. He was one of the founders of 107 Hoover Crips. When we saw each other, we embraced like brothers.

That association increased my clout even more. When Moomoo spoke, everybody listened. He probably had more juice on the street than anyone. I had myself a powerful ally in Moomoo, one I could trust. After all, he was the one who'd gotten me a pass from the Crips at Bret Harte. It was the least I could do. I made it clear to him that I was going to put him down.

For the next two months, things went well. It was all about the grind, 24 hours a day, seven days a week.

On 81st, we were rolling, doing $3,000 to $4,000 a day. I could see the operation turning into $10,000 a day. But the homies still talked about retaliation against Richard and Will. Having Moomoo on my team made it easier, but I was looking toward those $10,000 days, trying to put anything that didn't turn into a profit out of my mind, even though I knew it wasn't over with Richard and Will.

Then I got a break.

I was at Taco Pete's getting lunch when I ran into One-eyed Kenny, whom I knew from my low-riding days. But his brother stayed down the street from Will, so I wasn't sure which side he'd be on. I was cautious when we started talking about the incident.

"Are you going to testify?" he asked.

"Hell, no. What would that do for us? Besides, we weren't witnesses to anything other than twenty seconds of gunfire aimed at us."

"Well, they still have Will and the others charged with attempted murder." Then he paused and said, "You know, Rick, Will ain't mad atcha. This whole thing falls on Richard."

I watched him closely.

"Will wants to have a meeting with you," One-eyed Kenny said. "He wants to pay for any damage that was done to your mother's car."

On the one hand, I was relieved. On the other, I got a whiff of something that might smell like a rat. I knew it was best for everybody to put this behind us. The last thing we needed was a war. I didn't want anyone getting killed, and I didn't want to kill anyone. Still, my guard was definitely up when I said, "Set up a meeting. Somewhere neutral. I'll be there."

"How 'bout Melvin Youngblood's crib?" One-eyed Kenny asked.

For me, that was almost like having the meet up in my own backyard: Melvin had been in my crew since I was about nine years old. Most people had no idea, because he seemed so square.

Then we set the rules for the meeting. We couldn't bring more than two guys with us, and no weapons of any kind would be allowed in. Melvin would make sure that his place was safe and that the rules were followed.

I took Donnie and Ollie with me as back-up, because I knew how they'd act under pressure should something happen. If there was going to be violence, Donnie would run toward it, not away. He was fearless.

I didn't know who Will would bring with him, but I did know it wouldn't be Richard, who was still sitting in the L.A. County jail.

We got to the meeting in Melvin's garage. Will explained himself. He said the shooting was all Richard's idea, and that he himself hadn't been there when Richard made the call to retaliate for Will's car being stolen.

"I'd never do somethin' like that," he said. "I have too much at stake to get involved in petty disputes."

I kind of believed him, but I couldn't help being skeptical. Then I thought about what motivated him, and it convinced me. I knew it was money and his business, which was exactly what motivated me. Moreover, he was probably the richest guy in South Central at the time and had a lot to lose.

I went with my instincts and decided to be straight with him.

"The fourteen hundred was all I had," I told him, "and I feel like I was fucked over."

Then I figured, what the hell, and dropped more salt on Richard's wounds. I repeated to what Richard told me Will had said the day he copped the coke: "Richard told me you said, 'Fuck those guys,' meaning me and my homeboys, and you sold us bad coke." I looked him right in the eye. "So that's why I chopped up your car like I did, because of what Richard said. That's why I did it, plain and simple."

"I understand," Will said. "It's cool. Hell, I had that Caddy insured to the hilt. I came out ahead."

It was over, he said, and we had nothing to worry about. He wanted to pay for the damages to my mother's car, so I accepted. He even offered to sell us drugs to get us going again. I told him I appreciated it and I'd think about it. I still wanted to believe him.

I even felt comfortable that he was being straight up with me. But going into the coke business with this guy was another matter entirely.

With that, we shook hands. At least the bad blood was behind us.

CHAPTER 12
BLOODS 'N TURF

We were back on 81st Street with no lack of clientele. I was a young man, coming into my own. My girlfriend Sharon, from Belize, was still with me. She was finishing high school, and her mother was strict, so I was only able to hook up with her once or twice a week. She was where my heart was, and with the cocaine game.

I was surrounded by women who would do anything, including have sex, for cocaine. My boy Ollie and our mutual homie Jonny Mumbles went hard at it. I don't know why, but I wasn't like them. I never felt comfortable with the idea of having sex with a woman I didn't know. I still spent much of my time hustling drugs. And I spent any free time I had with Sharon.

Getting to Sharon, however, wasn't easy. It was difficult to find time to be with her, especially alone. Women I knew started treating me like I was the catch of the century. Funny how money and power can do that.

My biggest concern was finding a steady supply of drugs. From the start, my game was open 24 hours a day, seven days a week. Nothing, including women who wanted to trade sex for cocaine, could get in the way of that.

I began talking with influential people who could make things happen. I got in touch with one of my old car-thief homies whose name was Buddy. I'd always done well with Buddy. His younger brother, Big Mike, who owned a bunch of liquor stores, did some jobs with me a couple years earlier. I set out to find Buddy. I located him sitting at the liquor store in his black luxury car with the top down, looking like a million bucks. I walked up to him and he was friendly. The thing about me, no matter what, I don't burn friends. He told me to get in. Rick James's "Super Freak" was blasting on the radio.

I explained my dilemma to Buddy. He said that he could take care of it because he knew people in powerful places. I explained to him how much money I had at the time, about $6,000 to invest. Still, I felt completely confident in Buddy. He had never played any games with me. Everything had always been straight up. He knew that if I said it, it was for real. I told him about my spot, and painted the picture in his mind of how it was jumping. I felt like I was on my way up, so I probably told him that too.

He gave me a note with the address to his house. I handed the note to Ollie, because I still couldn't read at that point. He told me Buddy stayed in Palisades. I was impressed. We'd played tennis against Palisades High. I knew the area would be nice.

We weren't disappointed. Buddy's house was a dream. I knew there was no way he earned it selling only stolen car parts. Buddy had a bar set up, just like in a restaurant. Everything was laid out well.

I'd never drunk before—a lot, anyway—but I had a margarita as we sat and waited for the drugs to arrive. Buddy said he'd charge us $2,800 an ounce. We watched his cable TV, which was something new to us. We'd probably been there an hour when in came Big Mike, Buddy's partner, toting a bag.

Big Mike stood about six-foot, four-inches and weighed about 300-plus pounds. He was an imposing figure, to say the least, but very low key. He remembered me, shook my hand, and asked what was going on. Knowing he was Buddy's partner, I told him the story, and then he counted out the money, and Ollie and I took possession of the drugs.

We got back and checked out the drugs and everything was OK. We preferred dealing with Mr. Foster. The problem with Foster, though, was that he was unreliable. Some days he was up for the sale, other days he just didn't feel like it. I couldn't run a business like that.

We were glad to have a backup. I didn't want to stop there, though. I got the operation running to a point that I didn't necessarily have to be there every minute of the day. It was flying on its own. I had stopped standing out on the streets selling. Now that we had Jonny Mumbles, he would hold the drugs and do the selling, and I would hold the gun and do the collecting. We also used other people's apartments and houses. We'd make deals with them for a 50-dollar rock to set up in their houses and sell. Believe me, it always cost more than that.

The 50 got them started, and each time someone came over to take a hit, they'd charge them to use their pipe. They sweated our customers. After the customers left, they'd turn and sweat us. Mumbles and Ollie had already taken the hard line: If they weren't sucking or fucking, they had nothing coming. The customers knew that about them.

Bad street cred fell back on me. As soon as I entered a house, the owner would run up and pull me into a back room and complain about the quantity of drugs that had been sold in the house, how small the rocks were, and how badly Mumbles and Ollie had been treating them. I'd throw them something to keep them happy. Ollie was always telling me I was too soft.

I went down to call on another old buddy who owned an auto-mechanic shop on 66th and Vermont. Back in the day, I did a few jobs for him. Our shops were side by side, before I got raided. Lloyd was

121

a real character. He had hair like Don King before Don King became famous. He used to write for black comedian Rudy Ray Moore. He had the Signifying Monkey character down to a science. Up in his office, I explained what I'd been doing business-wise in the game.

"I got you," he said. "Don't worry about a thing. It'll be three thousand an ounce."

That was 200 more than Buddy's. If it was good, so what?

We counted the rocks—two made from the two ounces from Buddy—and bagged up close to $15,000 worth. We were making up to $4,000 a day. I planned to go back to him and asked him to line it up as soon as he could. I couldn't have enough supply. It was an endless search; we never stopped looking for suppliers.

We locked in Lloyd. The next morning I got a beep from Buddy. He offered to take me out to breakfast, which I graciously accepted.

We went to M&M's. Inside, I saw some high rollers, one named Kino I hadn't seen since my bicycle days. He now wore tailor-made suits and both hands were loaded with jewelry and a lot of flash around his neck. I was surprised Kino knew Buddy. Buddy never took the time out to introduce us, but I was flattered just to be there. I couldn't wait to tell the fellas.

Buddy and I talked about another deal and getting me a quarter-pound.

"Line it up," I told him.

After I left, I called Mr. Foster. He asked me to stop by. Ollie and I counted our money, and we had at least $10,000 and drugs still on hand.

Once at Mr. Foster's, I told him that I wanted a quarter pound. He called Mark, his middleman, who was above Foster. Then Mark called Ivan, a guy who was above him. Ivan informed him that the deal could be made in three hours.

The transaction was set for a price of $2,400 an ounce.

We cut our sale price again. Ollie and I weren't tripping off the price, thinking only about consistency. People on 81st Street noticed the cash that cocaine sales were bringing in.

If they started dealing in it too, they'd need somebody to buy it from. I wanted to have a large enough supply to be able to do that.

The guys who used to buy it just to smoke were now saving their money to buy product to sell. At that point, an eight-track went for about $375 to $400 and was supposed to weigh 3.5 grams. But what Ollie and I figured out was that when we bought a small quantity, it had probably been stepped on so hard that it might only be one gram of actual coke. We could move three grams of clean, good-quality product. The dealers had never seen it before and didn't know what good coke was. We started selling eight-tracks to the hustlers. We could get a little over nine of the eight-tracks out of an ounce. We made $3,300 off of an investment of $2,400 with much less work than before.

Business was good. We'd become distributors as opposed to being just street dealers.

Then an idea came to me. I needed a couple more partners. I needed to expand. One way was through Ramon, who was considered the king of the weed. In the same way 81st specialized in PCP, Ramon used Fourth and Main for weed sales. It was like a drive-up supermarket. Thirty or 40 guys at all times of the day and night sold weed. The only problem was Ramon was smoking coke, which made him unreliable. After he collaborated up with Wimp, I decided to pay them a visit.

They had no idea I was doing so well. I didn't flaunt it. I picked them up and took them to M&M's. They still couldn't tell I had a lot of money, even though I was driving a new Volkswagen instead of an old Chevy. The thing I knew for sure was that I had to get them off of drugs. They already had money, because they'd been buying weed for about $4,500 a pound of Thai, Indo, and Skunk. The stuff sold for $20 a gram. I'd seen them sell so many 20-dollar bags, it wasn't even funny. I knew that smoking cocaine could bring them down. I'd watched people in those smoke houses who were once rich and famous spiral from getting hooked on smoking coke, so I came up with a plan for my homeboys to avoid it.

I first had to tell them they were hooked, that they were junkies. And they couldn't get off of it. I wanted to push them into quitting, just to prove me wrong. It worked. They quit. Ramon was always trying to outdo me. For him, it was like a competition to get off drugs.

I told them how many ounces I was buying. Ramon said he could match my buy, if we bought together. So, we made a deal. To me it was no problem. I already knew that the more I bought, the cheaper it would get.

Another homeboy I hooked up with was Rich Ronnie. The first time I saw Ronnie was when Ollie, Jeff, and I tried to steal his car. In those day, I was still new to the streets, into low-riding, and fresh off the tennis courts. Ronnie's car was a beautiful blue-and-white Cutlass with all the trimmings. He had Big Hub rims, which people have been killed over. They were true classics. We were dying to get our hands on some.

The plaque hanging in his car window, "Superiors," was prominent. We were familiar with the Superiors as one of the better L.A.-area car clubs. The Superiors' cars were everything we wished for.

As we walked around the car, casing it out, the door of the apartment opened and Ronnie walked out. Somebody must have alerted him that we were trying to break into his car.

He was a stocky dude whose complexion appeared to be mixed with Samoan, or maybe Filipino. We could tell by his nice swoll that it hadn't been long since he'd been in the penitentiary. He walked right up to us and started a conversation.

About the same time, a red-and-white Caddy pulled up. The driver was Tate, another Superior. We all knew exactly who he was: an O.G. from the 'hood. Everyone had mad respect for Tate. He was one of the first dudes in the 'hood to have Zenas on his car. In those days, they had a price tag of about $3,500. When Ronnie saw Tate, his whole demeanor changed. Not that I think Ronnie was scared, but Tate was way more cocky than Ronnie.

Tate parked, jumped out, gave Ronnie some dap, and addressed the rest of us as "lil' homies." We tried our best to hide the fact that we'd gone there to steal Ronnie's car. That was my first time meeting Ronnie.

It couldn't have been more than a year and a half later when Whim called me over to 84th and Main. "There's somebody I want you to meet," he said.

"I'm on my way, homes."

Whim stayed on 84th Street and Ronnie stayed on 88th Place. As soon as we pulled up to Ronnie's house, I saw the car and knew exactly who I'd be meeting. I doubted he'd remember me, though, because within that year and a half, a lot had changed. The last time he saw me, I was flat broke and casing his car. By now, he was probably one of the richest black men in South Central.

We knocked on his door.

Ronnie's trippin' ass opened the wooden door. A light was on inside the apartment, making it easy to see him through the wrought-iron screen door. Ronnie stood behind the screen, no shirt on, holding a gun that looked like a cannon.

Whim was in front, but Ronnie acknowledged me first. I was surprised Ronnie remembered me, because I wasn't the only one there that night. "Freeway, it been a while. What up?"

Then he opened the door and let us in.

Inside sat a plate with rock cocaine, powder cocaine, weed, and cigarettes on it. Ronnie told me he'd been selling weed and PCP. Now I understood how he got his car so fly.

As we talked to Ronnie, we heard steady taps on a back window.

A small parking lot behind Ronnie's house led straight to an alley, an ideal spot for selling, because people could walk unnoticed to his apartment through the alley. From the looks of it, Ronnie had been running drugs out of this place for years.

Ronnie was a shrewd negotiator. It was rumored he'd done some pimpin' in his day. He was street savvy. We agreed to $1,800 an ounce. He'd buy two and I would front him two. It was set. We shook hands and I said I'd be back in less than 30 minutes.

The drive from his house to my spot on 81st was about five minutes. I returned in no time at all. The deal went smoothly. Ronnie became one of my close friends. Even though I was younger, he treated me like his big brother. One after another, the guys who were once players were calling on me.

Next on my list of networking to pull in another partner was to drive to Nickerson Gardens. It was risky. The Nickersons were loaded with Bloods. I knew only one person in the Nickersons and that was Tyrone. I hadn't seen him in a few months, but I needed to talk to him, and urgently. Tyrone sold "water," the street name for PCP. He did pretty well at it, too. I headed for Nickerson Gardens, a public housing project with more than a thousand apartment units. Tyrone lived in one of them.

When I got out of the car, guys on the sidewalk near Tyrone's building could tell I wasn't from there. They started to "Blood" me, but I felt sure I could get to Tyrone's apartment before anything happened. When they saw me walking toward his door, the mood changed. When I knocked, they backed off.

Tyrone looked down from of an upstairs window and told his wife, "Let Ricky in."

Tyrone was older than me. His younger brother was a Freeway Boy, so he treated me like a homeboy. Inside the apartment, I told him about my drug venture. He smiled. He said he'd been hearing about cocaine, but he hadn't jumped in yet. I invited him to go with me to 81st and see for himself the cash being made there. "Nickersons could be the same," I told him, "a supermarket for cocaine."

As I walked out of the projects with Tyrone, it was an about-face from how I was treated when I walked in. *So that's what it's like to be with somebody who's respected by all*, I thought to myself. I was learning fast.

When we got to 81st, I took him to the spot where Ollie and Mumbles were waiting for us. Tyrone and Mumbles were real cool. Mumbles had smoked PCP with Tyrone's younger brother. A couple of other guys in my crew had tried it a couple of times too. Another was Cruz Dog. I'm not sure whether Ollie ever smoked. I know that a couple of my other guys did. I was hard on all of them when they did it. I wanted them to stick to the business of selling.

I was never appointed a leadership role. It was just something I fell into. The guys gave me the respect for it.

Tyrone liked what he saw on 81st. As he and I walked to my car to take him back to the Nickersons, we saw King Flea standing at a nearby apartment building holding a big pipe. He wasn't wearing a shirt, and in place of it was a chest full of gold. When he saw me, he took a big drag, and then saluted me with his pipe. He'd given himself that crazy name because he claimed he was going to "suck the blood out of the game."

There were about 40 apartments in the area, split into two rows. One was pink and the other was lime green. This was before the city put up barbed-wire fences and locked gates to keep people out. Or maybe the gates were to keep people in. Sometimes it was difficult to tell which way it was intended.

We walked down the street, talking. There was no doubt in my mind that Tyrone was in. He assured me he had all the money he needed for me to set up a deal right away.

As I drove back from dropping him off, I thought about how well things were falling into place. I felt like an entrepreneur building a business. I speeded back to get to Ollie and give him the new deal. When I got back to Ollie, we told each other, using our typical words, "Nigga, we fixin' to be on top." I talked him into taking a break and going with me to M&M Soul Food to get something to eat.

Once we got there, we got a table, and then, man, was I shocked. Kino walked up to our table and said, "What's up?" He picked up our check and paid for our meals. I knew I was doing something right. We definitely were on the fast track.

Ollie and I made plans at the table to do our deal that night. It would be the most dope we'd ever seen in one place. Situations like that could be nerve-wracking, but in a good way. There wasn't much to do in preparation but to hope for the best.

I learned that as you move up the ladder in the drug game, when a particular deal is your first time, it plays with your nerves. The more you do it, the more you get used to it. The fear of handling that large quantity dissipated with each transaction.

Ollie and I didn't want to be the ones to carry Ramon and Tyrone's money. They'd have to ride with us. That way, if something happened, we wouldn't be responsible. The plan was to get the van and then ride over to Mr. Foster's house. We left Ramon and Tyrone in the van.

From the first deal, we weren't going to make a profit. It still hadn't sunk in yet that the more we bought, the cheaper things get, especially when it came to ounces. We also had a bunch of different suppliers, and some of them offered us better prices. Not that the quality was as good, but this got me to thinking that we should actively pursue better prices.

We arrived at Foster's house and Ollie and I went inside to do the deal. Foster made a phone call to his contact Ivan and his brother-in-law, Henry. They must have been nearby, because they showed up at Mr. Foster's in less than five minutes. Both Ivan and Henry spoke broken English. From their accents and attire, they appeared to be from somewhere south of the border, in Central or South America. They wore-ostrich skin boots, jeans, and plaid shirts.

We sat down in the living room and put the money—somewhere in the area of $45,000—on a coffee table. It translated to 16 ounces at about $2,800 apiece.

This was before we knew how to count money. Money was everywhere in my houses, because we didn't separate the different bills; we made piles that equaled hundreds.

We shook hands with Ivan and Henry. There was careful skepticism on both sides. We had to respect the chain of command, so we didn't interact with them much. This was before we realized that Mr. Foster was smoked out.

After they counted our money, which took about a half-hour, Henry walked outside to meet up with a guy named Poppy, in his car (who we later learned was Ivan's driver), and he gave the coke to Henry. These guys had been rollin' for a while; I could tell this wasn't their first rodeo.

Henry returned and showed us a bag. It was a large chunk of rock with a little shake, in a big Ziploc bag. Henry handed the bag to Mr. Foster. We all nodded at each other, and then Henry and Ivan walked out the door. After they left, Mr. Foster stuck a piece of paper inside the bag and pulled out the shake, which was probably an eighth of an ounce. That was his piece for hooking up the deal.

Seven grams probably doesn't sound like a lot, but Ollie and I could make $300 off of each gram. Even though Mr. Foster put us through hell, because he was wishy-washy, that was just a part of doing business. He still had the best deal in town. We took the bag and rolled out.

We got in the van and immediately passed the bag back to Tyrone and Ramon to inspect it. They looked at it, but they relied on our judgment. The deal had already been sanctioned, so we headed back to my mom's garage, where Tyrone and Ramon had left their cars there. It was our former hangout where we now kept a triple-beam scale. It was a place to chill and relax. I asked my cousin Kenny and Cruz to stand guard while we took care of business.

We went into the garage and weighed up everybody's stuff. We separated the bag into three even portions and put them in Baggies. When that was done, Tyrone and Ramon went on their way. From my point of view, I'd just distributed drugs to a new dealer at Nickersons on Main Street.

Ollie and I stashed our stuff. We used my mom's house—or, rather, her iron pipes—to hide our load. The house behind my mom's was vacant and our neighbors had been living there since we'd had the house, so it was a safe environment for us. We didn't sell drugs out of her house.

We headed back to 81st and before we could even get the car stopped, people ran up to us. We'd been getting mad props coming from everywhere: the women, the gangsters, the old folks. It was snowballing. We were growing so fast, we almost couldn't believe it. Ollie didn't usually talk to people very much, so I was the one answering all the questions. I told everybody we'd holler at them in a few minutes. Ollie made his way up the steps, and I told him I'd holler at him on my way up.

A guy on the street yelled out to me, "Hook me up! I've got $400."

When I was halfway up the stairs, Keith walked out the door, clowning and saying, "There goes my main man. What up, boy?"

By his expressions, I could tell he was ready to score. He felt I owed him and I should treat him differently because he'd schooled me on the game. I suppose he had.

I knew that things were going well for the block. But when we got upstairs, where Mumbles was waiting, money was all over the place. It looked like Ollie was shaking him down. Money was in every pocket, sock, shoe, and orifice. I didn't know exactly how much dope we had left for Mumbles, but he'd sold it all. Every crumb. He was ready for more.

"We're straight," Ollie told him.

With Mumbles out of drugs, traffic flooded to other areas. Everybody was getting in on the action.

The first people to catch on were the sherm sellers. Instead of buying after every sale, they saved their money and came to me when they had, say, $375. They wanted to buy eight-tracks. You could get eight or so eight-tracks out of an ounce. That came to about $3,000 an ounce. It made good sense.

By now, 81st had turned from a sherm track to a cocaine track. Hardly anyone sold PCP anymore and it became scarce. I still remember the look on Waterman Tone's face as the change took place and I took his track over. It took him a couple of months before he woke up to what was happening. When he did, he came to me and asked if I would put him down. That happened a lot. Guys who I thought were doing better than me were becoming my workers. There was plenty of money for everyone on 81st Street, so I put them down.

Just about all of the mothers in the apartment complex a couple days before the first of the month asked me about investing their welfare checks. It looked like an organized plan, because so many of them voiced interest. Welfare checks for coke. I knew it was going to be my biggest day ever, because I had so many prepaid customers. My network was growing.

Ramon called me after a young woman wanted to buy a quarter-ounce. He refused to sell it to her. She wanted it for $700. We were still able to take one gram and make $300 to $325 off of it. He felt he'd be working at a loss if he sold it for that. I'd already caught on to selling quantity. If I sold seven grams and made a hundred dollars, with little or no effort on my part, then it was a good sale. I figured if she was buying seven grams today, who knows? Maybe next month she'd buy two ounces. That would go from purchases every other day to sales every day. The frequency increased with the demand. It was only a matter of time and basic statistics.

Ramon set up the meeting with Ingrid, the young woman better known as Goldie, or Red Goldie. She had an apartment that backed up to the rear of M&M's on 96th, a great location. Her traffic easily blended in with the restaurant. Ingrid had a body that was out of this world and wasn't bad looking either. The down side was that she was gangster to the core and had a reputation for a lot of gangster stuff. I'd heard about her but hadn't met her. We got her started.

I sold her the seven grams and she paid in new hundred-dollar bills. I thought about hitting, but I thought it might interfere with the money. I did take special interest in her. There was no ego with her, so that was the beginning of our relationship.

Man, did our relationship grow. I think she came back the next day and bought an ounce. Whenever she bought one, I would give her one on credit. I only dropped her price a few dollars. The next time when she came, she brought her two sisters with her. It was starting to get fun, because her sisters were fine. One was named Ladybug and the other was Charmaine. They both sold drugs. The youngest couldn't have been older than 14, but she was already packing a pistol and kept $400 in her purse. This stuff amazed me. I didn't know that kids that young handled business like that. Not only was I enjoying the relationship with Ingrid, but the homies were too. This was like moving up a notch for all of us. Not surprisingly, Ingrid's crew had a bunch of tag-alongs.

Ingrid had become my biggest customer, and our relationship was growing. She and Ollie got involved, and that was cool with me, because whatever Ingrid wanted, she got.

By then, I was up to $200,000 and $300,000 and could do whatever I wanted, whenever I wanted. A bunch of us hung around one day with nothing to do. Somebody suggested we go to Magic Mountain. We all said, "Cool." I arranged to leave. We got gas at a station outside of our 'hood. While we were in a circle, having a ball, or what I called "baller's game," three guys slipped up on us. Or so they thought.

To everybody's amazement, Ingrid had drawn down and told them not to move. I was shocked. We were all strapped; everyone was back then. We weren't looking for trouble. We were all about business. I don't know what those guys were up to. Maybe we'd been stereotyped. They were three young black men dressed in gang attire. Ingrid got them to back off.

We headed off to Magic Mountain and had a great time. Money was not a thing. We played all of the games, ate, and drank. I was after Robbin, one of Ingrid's friends. She was gorgeous and worked at Baskin-Robbins. I bought a lot of ice cream the next couple of weeks.

After a day at Magic Mountain, the next day it was back to work. We had so much money we didn't even count it. We'd only count enough to re-up our supply. It cost about $32,000 for a pound, or $2,000 an ounce. It was good money for us. Ingrid bought an ounce a day, plus what I fronted her. Ramon and Tyrone came by every day to get quarter-pounds, and we made $450 off of each one.

We still used my mom's house and my old bedroom as our stash. We threw the money in the back closet and covered it with old clothes. We'd long given up on using shoeboxes because we didn't have enough.

My mom had put me out of the house. I figured she suspected what we were doing because of all the trips we made. It didn't seem suspicious to us, but then we were making drops every time we had $1,000. That was probably every 30 minutes. It added up fast.

On one of these trips, my mom stopped me. She told me to go into her room. I went in and she asked me, "Where all that money came from?

"I made it," I told her. "I earned it."

I was sure she thought I was using drugs. I'd sold the accessories off of my car to buy drugs, but not for me to use. I thought it was a waste to have money sitting on my car in gaudy accessories when that same $6,000 could make me $1,200.

Mom was kind of a den mother to all the fellas. They slept and ate at her house, and my mom demanded respect. She told me to go and get Ollie and Mumbles. I knew we were in trouble.

I left her house and went to 81st. I ran up the steps and told them what was going down. Ollie scratched his head, curiously, as he typically did. "Amigo," he said, "so Mom's trippin'?"

"Yeah," I answered as we got into my car.

We headed back to the house and into her room.

"How much money is in your closet?" she asked.

We looked at each other, clueless.

"You need to count it," she said. "I'll help."

When we'd finished counting, it was $100,000.

That should have been the day we walked away. We originally only wanted to make five grand. Before we started in the game, we couldn't even buy gas. We were poor.

It was too late, though. There was no looking back. After we counted the money and stacked it, Mom gave us a religion speech about gaining and losing your soul in the process.

She cried and pleaded with us that if we were in the mob and we could get out, now was the time. I love my mom dearly and I hated to see her like this. I tried to tell her in a polite way, without lying to her, that we were going to get out soon. There was no way I could give her a date, nor did I intend to quit any time soon. I'd finally found my niche in life.

I was proving wrong those people who said I'd never amount to anything. Here I was, after only six or seven months, a major player in the city with $100,000 in cash.

Once we knew we had a hundred grand, the game stepped up and our perspective changed.

I made phone calls to guys I thought could be potential suppliers. I informed them that I had a hundred grand and my intention was to spend it.

After I talked to everybody, I went to see my old friend Monk. He was one of the shot callers, if not the main man, from the Main Street Mafia. He sold a few dime bags of weed and worked at the alternator shop on the corner of 98th and Main. I knew he'd be an ally, just as good Ramon and Tyree. Who knew? Maybe even better.

I rolled up on 98th and Main and the fellas were standing outside. T.C., Fish, Psycho Mike, Baby Boy, Little Monk, and a few other cats I didn't know. I already had love on Main Street, because they knew Monk and I were homies. When I called out his name, he stuck his head out of the generator shop's garage door. Monk was a couple years younger than me and he always called me O.G. I walked over to the door and we gave each other fives.

"My man, O.G., what you been up to?"

"I been rollin'," I told him.

He said he'd been copping a few ounces of weed and the money had been good. I laughed to myself and then told him I was selling cocaine.

"With coke, the money's great," I told him.

"O.G., put me down."

"You know I got you," I said. "When do you get off work?

"Three in the afternoon," he answered.

It was funny, because not that long before I'd go to that same generator shop and sell him old generators off of stolen cars, or ones that we'd steal from the junkyards, for a couple of bucks a piece. As I watched my boy Monk go back inside and back to work with big greasy gloves on, I said to myself, *I could probably buy this joint.* As I headed to my car to leave, I thought about those times spent at the shop with Monk and got a little nostalgic.

When I got back to 81st Street, police cars were everywhere. I noticed, though, that it wasn't a regular raid, because the cars were black-and-whites, and couple of Metros, not the kind of cars that were characteristic of drug raids. I pulled up and saw Ollie and Mumbles standing near the street, so I was no longer worried about them being arrested. I parked the car down the street and walked back toward Ollie and Mumbles.

They explained that my cousin Evita had just shot up the block. They said her boyfriend had slapped her and since she knew where our guns were stashed, she wanted to do some redecorating with the M-1. Luckily nobody got hit, so her bail was only $5,000. We had no problem posting her bond. As the days went on, living with Evita was getting more difficult. She needed more and more money.

We didn't sell drugs out of her house. It was more of a combination stash spot and a place where we could sleep. We noticed our stash was coming up short. I had the utmost respect for and trust in Evita. She was my favorite girl cousin, and she taught me a lot about doing business. Her daughters were like my kids, and since I didn't have any kids of my own at that time, it was personal for me. We'd smoked primos together, but it was supposed to be a one-time thing. For me, it was just another experiment. I later found out that Evita hadn't quit—and hadn't planned to.

Things were rocky at our spot, to say the least. When she got out of jail, she raised all kinds of hell and made lots of noise. "Why did it take you so long to get me out?" she asked.

After bailing her out, I met with Monk that same evening. I rolled back to 98th and Main. This time I took an eight-track with me. It was my gift to Monk. It was a wise investment. He had a crew of about 50 under him and that meant I would be able to put product out that much more efficiently. He had a homegirl who stayed on the corner of 98th. Her name was Louise, even though I didn't know it at the time. We headed into the kitchen and I cooked up the coke for him. I showed him how to add the baking soda, how to put it into a pot of boiling water and watch it turn to gel. Add some cold water, shake gently, and it forms into one big rock. Once it turned hard, we took it out of the shaker bottle.

Then I started to cut it up for him. I cut him $1,100 worth. I told him all he had to do was offer it to all of his marijuana customers and it would start to move. I could see the skeptical look in his eye. I'd seen that same look many times before. He knew I'd never lied to him before.

"I'll see what happens," he said.

Monk was not your everyday, average thug. He'd been in jail for shooting at cops, for manslaughter, and, I'd heard, for rape. He couldn't have been much older than 18. He was big; he'd been hitting the iron hard. He commanded respect throughout the various 'hoods.

As I walked out his the door, I thought to myself, *What a move I just made.* Because Monk's place wasn't far from where Ingrid stayed on 96th and Avalon, I decided to swing by and pay her a visit. And, man, was she doing.

When I pulled up to her house, the line was around the block. Ninety-sixth was starting to look like 81st. There must have been somewhere around 50 or 60 people in line. She served through a hole in the door, which was a security tactic. She was a woman doing all of this on her own. She was smart about it. And careful.

When I walked up to the door, she recognized me, and, with pistol in hand, she opened the door. Her coffee table was covered with money. Some little skinny kid in the house was with her. He had a Jerry curl and I could tell he was a pretty boy. She ordered him to the back bedroom when I walked in. I wasn't trippin' about it, because she wasn't my woman.

She told me she wanted to buy 16 ounces. I'd never sold 16 ounces to anyone. My biggest two guys were Ramon and Tyree, and she just went past them even though I hadn't been working with her for more than a month and a half. I explained that it was cool and I'd set it up. I didn't quote her a price right off the bat; I needed time to consider it. Plus, I wanted to run it by Ollie and see what he thought.

While Ollie and I were up at the spot discussing Ingrid's deal, one of our female customers stopped in with a friend. I took one look at her and couldn't help myself.

"You're beautiful," I told her.

She was a little embarrassed, but she said, "Thank you," and we started talking. The customer said she was her niece, that I knew where she lived, and that it would be all right for me to visit her there. She stayed on 82nd, which was convenient.

Ollie and I finished discussing Ingrid's deal. We were buying two to three pounds at a time and getting them for around $2,100 an ounce. This Ingrid deal was going to be our biggest single transaction. It made me wonder about Tyree and Ramon. Why weren't they buying bigger quantities?

I made a point of going by Ramon's spot. He had a brand new Maroon Cadillac, a Fleetwood Brougham with all the fixin's, sitting out front. He paid $16,000 for it. His traffic was so heavy, he was buying quarter pounds just about every day. It was the same scenario with Tyree. He drove a brand-new van. I saw their new wheels and understood what the hold up was. This turned them into my workers. Because they were spending their profits as opposed to reinvesting, they'd never be able to catch up to me. I didn't say much about the cars, but it was the last time they rolled with us to go out and cop. We didn't need their money any more.

On my way back, I ran into Little Pete. He was from Watts and ran with the Grape Street Crips. He was a low ranker, but he was somebody I'd always had respect for. I heard he was in the water game. He had some cars too. I saw him at the gas station and we talked. I'd learned a valuable lesson on 81st Street: PCP guys and weed guys could all be converted. It's the old saying, "Go with the highest bidder."

Cocaine had become the new king. Pete started with a quarter-pound that same day. His watering days were over. I gave him a deal, $2,600 an ounce, and I knew he'd gotten the best stuff he'd ever had.

When Pete stopped by to pick up his quarter, he brought Albert Griffin, better known as Benzo Al, with him. Al was a water guy too. And he had one of the flyest Cadillacs around. Ollie and I had gone to Albert in the early days to get some PCP. I knew he didn't think I had money, because he'd told a mutual friend I was trying to get dope on credit. That hadn't sat well with me, first because it wasn't true and, second, because I'm all about putting money on the table. Now the tables had turned.

I taught Pete how to cook up the coke. We did it in my mother's garage. Everybody knew where that spot was and it had gotten to be safe. We'd gotten out of the car-stealing business because it because there were too many risks.

We finished up with Pete, and he was yet another happy customer. I also knew we had Benzo Al. I could tell by the look on his face that he was sold. But I knew that it wasn't right for him to crack on me in Pete's presence. I'd make myself available to him later that day.

Then there was Little Tommy. He used to be in my low-rider club. When I first met him, he was about 14 years old. He had the most raggedy '63 Chevy that I'd ever seen. But one thing I noticed about him was his determination. He was in high school bench-pressing about 350 pounds. We were all heavy into the weights, and putting up 350 was something very few people could accomplish. I had dropped out of the low-riding scene, and I was probably a little hard to find for people who weren't in the loop.

As it was, Tommy wasn't in the loop. On one of my trips to my mom's house, I noticed the bright orange '63 Chevy parked in the driveway. The car looked like it had been painted with a paintbrush. I was glad to see him because he was like one of my little brothers. I knew that he had been working at his uncle's liquor store. What I didn't know was that he was already dipping in cocaine. Tommy seemed mature for a youngster. I saw him and asked what he had been up to.

He told me that he'd been getting 50s from Ramon, five or six at a time. He was selling them over the counter at his store. At the time, most liquor stores had head shops in the back. In these shops, they sold pipes, scales, and shaker bottles, all kinds of paraphernalia for making and using drugs.

While I was building an empire of employees and managers for the street, to move the cocaine, I was also creating my future competition. Once everybody starts to get rich and successful, they may decide that working under someone else, like me, is no longer economically viable. Then they'll buck and take a shot at controlling the game. Eventually, that's what started happening with some of my workers.

After Tommy explained to me what he'd been doing, I told him to stop by later on that night and I'd hook him up. I already had more dope than I could sell, so I was looking for people to sell it for me. Later that night, I gave him a half-ounce. I told him that he'd have to bring me back $1,400. He didn't understand what all of this meant, but I told him that he should be able to make at least $3,000 off of it. He smiled from ear to ear. I knew he'd be very pleased with what I gave him, because Ramon wasn't looking out for anyone other than himself.

We made the transaction and the next day Tommy comes back with $2,800. I gave him two ounces this time. One paid in full and one on the front. I wanted to cut down on the amount of times that I was making transactions. Safety first. I also told Tommy where he could find me on 81st if he needed me. Aw, man, I could see the potential in this kid. He's one that looking back, I probably should have locked in as a partner.

I can't be certain, but it wasn't more than two or three days before he was back again. This time he came with $12,000. Worse than that, though, he saw 81st Street. He must have seen that Ollie and I'd been very relaxed with it. He zeroed in on its potential. This time I served him up a half-pound.

The next time I saw Tommy, he told me to go to his spot on 82nd Street. That was strange, because just weeks earlier he didn't have a spot on 82nd. When I walked into the house, I just shook my head. He was getting all of our leftovers, all of our walk-in business that might not catch us. He was drinking out of the same well we were. That was cool with me, because I was charging top dollar for ounces and it was all my dope. I still didn't see the threat.

During one of those trips, Tommy brought Haney with him, who was another one of our low-riding friends. Haney wanted in. Tommy was the kind to flaunt his wealth. We couldn't have been working together for more than three months before he had his first Mercedes. I guess that worked both ways because a lot of the young guys in the neighborhood would come up to me and say they knew that I had Tommy rollin' and that they wanted to roll the same way. I was always looking for workers. Ollie, Mumbles, and I could only do so much. It was getting harder and harder to keep Ollie and Mumbles on.

That's when I got a bright idea: If I could give Tommy a half-ounce, and he did well, why not do it for the whole Freeway crew? I called a meeting. I arranged for the Freeway Boys to meet at Manchester Park, because I wanted everybody there and it would be too big to have it at my mother's house. There were at least 20 to 40 people, but that would only be 40 ounces—maybe a bit more.

None of these guys had ever sold cocaine before. I had some concerns that some of them would smoke up the product, so I put the rules on the table.

There would be no smoking. What I was giving them was theirs to keep; to do with as they pleased—which was probably another mistake. I explained to them that we would drive traffic from 81st to Denver Street. That was a similarly set-up neighborhood, but this was our stronghold.

Other sets came over there, but everybody recognized that it was our turf, without a doubt. It didn't take Denver Street any time to get rolling. Maybe one week. The customers preferred it to 81st Street. And even though some of the Freeway Boys were into gangbanging, or, rather, claimed the Hoover set, we dressed more casual, they all played tennis, rode motorcycles, and did recreational activities like that. Nobody was getting robbed on Denver Street, which wasn't the case with 81st. So Denver was on and popping!

At least a dozen of the homies were coming up. Not like they should, but I was still proud of them. These guys were, and still are, like my brothers. We shared sodas, slept in the same beds as kids, and if somebody did something to one of them, they did it to me and to all of us. It was like a brotherhood.

Denver also touched Manchester Boulevard, which was where the Forum was located. People started telling me that we had it popping so hard, it looked like there might be a Lakers game going on every day.

After Haney dropped by with Tommy, he cracked on me. He said he wanted to be put down. I liked him a lot. I thought he'd be an asset to the team. I threw him two ounces and he started to roll. It didn't take any time before he started to look like Mr. T. He and Tommy were the first guys I ever saw who wore hubcaps on their chests, covered in diamonds.

When I saw that, my reaction wasn't subtle. "What the fuck is that shit?" I asked them.

Tommy said that his was worth around $50,000 and had "Young Tommy" written in diamonds across it.

Haney had some of the finest women with him I'd ever seen and I wanted to know where they came from. He told me he was meeting them from the skating rink. So, I said, "Let's go to the rink."

I'd never been to World on Wheels. It was like a candy shop. Chicks were everywhere. That's the first time that I ever saw Whitey, from Whitey Enterprise. There were about ten of them there with jackets bearing the same name on the back. They had been in a big war with Third World. This was a turf war between drug dealers. Haney was getting action from everywhere. You would have sworn that he was the richest guy in the building.

Me, I couldn't get any action. I had been dressing casual at that time. Levi jeans, sweat shirts, tennis shoes, and absolutely no bling. But my pockets were stuffed with cash. Girls, though, didn't check out guys' pockets. I went around and hit on a few chicks. But Haney was getting all of the action.

Finally, one chick, whose name was Marilyn, came up to me and said, "Hi, Rick," which was surprising. Nobody there should have known me. For the last 10 months, I'd been underground. She had on skates, Levi jeans, and a tank-top blouse. She couldn't have been more than five-foot one, maybe five feet even. And she had a fat ass. Her hair was in finger rolls, tight to the skull. I'd never seen that before. We started to talk.

I still wasn't quite sure how she even knew me, but it didn't really matter. I was just looking for something to hit. We talked and I asked her who she was with. She said she and her girlfriend had rolled together. I asked her where she was from and she said 98th and Main Street. But I still hadn't put two and two together. I told her she could ride home with my boy and me.

"It's all good," she said as she went back to skating, I went back to my boy. I explained to him that I had come-up.

When the end of the night came and the skating rink closed, we all rolled out. Ollie and I had just gotten our first apartment. It was an old wooden duplex we spent a little money on cleaning up. The guy who rented it to us charged just $300 a month. The situation with Evita had blown out of control, and we moved.

Evita's using had become obvious to us and everyone around her. We were paying the rent, plus we had to give her a couple hundred dollars a day. It was practically extortion. But the deal breaker was when her mom, who was my auntie, dropped by and gave me the blues. Her mom accused me of getting my cousin hooked on drugs.

Evita stuck up for me. Right after that, the landlord came over with a county marshal. It turned out Evita hadn't been giving the landlord the money we paid her for rent and we all got evicted. That's how we wound up with our own place.

On our way home, I told Marilyn I wanted to roll by my place and get my car. She was completely cool with that. We got to the house, went in, and homies were scattered all over the place as if it was a refugee camp or something. People were everywhere, just hanging out, watching TV. I decided to invite her into the bedroom, away from all of my homies. It was time for me to make my move.

She wasn't going for it—not that night, anyway. I took her home and found out that she lived just two doors down from Big Monk, one of my guys, and when I pulled up in the driveway, I asked her if she knew him. She said, "Yeah, that's my homeboy." She asked if I remembered going to her house with Monk. She said that she'd gone half with Monk on an eight-track and did a little rolling on her own. I figured it was all good and told her as much. It was getting late. "I'll holler at you in the morning," I told her.

What I really wanted to find was somebody to lay up with. The next day, I rolled back to Marilyn's place. I'd already talked to Monk about it. He told me that the homegirl was cool, didn't get high, and I was with that. She had good potential.

I drove the van on her street and she walked up to my window. She had this kind of walk where she twitched her ass. Doc Rob was with me and we both noticed it. I told him how much I was looking forward to hitting that. I felt, sooner or later, it would happen. I could see that she had heart. I asked if she knew of a spot where we could cook up some drugs and she said, "Yeah."

"I'll be back in fifteen minutes."

When I returned, she jumped in the van and pointed me in the direction of the spot. We pulled up to a fourplex apartment building. She got out and knocked on the door. A familiar face answered. It was Rene, an old friend from school.

We went in and put everything together so she could start rolling. I asked her to bring me back $2,400 on an ounce. Soon, 98th began picking up traffic. Monk and Little Monk had been doing a good job. Now the entire neighborhood was waiting to get in on the action. Little did I know how much they were waiting in anticipation.

It couldn't have been more than three to four hours before Marilyn called me. She had more heart than Monk, or maybe she felt that because she was a woman she could get away with more. Maybe it was a little bit of both. She was selling quantity. I was excited at what she might accomplish. She arranged for me to pick her up at the skating rink, which I was happy to do.

I pulled up to the rink early that evening, just to look around. I felt safe because nobody knew me around there. Since I wasn't with Haney, nobody paid attention. The snack bar was at the back of the skating rink. There was one way in and one way out.

I walked back to get a hot dog and a slushie, and when I turned around, there was Wayne Day, better known as Honcho. The last time I'd seen him was when I pulled a gun on him. Honcho was strong as a bull and could easily bench 500 pounds. On this night, he had two youngsters with him. Honcho was a shot caller for the Grape Street Crips and the president of the Majestics Car Club. Some people can hold onto a grudge for a lifetime.

When I turned around and saw Honcho, I was surprised. He was the last person in the world I wanted to see that night. I had hitting on my mind—and not the kind that involves throwing fists. When I looked him straight in the eye, he kept his mean mug on, just for a second, and then he put on a wide smile and said, "What up, cuzz?" Boy, was I relieved to see that. I'd seen Honcho and his guys drag people out of their cars and whoop them at street races. Back then, probably nobody else on the street had a reputation bigger than his. If there was an O.G. left on the street, it was him. Ultimately, he was featured on "America's Most Wanted" TV show, as a wanted fugitive, before police brought him down. Honcho and I'd done a few car jobs together in the past, but I'm certain he always looked down on me. But not that night. He gave me my props. Maybe my reputation was bigger than I'd realized.

He asked for an invitation, but without coming out and saying it. His actual words were, "I done heard that you the man, now."

I brought him into the fold. I also met Chubb, Honcho's first cousin, who I found out later had just gotten out of the Youth Authority. We started walking together around the roller rink. As we walked, Honcho said he'd heard rumors about what I was doing. Everybody at the rink watched Honcho as we walked. We stopped and stood next to the dance floor. I was careful. "Yeah, man," I told him, "I'm doing pretty good."

I asked if he'd gotten down with the cocaine yet. He told me he hadn't, but he heard it was a good business. We arranged to meet the next day at Ollie's mom's house. Ollie and I had taken it over and were in the process of renovating it.

Our game was up to about $250,000, maybe $300,000 a day. Things were going so well that when Honcho and Chubb stopped by the next day, I handed Honcho eight ounces. He was in a gray Fleetwood Brougham with a bumper kit and big grill. He already had money, but not the kind of money he was about to get. I walked him and Chubb out to the car and he stuffed the eight ounces inside his moon roof. I thought, *I've just scored a big one*. Having Honcho on the team was unreal. He didn't disappoint.

It wasn't two or three days later that Honcho was back. He had $45,000 and was ready to cop. Honcho ruled with an iron fist. He was the kind of guy who wouldn't let anyone sell drugs in his projects unless it was *his* cocaine. He had a crew to enforce the rules. He was in the game, and he worked for me.

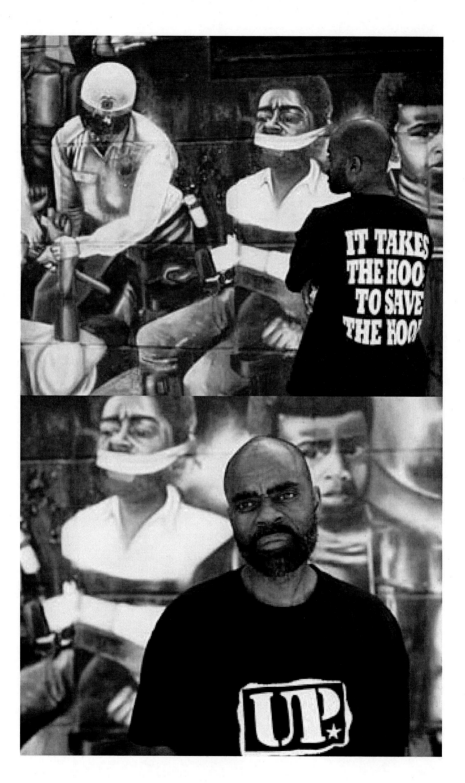

CHAPTER 13
WHEELING AND DEALING

People were lining up to join my team. I was enlisting more dealers every week, and not just any dealers. Two in particular stood out. Doc Rob was a Bakersfield police officer, and Dee was a California Highway Patrol trooper. Ollie and I were tight with them; we'd grown up together. We weren't surprised when they showed up and said they were ready to get down. Their contacts on the street gave them the potential to make some serious money. We were happy to have them on the team.

One day as I was chilling in the front room, I heard banging on the bar doors. I walked out and saw that it was Moped Greg, who rode around on a worn-out moped. He was an O.G., and he had two youngsters with him, Monty and Inky. I invited them in. They each wanted to buy a half-ounce.

Then my boy Dean told me he had a friend, Stacy, over in the Pueblo Del Rio housing projects in a Watts community known as the Low Bottoms. Stacy, he said, had the heroin market sewed up, and she knew how to bring in money. He wanted me to met her.

Dean took me to Pueblo, at Holmes Avenue and 54th Street. At the projects, kids tooled around in Mercedes Benzes and Chevy trucks with the tops cut off, all supercharged and decked out. Homies paid $5,000 for paint jobs. It seemed everybody had new low-rider wheels called Daytons that could set you back $3,200 a set. Obviously, the youngsters doing *that* well had to be selling something.

This was the territory of the Pueblo Bishop Bloods. Dean wasn't banging, but he was dressed in cherry red, the Blood color of choice. We pulled up and got out of the car while a fight was going on, in which a chick who looked to be about 6-foot-one, 200 pounds, and all muscle, was whooping on a guy.

When Dean saw her, he said, "That's Stacy right there. She carries it like a man."

"I can see that," I nodded.

The guy managed to get out from under Stacy's grip and run off. Just as we approached, Stacy walked to the edge of the parking lot and bent down to pick up her shoes, which apparently had flown off her feet as she beat on the guy. Dean, standing in the parking lot with me, called her over to us and introduced me.

"What up, man?" Stacy asked in a husky voice.

"Nothin', nothin'," I said. "Good to meet you."

She explained what had just gone down. "These niggas better realize that I'm all about my money." She said some guys thought that, because she was a woman, they had a right to fuck her over. She was having none of that.

I was really digging what I saw—at least with her. I wasn't all that comfortable standing in a parking lot at projects where it was an open market for drug sales. The Pueblo projects were rough, right up there with Nickerson Gardens. I wouldn't have ventured inside without Dean. Even then, I carried my 9-millimeter. Everyone hanging around the lot no doubt had guns on them too. There'd been some recent friction among homies there, which led to a few drive-by shootings. Gang unrest, the cops called it.

I wanted to get to know Stacy better. We agreed to meet, sit down, and chop it up. She was one more contact I wanted to pursue.

Ollie and I were now living in his mom's house, fixing it up as if we'd live there the rest of our lives.

The contractor kept adding to the house as the remodel continued. We spent around $150,000 on a home that probably cost no more than $65,000 new.

I'd never ever heard of sod until the day a truck pulled up with pallets of the stuff. It came with its own forklift.

The same people who installed the basketball rims in the Forum arena installed fiberglass backboards on our personal court.

The maid worked full-time at our place, we had barbecues in the patio at all times of the day and night, and our $35,000 stereo system could be heard blocks away. We had all the latest DJ and rap equipment, and the youngsters rapped and scratched music on our turntables. It was a nonstop party and *the* place to be.

We were out of control.

At first, I was proud of the house and its improvements, but gradually, I became leery of the attention it brought. As the work progressed, it became a problem. The house stood out like a sore thumb, which was exactly what we did not want.

To top it off, our guys were blowing up overnight. People stopped by the house driving Porches, Mercedes Benzes, Rolls Royces—you name it. We were looking increasingly conspicuous.

I was surprised when the gardener, a guy called Tweet, told me about a newspaper article he'd just read about the police and drug dealers.

"I read this story in the newspaper that said the cops were protecting the big drug dealers. I figured you to be one of 'em."

For the life of me, I couldn't tell if that was good or bad. Even so, we still felt secure in that house, which sat on the corner of 88th and Grand on the I-10 freeway side. We didn't have neighbors on one side, plus our friends and families lived across the street and down the block, and many of them hung out at the house.

That was the way life went for us for a while. Every day we had a new hook-up and every week a new buyer. The money continually flowed.

Then one day I paged Ivan, one of our Nicaraguan suppliers, and he didn't answer, so I paged him again. Still no answer. That went on all day, then the next day, then for a week. We started to get desperate. We couldn't see ourselves going back to our previous connections because the prices didn't compare. Ivan gave us a good deal. But our people were going nuts without cocaine to sell. We'd created a monster. I had a clue where we might find out about Ivan. We'd once met him with another Nicaraguan, Tony, who owned a small clothing and manufacturing shop.

"Let's go to that clothing shop and see what happened to Ivan," I told Ollie.

When we got there, Tony said he hadn't seen Ivan in months. He volunteered, though, to hook us up. The price was high: $34,000 a pound, which was slightly less than what we were selling it for, and that was after breaking it up into 16 ounces. But we agreed to buy two, to get things rolling. We had to have coke for our dealers, and we figured the price would come down.

Tony made his calls and we left to go get the money. We got back to his shop and he said the deal would go down at his house. We went there and let him count the money; then he made a phone call to the contact. Fifteen minutes later, another Latino guy knocked on the door. He was holding a brown bag that looked like it held two pounds of cocaine. And he was acting paranoid.

"Where's the money?" the guy asked me.

"Where's the dope?" I countered.

He held up his bag to show me, and I held up mine. I felt safe with my guys, Grump and Zo, sitting in a car out front.

"Man, just give 'em the money," Tony told me. Tony's family was upstairs, so I couldn't imagine anything dirty was going on. It was too much of a risk for him.

Tony took the bag of money from me and handed it to the guy, then he grabbed the bag of cocaine and handed it to me. I opened the bag and could tell instantly that it wasn't cocaine. It would probably bake a nice cake, but it wouldn't get you high.

I looked up and Tony's connection had burned off, out the door like he was on fire.

I jumped up and took off after him. Ollie ran after me. I saw the guy jump in his car, which was already running. When I got to Grump and Zo, who hadn't been paying attention, we fired up our car, and the chase was on.

It started on Washington and Vermont and we chased him into downtown L.A. before we lost him. When we got back to Tony's house, Ollie had already called the rest of the homies, who went to his house and beat him up pretty badly. Tony readily agreed to take us by his connection's house. There was no doubt in my mind that Tony didn't know that his connection was going to burn us and had nothing to do with the scam.

We got to the guy's house and it was vacant. The neighbors said they'd moved out a few days before. Now, I had to figure out what to do with Tony, who was still with us. My homies wanted to exact revenge. They all screamed, "Murder!"

I took him home myself because I knew he was innocent, duped just like we were. I didn't want anything more to happen to him.

Still, Tony was scared shitless. He offered me everything he owned to make sure no one laid another hand on him. I reassured him that everything would be all right. He got out of my car and walked away holding the side of his head, but with a much calmer look on his face. He was obviously relieved and thankful to be alive.

During the ride back home, all kinds of things went through my head. Even though I'd just lost $68,000, I felt lucky that Tony wasn't hurt too badly. They'd bruised him, but that was it. Also, even though Tony's contact had pulled a switcheroo—the oldest trick in the book—I felt good that I still had money left. Like Tony, I had plenty to be thankful for.

Still, my dealers were begging for more product. It was late and I needed to go home and lie down. I'd sleep on it and figure it all out later.

I got up early and called one of my old connections.

It's a funny thing about the dope game. The second you relax and let your guard down, someone will surely take advantage of you. Or at least try. The prices the contact quoted were high. I wasn't ready to raise the prices that all of my dealers and workers were accustomed to. I said, "No thanks."

Then I got in touch with Buddy. We hadn't been in contact for months. I told him how much money I had—right around $350,000, give or take a few thousand, not to mention what I had out on consignment. He arranged for me to talk with his brother, Big Mike. Mike told me that his friend, Chinese Dave, had just gotten out of prison and was a major coke boy.

Chinese Dave was a crazy-looking mother. He resembled a sorcerer—dark enough to be black with his hair in a perm in a kind of fake afro. Also, Chinese Dave was flashy: cars, clothes, toys. You name it, he had it. I talked to him and he said he'd start me off at $2,100 an ounce. I didn't like it, but at least we were working. We started with two or three pounds. After we did a couple of deals, he threw me a couple extra pounds on the front. We didn't need it because we already had the money. But it showed the trust factor, and that was important.

Although the money wasn't increasing as fast as it had been before, it was still growing. It must have been obvious to Dave that he couldn't keep up with our pace. I was sure I had more cash than he had.

One day, he said that his dope came from Miami and if we went there to get it, it would be much less expensive. I'd never considered going out of state to get drugs; the idea didn't sit well with me. It was risky enough carrying cocaine across country, but carrying all that cash was even more nerve-wracking. On the other hand, the price Dave was talking, $38,000 to $40,000 a kilo (a little more than $1,100 an ounce), was too good to ignore.

Dave had been in the game a while and knew the ins and outs of the cocaine business. The Nicaraguans had kept us at a distance, but Dave had opened it up to us. We could drive any of his cars and go to his house any time. He was like one of the homies. I felt comfortable with him, especially after we'd worked closely together on a number of deals.

We began making plans on how we'd get the money to Miami. I'd never carried drugs out of town before. I'd sent it to Texas with my twin cousins, but that was only four ounces. I could take four ounces anywhere. This time, though, we were talking nearly 50 pounds.

With me were Ollie, Dave, Ton-ton, and Nevel as we flew to Pensacola. There, we got a rental car and headed to Miami. We taped the money around our waists and put some in our carry-on bags. We had money everywhere. We didn't book a flight home; it was way to risky. It was Ollie's, Ton-ton's, and my job to get the product back without incident. Going through LAX was no problem. We made it from one airport to the next, and then to the rental car. Everything was fine.

Dave kept two ounces of snort on him at all times, for personal use. All the way to Miami, in our rented four-door Lincoln Continental, he snorted. I needled Dave in the car about snorting so much. I had a lot to lose if this thing went tits up. We made it to Miami, checked into a motel near the airport, and waited for a call. We rode around town checking out the scenery and had fun. Ollie, Ton-ton, and I took a ride down to the beach, near where *Scarface* was filmed. I hit on some chicks. That's how our day was spent: Driving around, spending money, trying to pick up chicks. I was tired and ready to head back to the motel and rest up.

When we got back, Ollie ordered pizza, and I went to holler at Dave. When I got to his room, he was doing what he loved best: putting snorting powder up his nose and talking on the phone. Nevel was kicking back watching TV.

I didn't mess with Nevel very much. He'd popped onto the scene and Dave handed him the right-hand man position. I was a little jealous.

In fact, the first time Dave brought him to my house, we had it out. Nevel was a black guy, but he looked white. When I first saw him, right off I figured him for a cop.

"The only white guys who come over here are cops." I told Dave. "What'd you bring him to my house for?"

Ten years later, Nevel and I ended up as cellmates at the Federal Correctional Institution in Phoenix. But in Miami, he didn't hang with us. I steered clear.

Dave said everything was set for the next day. I was glad, because I had no idea what was going on back in the 'hood.

The next day, we left the motel to make the score. At the location, a two-story apartment building, I got nervous. I'd heard all kinds of stories. We were down there without straps. Dave wouldn't bring all the money until we saw the product. He was a veteran at this, so I followed his lead.

The score ended up going down without a problem. I got myself 20 keys and Chinese Dave got 12.

Off we went to Georgia, our first stop. Chinese Dave had the big idea to use Florida plates till we got out of that state, and then change cars. We rode down the highway, the four of us, with 32 keys, stacked like bricks. One of the ounces broke open, causing dust to blow everywhere. I honestly thought there was no way this was going to end well.

I was so relieved when we pulled into a hotel in Georgia for the night. I immediately called California. The guys said they'd be driving out in a motor home to meet us in Indiana. If we made it home with the cocaine, then it was the come-up, the big score.

The next morning we went car shopping. Dave picked out an '83 Toyota van that was loaded. It looked like a breadbox. It had tinted windows and was nothing if not inconspicuous. The trip would definitely be more comfortable than in the Lincoln. Dave had agreed to pay $28,000 in cash for the van. We headed to a couple of banks, got a cashier's check, and I drove that baby off the lot.

It took us another 12 hours to get to Indianapolis, where we hooked up with the homies. We put the drugs in the ceiling of the motor home. It was smooth sailing from then on. No cops. No problem.

CHAPTER 14
MIAMI OR BUST

The minute we got back to Los Angeles, Dave wanted me to give him a kilo of coke in exchange for the van—a duplicitous act on his part, overcharging me at least $10,000. I could have sold the key, paid him for the van, and had five figures left over. Then he wanted another kilo for hooking me up with the connection, telling me that he hadn't added any "taxes" to the price. I was pissed, but I understood that this was how the game often went—all part of the game of moving cocaine. In the end, I had 18 keys instead of my original 20. Plus, the van made a nice gift for my mom. Kind of like making lemonade out of lemons.

I could still make close to $100,000 off of a key, so we were talking about nearly $2 million in profit. We came out of it in fine shape. Once again, we were rollin' good.

In a month and a half, we'd gotten down to our last five keys. Money was all over the place. That's when Old Man Murphy and his law "anything that can go wrong, will go wrong" cropped up and we had what I called our first "accident."

It was the day before the first of the month, sometime in the summer of '82, when we took two keys to the house in Norwalk, a suburb of Los Angeles about 20 miles northeast of downtown. We spent the night cooking and cutting it up for the next day's sales. I was hoping to clear $200,000 from the two keys. We ended up with two Ziploc bags of rocks, all cut up into dice-like shapes.

We woke up early the next morning and Marilyn drove my car with the drugs in it back to L.A.

On the freeway, I followed behind her in one of my partner's trucks. When she got off the freeway on El Segundo, I was furious, because she hadn't taken a direct route to the drop-off spot. Besides that, she'd exited in the worst possible area where three different groups of deputies regularly patrolled. I caught her attention and got her to pull over.

"Where the hell are you going?"

"I have a doctor's appointment."

I instructed Don Vey and Baby Crim to get that car back on the freeway. As fate would have it, as soon as they pulled away from the curb, a Los Angeles County sheriff's deputy turned the corner.

When I saw that, my immediate plan was to get between the drugs and the deputy, but I was too late. The chase was on. Don and Crim punched out, with the sheriff's deputy behind him in hot pursuit.

Marilyn and I jumped in the truck and followed the chase for a couple of minutes, then I thought it'd be best to switch cars. We went home, dropped off the truck, and took a different vehicle.

When we got back to the area where the chase had started, it was cordoned off with yellow crime-scene tape. I found my Lincoln with its doors, trunk, and hood wide open, obviously searched by deputies. I was not only sweating losing a couple hundred grand in drugs, but the possibility that these guys just might sing. It was a stressful morning, to say the least.

Marilyn and I talked to neighbors on the street that saw the arrests go down. They gave us the rundown. My homies had tried to get away by jumping out of the car and running. A police dog—a

K-9 unit had been dispatched to the scene—tracked them down. One of my homies was bitten pretty badly.

I hadn't dealt with a problem like this before. I went to Chinese Dave and Big Mike, guys I thought would know how to work it. Don and Crim were back out on the street in less than an hour. Their bond was only $50,000 each.

It was the first time I met defense attorney Alan Fenster, a big-shot L.A. drug lawyer. He'd practiced law under Howard Wiseman, who'd represented automaker John DeLorean in his notorious cocaine case. Alan had a big office in Beverly Hills and I was impressed. The criminal legal process was relatively new to me, but Dave was familiar with it. He walked around Alan's office like he owned the place. Who knew? Maybe he'd paid the rent on the office several times over.

We arranged for Alan Fenster to represent Don Vey and Crim. I insisted that they do no time. These guys were like my brothers. They'd do almost anything for me. And I wasn't going to let them do time for a drug possession they weren't even profiting from. I told them that money wasn't a problem.

I won't say exactly how much I paid Fenster, but I can tell you, it was the largest sum I'd ever paid for anything besides drugs.

With the drug sale, we would have been fine. But with the arrest and the confiscation of our Ready Rock, when all was counted up, we were worse off than before we left for Miami. We still had money on the street, but our drug supply was bone dry. It was time for another meeting with Dave.

It was around that time I had my chance to meet my drug hero, Thomas E. "Tootie" Reese. His name was all over town as *the* man for selling drugs. He'd just been arrested and made the front page of the *Los Angeles Times*, which was no small feat. I was very careful, but I wanted to meet him and have a chance to talk to the guy who the streets said was the real Super Fly. People had pointed out his car, a red turbo Porsche, from time to time when we were out.

One of the guys working on my house said he could set up a meeting between Tootie Reese and me. I met him in Inglewood. It was a nice middle-class neighborhood in the South Bay region of L.A. The house looked like it could be one of his stash spots. I also met Flint for the first time. We all sat down to talk.

Tootie told me he'd heard a lot about me, that my name was starting to carry some weight. I quickly decided against telling him that I admired him coming up, because I was starting to feel like maybe I was the man too. Besides, he'd just made the crucial mistake of selling to an undercover agent. Rumors were also on the street that he'd started using, so maybe that's why he'd been caught. A dealer using always spells disaster. For those reasons, he dropped a couple of notches off the pedestal I'd put him on.

In fact, I did not intend to do business with him, no matter what he offered. I had to establish, for myself, that I was on an even footing with this guy. I had to humanize him, take away his status as an idol. Then I'd be able to understand where I fit in among the heavy hitters. On the other hand, he was the man just the same, and I was happy to meet him.

We talked, he showed me some drugs, and we discussed prices. He inquired as to how much I was moving a week. I told him. That was the extent of the conversation. Then I left, walking out with a sad feeling. He looked to be around 50 years old, but he was in his 40s. From the back of my mind, a nagging question emerged: Was this my future too? But I dismissed such notions because I didn't use drugs. That line separates the ones who last from the ones who eventually go down.

The meeting also crystallized exactly what I wanted to be, not only the biggest, but also the best, drug dealer in the City of Angels, if not in all of America. Nothing else would do for me. I guess it was something I'd gotten from tennis, an overbearing need to be number one. When you have a goal like that, and you can visualize it, feel it, almost smell it, you do whatever you can to get there.

———◆◆———

It was time for another trip to Miami. Ollie and I wanted to see Dave.

We stopped off at Taco Pete's. Even though we had money, we still preferred 99-cent burritos. Chinese Dave stayed up in the Los Feliz; back then, it took about 30 minutes to make the drive. I was still on a high from my meeting with Tootie Reese. When we arrived at Chinese Dave's house, I mentioned the meeting. Dave blew up.

I didn't know they were rivals. I also didn't know they were sharing the same woman. Chinese Dave may have felt that Tootie Reese was trying to steal me away from him, too. I assured Dave that I was loyal. I kept to myself that Tootie's prices were too high anyway. My main concern at that point was getting back to Miami to resupply.

So that was where we went, to Miami, with the same amount of money as before: $600,000. This time, though, the full 20 keys would be mine. Chinese Dave got a better price this time (about $850 an ounce). Of course, I had to factor in the price of the trip, plus buying a new car back east, but it was still a better deal than I could get in L.A.

We flew to Pensacola—Ollie, Ton-ton, and me. The buy went smoothly. Then we made our way up to Georgia to pick up a car.

We'd started looking in the newspaper to buy the car in advance, so it would be waiting for us. We found a '75 Suburban. They wanted $2,000 for it, but we negotiated it down to $1,500.

The car was a financial burden, because my funds were so low. We had only about $3,500 left after the dealings were said and done, cutting it very close.

Luckily, the Suburban wasn't in bad shape. It had plenty of room, and if we took our time, we could make it. We paid up and hit the road.

Suburbans have three rows of seats. Ollie and Ton-ton had been asleep in the back for a couple of hours when I heard it.

It started innocuously enough, a tick here and there. Nothing that sounded serious. I thought, *We probably should have checked the oil.* It was about two in the morning, pitch black outside, and in the middle of nowhere in Tennessee. I woke up Ollie first.

"Man, listen. Do you hear that?"

"Amigo, how fast you been going?" he asked.

"I wasn't going fast, only about seventy-five or eighty."

The car was losing steam. We had a problem. I looked for the first exit. We paid close attention to the highway signs as the car crept slowly to a stop. I pulled over on the side of the highway. The first thing we had to do was get the suitcase of drugs out of the car and hide it. Ollie and Ton-ton took care of that, while I waved down cars, trying to get us a ride. Finally, a guy pulled over, cracked his window, and told us that at the next exit, he'd let a tow truck driver know where we were. The guy was true to his word. No more than an hour later, a tow-truck driver pulled up. Boy, were we happy to see him.

It was during the winter, and we were dressed for California and Miami weather. The truck wouldn't start, so we'd been without a heater while we waited for the tow truck.

The driver pulled up, got out, and asked what the problem was. I answered that I thought we blew the engine. I asked what he'd charge to tow us to a gas station. He worked at a police impound and junkyard and said we could get it fixed there. The price would be $125 for the tow.

At that point, I was so cold, I didn't care where we were going or what it cost. The deal was affirmed.

While he hooked up the Suburban, Ollie slipped back into the woods without the driver noticing, and threw the suitcase back into the Suburban. We didn't worry that we were going to a police-impound yard.

We arrived at the yard and met the owner. He was cool. To this day, I believe he knew what we were up to. He learned we didn't have licenses when he offered to get us a rental car. Without licenses, that wasn't an option. He asked us a few questions that sounded suspicious, like why none of us had driver's licenses, where we were from, that sort of thing, but then offered to sell us a car. At that point, we had only $1,200 left and we didn't want to be stuck with another lemon.

We had no cash, but we did have a bag full of cocaine worth millions. And no way back to California.

Finally, we wound up with a U-Haul box truck, the smaller variety, which the owner of the yard drove us to pick up. When the three of us climbed into the front seat, there was barely enough room to shift the gears. Ollie was around six-foot-two, a solid build with broad shoulders. Ton-ton was somewhere in the neighborhood of six feet and stocky. As expected, I landed the luxury seat, in the middle.

We drove back to the yard to retrieve our bag from the Suburban. We threw it in the back of the truck. We said goodbye to our newfound Tennessee friends and headed out. The owner volunteered to escort us back to the freeway. Before we left, I phoned home and instructed my brother David to let Dave Chow know, if he saw him, that we were en route to L.A.

Homies from the old neighborhood joined the team as workers, but my brother David played a small part in the drug game. He wasn't good at it, but he was good at transporting the drugs and protecting the money and me. He had that big brother mentality. To him, I was still his baby brother. He watched over me.

The truck had a governor on it, so it wouldn't go more than 50 miles per hour. Our plan was the same, to take the long route around. We went through Cincinnati, Kansas City, Denver, and then, finally, we rolled into Las Vegas. We were lucky the police never pulled us over.

It was the first time I'd stayed in a Las Vegas hotel. We enjoyed it. We didn't have any money on us, but we felt like millionaires. Technically, we were. At that time, we could fetch $200,000 per kilo, so we had a bag of cocaine with us in Vegas with a street value of about $4 million.

We took showers and got a good night's sleep. The next day, our homies arrived. They drove in two cars and the motor home. We stuffed the cocaine in the roof again and headed for L.A.

All told, it was one long trip.

———————◆◆———————

Once we arrived home, we went right back to work. Business started jumping again. Things couldn't have been better.

It was becoming obvious to friends, neighbors, and relatives in the 'hood that we were doing well. They'd hit me up for cash. I carried $40,000 or so in my pocket just for those occasions. I was the guy in the neighborhood with the money and they were my friends, so I gave it to them. Whether it was to pay rent, a car note, the mortgage, or groceries, they came to me. It's probably one of the best feelings you can have, helping them out. That's what I would want someone to do for me if I were in trouble.

One day Lorenzo "Zo" Murphy told me his mother needed help. "She's dying," he said. He broke down. "She needs surgery and she doesn't have insurance." I paid the $40,000 to cover her open-heart surgery and his mother lived. Zo never forgot it.

For the neighborhood church, I bought new pews and replaced its broken-down air conditioner.

For the kids, once a week my homeboys and I'd drive our van to Manchester Park with Sparklett's water jugs that we'd collect our loose change in—quarters, dimes, and nickels. The jugs filled up quickly and, man, were they heavy. At the park, we'd pull into the parking lot and the kids would see us coming. They'd run to the van as we opened the back to set the jugs of change on the floor near the doors. "C'mon," we'd tell them, "dig in. Take all you want." The kids filled their pockets to overflowing with change. I heard rumors, but never to my face, that people had started calling me the Robin Hood of the 'hood.

Los Angeles probation officer Jim Galipeau told the *Los Angeles Times* that I was "the biggest-time dope dealer to come up from the streets of South Central" and my reputation was enhanced by my avoidance of flashy jewelry, body tattoos, luxury cars, and designer clothes. "You never heard of him getting high or drinking or beating women or dealing dope to kids," he told the newspaper. "The guy really had a reputation for helping people out and giving money back to the community. He was more like a Robin Hood-type guy."

One day, as I was leaving my mom's house after dropping off money, standing next to a car waiting for me was Henry, a Nicaraguan from my past.

Henry was Ivan's assistant, or at least that was the way it appeared to us at the time. We later learned he was Danilo Blandón's brother-in-law and, in actuality, a partner to Ivan, our missing Nicaraguan supplier. Henry called me over to his car in his half-broken English, "Hey, Ricky-man," he said, "I need to talk to you." He put his arm around me and asked where I'd been.

I looked at him incredulously, because he was the one who'd disappeared for several months while we worked night and day trying to earn back what we'd lost from their contact, Tony, in the snatch-and-grab bad coke deal. He told me Ivan wanted to talk to me.

"Well, where's Ivan?" I asked.

"He's in the hospital. He got hurt bad."

"What happened?"

"His wife shot him and he's paralyzed. He can't walk.'

Henry asked if we could go to a phone booth and call Ivan right then. I agreed, and we made a call to the hospital.

On the phone, I heard the weakness in Ivan's voice. Ivan was a big man, six-foot-three and about 230 pounds, and he was both stocky and confident. But now he sounded like a different person, someone who was in bad shape. He asked if I could visit him. I told him I'd be there anytime.

"Come today."

"Okay," I told him, "but I need to pick up Ollie, and then I'll drive out to see you."

Henry gave me the address. It was in Bellflower. Blacks didn't live in that part of town, but homies went there to steal cars and burglarize houses, so the sheriff's deputies were on you quick over there. Ollie and I were careful as we drove in. We didn't want to break a law and give someone a reason to pull us over.

At the hospital, Ivan was sitting in a motorized wheelchair. He was partially paralyzed and could hardly move the remote stick that controlled the chair. I felt his pain. He told us he didn't want to talk inside his room, and asked us to follow him outside.

Once outside, Henry stood nearby holding Ivan's drink, while Ivan took sips of soda with a straw every so often. He told us that in his condition, he couldn't work and that Henry would be taking over. It would be business as usual, he said. We told him we no longer bought pounds, that we were buying strictly keys. We also claimed to be getting them for $2,000 less than we actually were. We didn't tell him that we'd been going to Miami to get them.

"Give me some time to make a few phone calls to check out the prices," he said. "I'll get back to you."

"We have six hundred thousand dollars in cash," I told him. "Business has picked up."

He smiled and said, "I knew that. That's good."

Ollie and I were pleased with the meeting. We were glad to see Ivan, because we considered him a friend. I mean, we felt bad for the guy, getting shot in the back by his wife and all, but we were happy we had a source closer than Miami. We wondered if he could match the prices that we were getting through Dave. We had plenty of cocaine, so we weren't in a bind. We just wanted to set up more.

I got up the next morning and saw a big yellow van sitting in front of my house. A white-haired man was sitting in the front seat. It was Poppy, Ivan's driver. I walked outside and Poppy said, "Get in."

Inside the van were Ivan, Henry, and another guy I'd never met.

"We have three hundred keys that have been crushed, dropped, and in disarray," Ivan said.

"I don't care about packaging," I said. "Coke is coke."

"I'll give them to you for thirty-four thousand a kilo."

This stuff must be garbage at that price, I thought. Other than Miami, I was used to paying 40 or 45 per kilo.

"We need a sample," I said. "I'll go inside and get thirty-four thousand. You can drop off a key tonight."

I got the money, which was no more than pocket change, and gave it to them. If this was truly good stuff, then our business was fixing to explode.

That night, Poppy dropped off the package.

Ollie, JJ, Zo, and I hit the spot and did a cook test. It passed but it created yellowish rocks. To test further, we took it to some smokers. They loved it and gave it a new name. They called it "Piss Yellow." I could visualize my future improving enormously.

I contacted Chinese Dave and Big Mike and told them that we had a better price. It finally felt like we had the upper hand on Dave. He was curious about who I was getting it from. I told him it was an old connection. Ollie'd already nicknamed Ivan "Ironside," after a TV lawyer played by Raymond Burr (he also played Perry Mason) who sat in his wheelchair barking orders at people.

Dave wanted to see the product, so we set up a time. I didn't tell him it was shake, so he'd do his test without thinking it wasn't good quality. Dave was a customer I didn't want to lose. He was buying anywhere from 15 to 20 keys at a time, cash money. I figured he'd be happy to pay between $35,000 and $38,000 per brick. That would squeeze off anywhere $7,000 to $8,000 per brick for Ollie and me. *Not bad for a few hours' work*, I thought.

Over at Dave's, the first thing he did was give it the old nose test. He snorted, then snorkeled, meaning his facial muscles twitched slightly. The look on his face told me it had passed with flying colors.

Then he had Nevel cook some up. I already knew that it was all coming back. If you put a certain amount in, after you cook, you can see what comes back out of it; that tells you how much cut there was in the powder. This powder had no cut, none, zero. It was as pure as I'd ever seen. It couldn't have been any more pure than if you'd been on the farm in Nicaragua.

We haggled over the price. I always tried to take a laid-back attitude. I wanted them to think they were running the show. Dave, especially, loved doing that. Of course, I knew the real numbers and I'd already done some figuring. I'd added in a nice premium on the Miami price, even though I'd just eliminated all the stress and hassle of those trips. I knew that without me, Dave didn't have anyone to go to Florida for him. Besides, with this new hook-up, when he released the money, he'd have his drug. Same hour even, sometimes.

As the meeting ended, being the wise businessman Dave was, he agreed to all of my terms. I felt good about that. With two guys I respected now working for me, it seemed like my time had arrived. Tootie Reese was in prison serving 35 years. I could, if I had to, control the flow of cocaine into the greater part of Los Angeles. I was really the man now. It did cross my mind, as I read about Tootie's lengthy sentence, there was always the possibility I could go to prison too. But not like Tootie. He used and that was his first mistake. Plus, Ollie and I cultivated our sources and dealers from the 'hood and treated them well. We made them rich. And if we kept making them rich, they wouldn't turn on us. That was the theory, anyway.

So, 1983 ended on a high note. I was making so much money, that money didn't even matter anymore. It got to be where I did it for the rush.

Then, the following year was off the charts. We moved 50 to 100 keys a week. It was early 1984, I was 24, and a kingpin with more than a dozen crack houses in South Central that each churned out $20,000 to $40,000 a day in profits. My network of drug dealers was able to peddle a staggering 500,000 crack rocks daily. By the end of 1984, I'd be moving 100 keys daily.

Word spread so far that my twin cousins in Texas had gotten the word. They lived 1,800 miles away and were doing well for themselves on their own. They came out to California to see my setup.

When I picked them up at the airport, they had on large cowboy hats and ostrich-skinned boots. It just so happened that the day I picked them up, I had the urge to see what a Mercedes felt like. I asked Maildog, one of my youngsters, to borrow his Benz, which was all laid out. My cousins thought the car was mine.

I explained that I stayed low-key and that the car belonged to an 18-year-old kid named Maildog. When we got to the 'hood and they saw Maildog, they said, "What?!"

Maildog dropped us off at home and it was the usual scene: barbecuing, rap music, plenty of drinks, and girls everywhere. I introduced them to everyone as my "cousins from Texas." They got the royal treatment.

"How long you here for?" I asked them.

"As long as it takes," they said. They were trying to get plugged in.

I had homies take them over to a house and show them how to work a triple beam and how to cook it up—kind of like a crash course into the drug game. After they went through the process, I suggested they visit the rest of the family. I also told them that once they were ready to return to Texas, I'd have a package for them and they didn't need to pay me for it.

When the time came, I fixed them up with eight ounces apiece, taped it to their sides, and put them on the plane. I told them to holler at me when they got back to Texas, which they did.

Around this time, I got a call from Henry. He was talking fast, and I could tell he was drunk.

"I gotta talk to ya right away," Henry said.

"Okay," I told him. "Meet me at Mary's house. I'll be there working on my racecar." Mary was like a neighborhood den mother. The homies and I played pool at her house and hung out.

I was leaning under the hood when Henry walked up the driveway.

"I have good news!" he said, excitedly. "'C'mon, let's go for a ride."

Someone was sitting in the front passenger seat of Henry's car as I stepped into the backseat. I'd seen him before, but he'd never done more than nod his head at me or wave from a distance. This time, though, he extended his hand to me.

"Hi, Ricky. I'm Danilo."

It was Danilo Blandón, a drug supplier of nearly pure coke straight out of the cocaine fields of Nicaragua.

CHAPTER 15
DRUG LORD

I'd officially connected with Danilo Blandón, a move that, unknown to me at the time, would change the course of my life.

It cost me $60,000 to meet Danilo, a stocky man with salt-and-pepper hair and a trim mustache who carried himself like a seasoned businessman.

Danilo paid 60 G's, too, to meet me. With payments from each of us, Henry and Ivan were out of the picture and Danilo and I were free to deal one-on-one. Ivan, however, didn't know about the introduction fee when it went down, and I didn't know that Ivan didn't know about it. It was a backhanded move by Henry to get some quick cash.

For me, it was access to cocaine directly from the source: Danilo.

During our first meeting, Danilo and I rolled around. We drove down to Rialto for dinner to discuss future business.

The price per key was fixing to drop into the 20s, which would be very good for business all the way down the line, and even better for profits at the top. In addition, Danilo extended credit to me.

Offers of credit lines were new to me. Not that I thought I needed it, because my cash was stockpiling. I was well over a million dollars and making so much money that I had a tough time getting to it. It's difficult to explain. The money was flowing in so fast and had to be counted so often that we couldn't keep up.

Meanwhile, I had houses all over town, motels, a junkyard, racecars, and motorcycles. I was living out my childhood dreams of being somebody. Money wasn't a "thing." But it was what made things possible. Everybody's heard the saying that money can't buy you happiness, but it was as close as I'd ever been to being happy. Money made me a ghetto superstar.

My first deal with Danilo was around 50 keys and took place just a few hours after our first meet-up. It was the biggest dope deal the Freeway Boys and I had ever done, and the easiest. Danilo put the coke in a suitcase in the trunk of his brown silverfish Honda Civic, a nice little 4-door model. The car looked brand new.

"The keys are in the ashtray, Rick," Danilo said. "I'll come by tonight to pick up the money."

We never mixed drugs and cash. Every deal after that first one went down the same way—clean, effortless, and far better than the deals done in Miami, and with Dave, and better than with Ivan. There was always a lack of trust with Ivan, until we went with Danilo. Then Ivan changed his tune.

He called, and I didn't suspect anything out of the ordinary. He invited me over to his house, so I went.

As I said, I had no idea that Henry had crossed Ivan out of the deal. Not that I wouldn't have gone with Danilo anyway, but I didn't have a say in it. As far as I knew, it was all above board.

After Ivan was made aware that Henry had taken money from both Danilo and me, in essence cutting him out of our business dealings, Ivan went ballistic, which was why he wanted to talk.

When Ollie and I got to his place, Ivan's son let us in and took us to Ivan's bedside, which was in a mechanically operated hospital bed. I felt bad for him. Here was my friend, a guy who'd helped me get rich, and he was never going to walk again. He'd lost weight and looked sickly.

Even though he wasn't well, he wanted to talk business. He laid it all out on the table. He felt Henry had crossed him and he thought I had, too.

"You took my people," Ivan said.

I explained what had transpired with Henry and that since he and Henry were partners, I hadn't suspected anything dodgy. After all, Ivan had told me himself that Henry was taking over their business, so I had no reason to think anything different. Before our meeting ended, he said he was going to make some new connections to get competitive prices again, which would work out great for us. If they started competing for our business, I'd reap the benefits.

His main concern was if I was still willing to work with him.

"Ivan, "I said, "I don't have any loyalty to Danilo and he doesn't have exclusive rights over me. It's all about the prices he's giving me. I've known you longer than I've known Danilo, so it's all good."

To prove to him that I was serious, I gave him a gift of $10,000 and told him that if he needed anything at all, just ask.

"I appreciate the effort, but I don't want your money," he said.

"It's good-faith money," I told him, "not charity."

Before we left, he repeated that he'd be back in the game competitively again, just like before.

I believed him. Ollie and I discussed it afterward, the way everything was turning out, and if it went the way we visualized it, the money was about to really start pouring in.

We sold nothing lower than ounces. We were totally removed from the streets. But that was about to change.

Things went as planned and the money flowed in. I felt like I was living in a dream world. I was working nonstop, so my homies took me on a surprise trip for my birthday.

They'd try to find something new to do, because they said all I did was work. I didn't consider what I did as a job or work. It was my big opportunity to make something of myself and build a future, and I enjoyed it. For once, I'd found something that just maybe I could be the greatest at. In tennis, everybody wants to be number one. Heck, in any sport they do. I brought that same mentality into the drug game, and I didn't want anyone or anything to stop me from climbing to the top.

One day as Ollie, David, and I were rollin', one of them said, "C'mon, man. We have to go and pick somethin' up at the airport. Ride with us."

Once we got to the airport, both of those jokers revealed that they had travel bags with them. I stared at them, wondering what they planned to do with the bags. None of them answered, except to say, "C'mon," and we parked and walked to the terminal.

If I'd known they were planning to catch a flight, I wouldn't have gone with them, but I was stuck. As we walked toward the gate, they told me we were going to Colorado. I wondered why Colorado. Maybe they had a new connect there or some other pressing business. Business is global, and so was I.

"We're going to Aspen to ski," Ollie said.

"Skiing? I'm not going skiing. You go without me. I don't have any clothes with me.

"You can buy everything you need when we got there," David said. So, I boarded the plane for Colorado.

We got to Denver just before dusk, hopped off of the jet, and caught a commuter plane for a 45-minute flight to Aspen. The snow-covered mountains were beautiful from the air. We'd passed through Colorado before, during one of the Miami trips, but it looked different now; we weren't paranoid that we'd get caught with 50 keys in the trunk this time.

When we landed in Aspen, a couple of homies were already there, waiting for us in a van. They'd planned this out. We got in the van and drove to a cluster of cabins surrounded by mountains. Inside, a big party was already going on. The song "If I Ruled the World" by Curtis Blow started playing and most everybody sang. *How appropriate*, I thought, as I listened to the song. My time had come, and I was feeling it.

Back then, I was still smoking a lot of weed. I'd slowly picked up the habit. I could try and blame Ollie because he was always smoking, but it just kind of grew on me. They had weed at the party. Our habit cost us around $30,000 a week. When I smoked, all the homies smoked, and it added up. And guess what? There was no weed in Aspen, Colorado. None. That wasn't the only problem: They didn't bring a homegirl for me. Everybody else had girls with them. I was the only guy without one. Even though I was having a good time, I was a little bothered by it. To top it off, only one telephone was in the area, and it was in the cabin office. To call out, I had to go to the innkeeper and beg to use his phone to place a call. I'd persuaded a chick I didn't know in L.A. to grab some weed and jump on a plane. Once that was handled, it was back to the party.

By then, most everybody had moved to the swimming pool, and they were naked. Snow was on the ground and the water was steaming hot. I sat back and tripped. Homeboy Cruz Dog went crazy. He'd always been a party animal, and once we got rich, it was no different. He'd stay perpetually high and drunk and occasionally went on smoking binges. He'd been one of my partners almost as long as Ollie and was welcome anywhere we went. Whenever I ever said,

"Cruz, let's roll," he was there in a second. So, his partying wasn't a problem in Aspen.

The night went down like that—fun and games. I was a little restless, watching everybody else hang out with a young woman, because I hadn't slept without a lady in several years.

But my homies had big plans for the next day. One was riding a snowmobile, which sounded like a good idea at the time. We'd all driven dirt bikes, three-wheelers, and quads, but none of us had ever been on a snowmobile. We didn't know they didn't have brakes. All told, there were about 40 of us, and we rented all the snowmobiles in the rental shop. We started racing, then we rode around the track to see who could go the fastest. Next, we played bumper mobile. Some of the girls had already wiped out, run into trees, or driven through fences. It was total chaos.

This went on for about four hours. After we finished, we went around picking up all of the pieces of the broken snowmobiles and fences. The owner was pissed. Half a dozen snowmobiles had to be towed back. I assured the owner that we would take care of all the repair and replacement costs. Everybody on the trip was ghetto rich or part of my personal crew, so money wasn't an issue. Those four hours on the snowmobiles cost me about $40,000. I called Mary and she sent a cashier's check via overnight mail. Mary took care of everything to do with money. I could always count on her. Her house was our first money-counting spot, at 88th between Grand and Broadway. She was also much more organized than any of us were. Mary kept everyone's phone numbers, and she knew who was short on their money and who was straight. Mary was like a mother to me, and her daughter, Karen, was like a sister.

When the check arrived, I gave it to the owner and told him we'd be back in the morning. The next day, he said there was no way he'd allow us back on his snowmobiles. I understood.

Instead of snowmobiling, someone came up with the bright idea to go horseback riding. We must have said it too loud, because when we got there, the guy refused to let us ride his horses. We ended up in Aspen with nothing to do. The cabins were meant for people who liked to get out of the city and go off the grid, disconnected from the outside world. No phones, no television, no radios. Just a fireplace, a bar, a bath, and a bed. With my guys all with me, we were leaving a lot to chance back home.

We put on our football jerseys and headed to a nice country diner for breakfast. The people were friendly. Still, some people stared and we could tell that they weren't used to seeing blacks up there. The football jerseys helped. We acted like superstars and were treated as such. We got invitations to Super Bowl parties. They loved us, because the homies had big appetites, ordered a lot of food, and gave nice tips.

Once we finished eating, we went to the ski slopes.

Everything was going well and everybody was having a good time until Ingrid, who everybody called Goldie, who worked for me, tried to catch her balance instead of learning how to stop on skis and headed down a slope, crashing straight into a building. Luckily, she didn't get hurt, but that was the end of skiing for Goldie. Because she was okay—just shook up—the rest of us continued on the slopes and had a good time. I fell in love with skiing during that trip.

Back in the city, things were booming. It was almost 1985, and this was when I came up with "doubling-up." It wasn't completely my idea; I stumbled upon it. Marilyn, my girlfriend from Main Street, had a group of girls working for her, and I'd give her about eight ounces a day, you know, to keep her out of my hair.

I'd been wondering where all of the dope was going, because she wasn't a junkie. It was obvious it wasn't going for personal use. She'd bring money to me, periodically, but I never counted it. I usually just threw it in the bag. To me, her money was free money, and she didn't have to bring anything, although I don't think she knew that.

One day when my chauffeur and I cruised by her spot, I noticed a line in her front yard. I'd seen those lines before, on the blocks. But this was my girl, so we stopped and I went in to see what was going on. I walked up to the spot and saw people buying rocks, fives and tens at a time. I asked Marilyn how much the rocks weighed. She didn't know. She was doing it all by eyeballing it, making sure she got 14 rocks out of each ounce. I figured the rocks were close to two grams each. I hadn't sold grams in a long time, not since they'd been 100 bucks apiece. She was killing other dealers on the prices. Because she wasn't paying for it—I was giving it to her—she could afford to offer it for much less than what everyone else was selling it for.

The main deal here was she'd made it so that anyone with a hundred dollars had the ability to get a rock. With that concept, anyone could afford it. The key to a good product is making it affordable to everyone, not just to the privileged few, and Marilyn had figured that out, mostly because she had small quantities and passed on the price break to her customers. Without realizing it at first, it was a model of economics, and we were testing it.

I liked this idea. I rushed out to round up the fellas and we headed back to Marilyn's spot at 97th and Hoover. One of the things I liked was that the customers didn't grumble, argue about price, or try to negotiate. They stood in line, bought their dope, and left. It was simple. A lot of the guys who I helped get started had gotten big by now. They had several hundred thousand dollars and would argue about pricing issues. It was a headache. But this way, I could put the squeeze on them.

I had a plan. This was going to be what I called our first "mega-rock house." Ollie, Renzo, Tootie, Little Steve, and I went in together on the venture. Once we got there, the fellas could see the line running from the side of the house as we pulled up. It made an impression. None of the homies cared for Marilyn. She often flaunted her influence, letting everyone know that she was Ricky's girl. Some of the guys took it wrong. There was a general sense of skepticism before we even got there, being that this was Marilyn's project. Plus, the guys weren't thrilled about decreasing down to selling $100 rocks. To them, it was like taking a step back.

Once we got inside and I pointed out the process to them, I could see them taking it in and realizing the potential, like I did. By doing it this way, I told them we'd be making $1,400 an ounce where we'd previously been getting a thousand or even less. It was simple logic.

I arranged for Joe, JJ, and Tootie to take over the house. At first, it angered Marilyn because she thought that she was being shut out. At the end of the day, my word was final. I told her I'd let her know that night what I had planned for her. My mind was racing.

That house alone could make up to $40,000 a day, and the rent was only $450 a month, which was cheap. Many of the homies still hadn't been able to stand on their own two feet. The house and its potential were going to make it easier for them. All they'd have to do was sit there, all day, watch videos, invite girls over, sit on plush furniture (which we were providing), take money through a small hole in the wall, and send the drugs out. It'd be done in shifts. We weren't worried about the police because the line of people outside wasn't made up of junkies; they were established, working-class people who had a weakness for crack. Sometimes the crack lines were 60 people deep, "Like waiting for a Magic Mountain thrill ride at Disneyland," my brother David used to say, except they were waiting for the thrill of crack.

That night, when Marilyn and I went home, I told her I was putting her in charge of finding the houses. She'd become my main girl. She'd still have access to all the money she needed, but she'd no longer be sitting in a rock house. I'd continue to let her cook and cut the dope, which Marilyn and her crew took time and great pride in so each rock was nice and even. They were good at it. Things were taking off for Marilyn and her crew.

One of the parameters for buying houses was that they be located near the tracks. A track was a street where all of the guys stood outside selling drugs. It was all about convenience and pricing. They were apartments in rundown areas and usually gang-infested. We wanted streets without neighborhood-watch programs in place. We liked to get near high-trafficked areas. But pretty much anywhere in South Central would do.

What I did was go by all the tracks and tell all the guys I knew—smokers and hustlers included—that I'd just opened up a spot nearby, give them the address, and use the term "double-up." What that meant was if they spent $100 on a two-gram rock, they could keep one gram and sell the other for a hundred. The smoking hustlers loved it. Those guys sold just enough to support their habits. I ran experiments with some of the guys I'd known since I started. They felt like I owed them. If they saw me out, they had no problem asking for money or drugs. Most of the time, they got it because they were the roots of my business; I couldn't turn my back on them. At the same time, I knew that the majority of my homeboys still didn't get the big picture.

On a couple of occasions, as a test, I'd give the guys a half-ounce or even an ounce. I'd do it around the first of the month when cash was plentiful. I wanted to see how long the drugs and money would last. It didn't take them long to run out of both. They might start out the month with $4,000, and 10 days later, they'd be finished. They'd tell me stories about how they had some out on credit, or other wild tales, but the reality was they were flat broke. I learned a lot about the clientele by doing those experiments. Those guys worked all night. It was amazing how when a guy was trying to support his habit, how hard he'd work and how determined he was, but in the end, the habit typically won.

I did the same experiment with 100-dollar rocks for those who smoked. The problem was that once they started, they couldn't get up from the table. The thing about cocaine is people feel like they've had more than they actually have. Some, for instance, think they've smoked all of their stash, and they knew it without a doubt, yet they still insisted on searching their pockets for more dope, which was never found. With the new 100-dollar system, they knew that every time they got a hundred, they could get a little to smoke and some to re-up.

The houses took off all over the area. We had seven or eight of them, complete with what I called McDonald's small drive-through windows, for fast, efficient service. As quick as we'd open the houses, they'd be busy.

That's when we started having meetings.

I wanted every house to be open 24 hours a day, seven days a week, including holidays. We had to come up with a formula—a system, really—to keep the houses supplied with both manpower and product. We also didn't want too much work in the house at any one time. We knew at any given time that these houses could get shut down, so we minimized our exposure and loss if it were going to happen.

I came up with a structure for the houses. All the main guys who'd been working with me since we started would be the heads of the houses. It would be their job to go to the 'hood and recruit three youngsters to work in the houses. We also made it a competition to see which house would bring in the most money. Each head of the house made $5,000 a week, and his workers made $400 each. Food and weed were free. We had another guy, Paul, who was in charge of dropping off work, or dope, and picking up the cash.

He delivered $4,000 worth of rocks in each bag to resupply the houses. Paul rolled around from house to house, all day long, picking up cash and resupplying product. He had numerous other houses for dropping off the cash. Things rolled quite well. The guys started reporting to me that, oddly enough, some customers were buying entire bags at one time. That's what pushed us into opening the quarter-pound house.

It was during this time that something weird happened. We were at a spot on 79th and Avalon, which was a quarter-pound house. I was talking to one of the young workers named "Dollar." Dollar had been coming up short without an explanation. While I was sitting there, we tried to sweat the guy into coming clean. There was no question about it; he was doing something. Dollar knew me well. He probably knew me all his life. And he knew that I was just pressing him. He wasn't about to give up anything. And that's when I heard a bang on the door.

"Who is it?" I asked the door guy.

"It's Honcho and three of his guys."

He walked into the apartment and heard the conversation we were having with Dollar. Honcho was a buyer, a client—one of my best clients, in fact. And he heard the gist of the conversation. He offered his input, being that he was a professional "sweater"—in other words, he knew how to apply pressure.

He threw two shopping bags of money on the table, and money rolled out and onto the table. He turned to me and asked, "How much does he owe?"

I didn't answer because Honcho was a customer; I didn't share the inside goings on of the business with clients. Honcho said, "I'm gonna pay his bill."

He told his two guys, Chubbs and Blue, "Grab 'im." Once they got Dollar, Honcho told him, "I haven't seen anything as pretty as you in a long time."

Dollar was in tears.

Then Honcho said, "I wanna kiss," and he unbuckled his pants and pulled them down around his knees.

Dollar cried like a baby.

I couldn't let it continue. I stepped in and said, "No, man. Don't do him."

Honcho put his clothes back on and Dollar took off to go back to work.

And, boy, did he go back to work. Dollar came back with extra. Needless to say, the problem fixed itself, and Dollar turned into one of our best dealers. He worked with me until he and my cousin Tootie got arrested in Dallas, sometime around the end of '86.

Then, we started having mishaps, one after the other.

Early one morning around six, I got a call. I was told that my cousin Eric had just killed his girlfriend, Joy, and that it happened at one of our spots. I got up and immediately did some investigating. I definitely didn't want the heat on us, plus I'd always liked Joy. She'd attended the same church as my mother, so I knew her well. Eric and

Joy had two kids, and she was like a part of our family. I was told that Eric and his homeboys had already dumped the body and made the scene look like a robbery. I didn't like it, and I told Eric so. While I was talking to him, I could see that he was drunk. A lot of my guys were starting to drink heavily. I didn't trip off of it because it was a typical thing. Looking back, I should have made a rule against drinking. There were rumors that he was smoking Primos, which were weed and rock cocaine mixed together. I had to handle a few of my crew members with a delicate touch, and Eric was the main one. These guys had hot heads, and were quick to grab a gun. And I knew, at the wrong time if I pushed them, they'd draw down on me.

We had to shut that house down. The cops swarmed the neighborhood, asking everybody questions. I'm sure that Joy's people probably told them who we were and what we were doing. Not that this is what eventually created the "Freeway Ricky Task Force," but it certainly didn't help matters. And incidents like this kept adding up.

The next incident was when I headed over to 81st Street looking for Big June Bug. He had taken over 81st, my original spot. He and Juda Bean were getting the Hoover Crips together. They'd given the gangbangers the new name of The Hoover Connect. It's curious how when the money flows, people look at themselves differently. When I arrived, they told me a car had just hit Big June Bug. The injury was the work of some Bloods, and it looked like Big June Bug wasn't going to make it. It was another blow to my network. But that wasn't the worst of it.

Little June Bug was one of the craziest little motherfuckers around. And the word was out that he wanted revenge. Stuff was jumping off the hook.

As if there wasn't enough heat, three people got killed in the same area a couple weeks later. Word on the street was that those three were the ones responsible for the attack on Big June Bug. Police and narcos were everywhere. I knew that my name was going to come up. No matter where they went, no matter who they asked, my name would have been ringing. Back then, I didn't understand it. But it was all part of the reality of becoming "the man." When you're in that role, everybody talks about you. I dressed low-key and drove buckets. But you can't hide yourself when you employ the biggest names in the business. They got their reputations by gangbanging. They worked for me in the drug business and anything they did on their own had nothing to do with me. But because I was associated with them, the cops automatically associated me with the violent gangbanging they did.

Looking back, I realize that incidents like those were what fueled the fire for law enforcement to create the Freeway Ricky Task Force with the singular goal to put me out of business and send me down.

Another problem was that I was sneaking in and out of the 'hood. I wasn't hanging out at the street level. I had a structure around me and everyone knew their jobs. Because of that structure, I was separated from the street. My name was all over the place even thought people didn't know me personally. Cops placed a surveillance team in front of another one of my spots. Although the cops couldn't connect us to the spot, because we were rarely there, it was one more house that had to be shut down. It brought too much heat.

Overall, 1984 was turning out to be a good year with lots of business, tons of connections, and plenty of women. Life was good for the Freeway Boys. The police, though, were still sniffing around, making it tougher to enjoy. We'd gotten to a stage where we moved anywhere from 125 to 150 keys a day and bought 40 to 50 kilos at a time, all from Danilo Blandón. The key prices had dipped into the teens, so that made it much more affordable for us, and we passed the savings on down to the customers. All over the board, things were going well.

Money rolled in by the bagful. The only issue was that I was starting to get bored. I wanted to expand into other businesses.

So, I opened the Big Palace of Wheels tire-and-auto parts store on Western Avenue and got a kick out of helping out. On hot days, I washed cars and flirted with women. This was one of those days.

Chris Young, one of my main guys, pulled up. Chris had a knack for hanging around money. He liked dealing with the big guys. The first night we ever got together, we hit a $75,000 lick apiece from one of his guys in Seattle. Now, it seemed like every time we got together, he'd have a 10- or a 15-sale lined up. I had a thing about making people feel special. And I had no problem showing Chris how special he was in my book.

He stepped out of his car with a phone to his ear. As we walked up and we gave each other dap, he handed me his phone.

I asked, "Who dat?"

"It's Dennis Thornton."

Dennis Thornton? *Hell, Den is in jail*, I thought.

Not long before, the feds had raided Den's house, along with four others. They found quite a bit of dope, money, and machine guns at Den's place. He was the last person in the world I wanted to talk to.

I didn't like talking to people who were in jail. Especially in for drugs. But this was my man Chris, and Den was cool, so I took the call. Den had always been a jokester. He started right off, laughing and playing. He didn't sound like someone who was in jail. But then he told me he was at Terminal Island and that my name was ringing down there. People saying stuff like, "Things must be flowing on the Freeway." He told me to be careful. I took his warning seriously.

Thoughts of going to prison ran through my head as I handed the phone back to Chris. Kenny Ray had been handling Den's business while he was away. I'd just seen him a couple of days earlier, right before he landed in jail too.

———◆———

I owned the auto shop, plus I was putting on the final touches of a 22-unit motel, called the Freeway Motor Inn, plus I had a junkyard that also sold used cars. The energy around those businesses wasn't the same as the drug game. Hanging out with my homeboys and talkin' trash—the things guys do—none of that was a part of the business world. I missed the camaraderie. I also had become a heavy weed smoker. It had gotten to the point where I couldn't function without it.

I started thinking about new frontiers. If this place didn't need me anymore and I could receive my money without any effort, then the goal was to obtain new territories. For quite some time, I'd been trying to get the fellas to go to expand into new territories. But they felt more comfortable being underneath my wing. So, once again, if there were going to be any ground broken, then I'd have to be the one to do it. It was surprising to me that my guys had all of the skills to go out on their own but they hesitated to do it. I mean, they knew there were places where keys were going for 60 grand a piece, and they also knew that they could get the keys for 18 to 20 grand, and on credit, yet they still didn't want to break out on their own. They were in their comfort zone, and they were making only five grand a week. These were guys, in my opinion, who should have known this business from start to finish. They should have had all the tools. I'm not sure if it was a lack of desire or ambition, or if they were scared.

I'd made up my mind that once I finished the hotel, I'd be moving to St. Louis, Missouri. I'd never been there, but I had a friend, Tony Wingo, who I played high school tennis with and he was from St. Louis. He was like a big brother to me. As a matter of fact, I'd gotten him into business. While we were still in school, he cut lawns to earn extra money. Every now and then, I'd work with him, and we'd always talked about starting our own service. After graduation, Tony went into the Army. We didn't have much contact. When he got back, I wasn't the same Little Ricky he used to look after. I no longer had a desire to have a lawn service, but he did. And, because he was like family, the same day he asked about starting a business with him, he had himself a lawn service. He also got the contract for my houses—an instant business.

My gardening bill alone was probably about $12,000 a month. Mr. Tweet, a gardening and landscaping service I used, was expensive. They'd done the landscaping for the places I'd built, including my house, Ollie's house, and my mother's house. He was the drug dealer's gardener. That left the ground maintenance for all the properties up to Tony.

Tony and I got tight again. We'd run into each other often at the houses whenever I checked in on the fellas and Tony was there working on the grounds. I ran into him again at one of the houses and he said he had a brother in St. Louis who was selling marijuana who'd like to get in on the game. I told him I was definitely interested in meeting his brother and to let me know when he could fly out to see me. I offered to buy his airline ticket. Soon after, the brother, Mike Wingo, arrived in L.A. and we had our first sit-down meeting.

I'd gained a lot of experience in how to get people started in the drug business. I'd learned through trial and error and understood some of the traps and pitfalls of both sides. But by now, I'd gotten the hang of it. When we sat down to talk, I explained to him about using drugs. I had no idea what a gram was going for in St. Louis at that time, but I took a good guess. They were worth anywhere from $150 to $200 a gram. I planned to bless him with two ounces as a starter kit—free of charge. I'd do it so he could feel out the market for me. We made the deal and he left for St. Louis.

He wasn't at home for more than two days when Mike called and told me he had a brother-in-law, Billy Stallings, who wanted to come out and see me. I talked to Tony about it and he said Billy was cool. He had a good job working for Busch beer and had some money saved. Later, though I found out that he was already smoking. This was a bad thing in this business. The prices that they got from me were so good that they were still doing really well. Billy, in no time, was doing better than Mike.

Then Tony's youngest sister and boyfriend wanted to get in on it too. They flew out on their own. His sister, Kim, got tight with Marilyn. They were close in age, so I thought it'd be a good way for them to get into the game. Marilyn was anxious to start, so it was a good little pairing. Marilyn started selling to Kim. This helped because I wanted to build up business in the St. Louis market. And since Marilyn would be living with me there, it'd give her something to do. The St. Louis connections were looking good.

At around the same time, Indian Tommy, Maicha's daddy, who lived in Cincinnati, approached us with his hand out. He'd been smoking when he lived in California. He and his girlfriend, Smoke, had moved to Cincinnati to start over. I'd always liked Smoke, because she took care of her business. Tommy must have known that because he brought her with him. I had a system where I set up workers wherever they lived, and in a short time, they were up and running. Because of that, business was exploding. The amount of drugs I gave them to get started didn't hurt the business. It ended up creating more businesses, only out of town. I hadn't been anywhere outside of California, other than to Texas and Florida. But a voice kept telling me I should visit St. Louis and Cincinnati.

With Indian Tommy and Smoke buying two keys a month, and Mike in St. Louis buying two keys, plus Billy buying about three keys a month, business was hopping. The money was good enough to justify a visit to see the operation. I didn't know it at the time, but the Midwest spots were the beginning of the end. And I didn't see it coming.

CHAPTER 16
DIRTY COPS

I found a nice condominium in downtown St. Louis to rent. I was waiting on the manager to finish the paperwork and prepare the condo for the move-in. Instead of hanging out in a hotel room alone, I stayed most nights at Mike Wingo's house. He had a beautiful wife and two of the prettiest little girls you'd ever want to see. I slowly learned my way around the town. My homegirls flew in periodically to keep me company. Things were going well.

And then JJ called me with bad news.

At this juncture, Ollie was doing my old job: checking on the houses, picking up the cash, riding horses, and flying model planes. You know, the important stuff. JJ was running the day-to-day operations. Everything went through him.

"The cops raided Marilyn's house," JJ said.

Man, they arrested Marilyn, her brother Steve, and my brother Tootie. It was puzzling, because Marilyn, along with the rest of us, never kept drugs in our houses. We kept the cocaine in a variety of stash cars parked a couple of houses away. That way, the cars couldn't be tied to the house. Whenever we retrieved drugs from a car, we pulled up behind it. The passenger got out, got into the stash car, started the engine, drove a few blocks, pulled over, opened the trunk, and grabbed a sports bag. He put however many keys the person wanted inside another bag, then tossed the bag in the follow car. He took the car back, but parked it in front of a different house. Nothing looked odd or suspicious about any of it. The cars were always low on the list for potential car thieves. And they were heavily alarmed.

On that day, JJ told me that 50 birds, or kilos, were in the car on the street near the house that was busted. It was a nice load and one we didn't want to lose. And nobody wanted to get arrested with 50 keys. I asked JJ if the car was safe. He assured me the car had been safely moved.

I didn't like the idea of any of my workers sitting in jail. I asked JJ to contact attorney Alan Fenster and get him on the cases, bail everyone out of jail as quickly as possible, and keep me posted on further developments. I also let him know that things were going well in St. Louis. Once I got my apartment set up, I wanted the fellas to come to St. Louis for a visit.

About three hours after that first call, I received another page. JJ had posted Marilyn's bail and she was released.

She was pissed off and in tears. The cops planted two ounces of dope on her, along with a gun. They also took around $14,000 off of her, which was her petty cash. Alan had already been down to the jail to talk to her, but Marilyn wanted to see me before talking to an attorney.

I jumped on the next plane out, and JJ and Ollie picked me up at LAX. During the ride from the airport, they filled me in. Stevie had been staying with Marilyn and our baby daughter, Rikiya. My cousin Tootie and his wife had gone to Marilyn's to pick up our daughter while the cops were still there. Steven and Tootie got their asses kicked by the cops. The cops also made them put on my clothes from my house, to see if they fit, to verify if one of them was Freeway Rick Ross. There were no photos of me in Marilyn's house; the cops didn't know what I looked like.

I met up with Marilyn. She was more concerned about me than herself. "Be careful, Rick. These guys are crazy."

"It's all good. It'll be a'ight," I assured her.

I planned to return to St. Louis within a week. She and I got a room downtown at the L.A. Hilton.

I'd been in L.A. for three days when Tony pulled up outside my body shop on 65th and San Pedro, in the big yellow Dually truck I'd given him. When I saw him coming, I knew something was wrong. He gave me more bad news. Mike had been arrested in St. Louis.

I told him it couldn't be that bad, because I'd only given Mike a key. We'd sold most of his stuff before I left St. Louis. I was thinking he couldn't have had more than 10 or 15 ounces on him.

As it turned out, Mike not only got caught with what he had, but also with four kilos I'd left in the trunk of my car. A few days before I left, I promised Mike's dad the car, because I didn't need it anymore. I only paid $4,500 for it and it was a clean title. After I sold those four keys, I'd have $400,000. The least I could do was give his father, who was one of my helpers, a car.

But Mike had jumped the gun. He'd taken the four keys out of the car and given it to his dad. He removed a brick from the wall in his basement and stashed the coke in the wall.

He thought that'd be a safe hiding place. It wasn't. The cops found the keys. What made matters even worse was that the feds were involved.

It got worse. Mike was selling drugs out of his own house, where his family stayed. This was unheard of in my circles. It just wasn't our M.O. It was a major blunder on Mike's part. Then I remembered that I'd been flying under my real name. There was a good chance I'd left the plane-ticket stubs at Mike's house, which could be used to implicate me in the coke.

I was sitting 2,000 miles away, wondering what was going on. I'd been called away from St. Louis with trouble in L.A. and here I was in L.A., hearing about trouble in St. Louis. I also was worried for Mike and his family.

In all fairness to Mike, though, he'd been set up by one of his high-school buddies. He never expected that, as people rarely do. What had started out to be a great come-up had now turned into a big loss. I wanted to put a safety net over Mike's family, so I asked his wife to post the bond and find the best lawyer in town. I was still making money hand-over-fist in L.A., so a $200,000 or $300,000 loss in St. Louis for bail wouldn't put me out of business. As for Marilyn, Tootie, and Stevie, their bail was set at $50,000 each, but I only had to pay 10-percent bond and put up property as collateral, so that wasn't too bad. My attorney Alan Fenster, on the other hand, had gotten to the point where every case he handled cost me $50,000 or more. My thing was that if I kept all of them out of jail, it would keep me out. So I gave Alan his hefty retainer. It was during this time that the talk with my lawyer about crooked cops came up.

Alan had a nice office building in Santa Monica. His practice thrived. Some people said his law firm grew because of my referrals to him. Some were indirect, rather than direct, referrals; guys went to Alan Fenster knowing he was my attorney.

I told Alan there were no drugs in the house that the cops raided. I could tell by the look on his face that he didn't believe what I was implying. "You mean to tell me the cops are planting drugs?"

"I'm sure there were no drugs in that house," I stated flatly and left his office.

Around the same time, my brother David had a strange run-in with the police, which told us we definitely were dealing with crooked cops, guys who'd do almost anything to get their man, dope, and cash.

A couple minutes after David and some homeboys left the Big Palace of Wheels, the driver said, "We're being followed."

"Take a right," David told him, just to see if the car still followed.

It did. He asked his homies in the car how much money they had on them. All together, they had about $3,000. The people in the car following them could have been getting ready to rob them, and David wanted to know where they stood with cash.

They finally lost the tail and stopped at a gas station on Ventura Boulevard. The gas station attendant motioned across the street at a parked Los Angeles County Sheriff's Department black-and-white car and told David, "That's the fuckheads."

"Fuckheads?"

"Yeah, fuckheads. Sheriff's deputies."

David didn't think much about it, got his gas, and left.

But as they rolled out, the black-and-white followed them to the freeway and pulled them over. Then they heard the cop on the radio saying that he had them. Just then, a trooper with the California Highway Patrol also pulled over behind them.

"What are you doing stopping a car here?" the trooper asked the deputy.

"These guys are drug dealers," he told the trooper. "They work for Ricky Ross and detectives are looking for him. One of these guys is Rick."

"Okay, but you're not supposed to stop them. You're out of your jurisdiction."

He was right. Police and sheriff's deputies patrolled roads and streets in their respective cities and counties, while the Highway Patrol policed freeways and interstates.

The deputy let them go, but followed them all the way to Sylmar, in the San Fernando Valley, where they turned off the freeway. He pulled their car over and waited for drug detectives. When a team of narcs arrived, they pulled David and his friends out of the car and had them spread their legs and put their hands on the car roof.

What happened next was another confirmation that we were dealing with dirty cops. A deputy searched the car without probable cause or a warrant, and emerged holding a bag of dope, even though David and the homies didn't have cocaine with them. The weird thing was, the deputies didn't arrest them.

David put it like this: "I don't know if they got spooked because the Highway Patrol may have been onto them, but a detective returned the dope to the cop car."

Then one of the narcos hit David in the back of his head with the butt of a gun. After the cops left, the homies called an ambulance, which took him to Valencia Hospital. He had a big knot on his head for a while.

Because of all the incidents with the cops planting drugs and hitting our rock houses pretty hard, and my guys going to court all over the place, the crew was a bit gun shy and wanted to lay back, take it easy for a while. But the cops had yet to find drugs on any of the homies—at least so far—except for what they'd planted.

People still wanted all the dope I could get, so I got my hands on 100 keys. One night, I decided to cook up the coke. Before I started, though, I got a phone call out of the blue from Danilo telling me to hold up.

I wasn't totally convinced I should wait to cook. *What does Danilo know that I don't?* I thought. But then I ran into Ollie and Doc Rob. They said they were on their way to the Comedy Club. I had Little Steve, Nigh, and June with me. These were my young cats. If I rolled, they rolled with me.

The keys of coke were safely in the trunk of a car, in our Brentwood apartment complex parking lot. I hadn't been to the Comedy Club in a while, so I thought, *What the heck? I'm not cooking tonight after all. I'll kick it with my homeboys.*

I told the little homies to stay low, and take the bucket and have fun, that I was going to the Comedy Club, and I'd page them first thing in the morning. We then headed for the club.

The place was packed, but Ollie had gotten it fixed with the door guy so we didn't have to stand in line. We went straight through. We got a kick out of going to the Comedy Club and messing with the comedians. A lot of times we'd make the show even livelier. And every once and a while I think that we might have gotten on their nerves with our banter.

I usually didn't drink, and it had been a while. I thought, *Why not live it up?* I ordered a Hennessy and Coke on the rocks. It didn't take much to get started. We were in this dark smoke-filled room, packed to full occupancy. Comedians who later became famous were just getting started there, taking a stab at stand-up. It was a hard act for anyone to follow Rodney Dangerfield, even though Robin Harris gave us a great time. He called us Sherm Heads and the whole building went crazy. He and I were cool with each other. The night was going super well.

As we left, I pulled the car onto Sunset Boulevard. The Strip was still buzzing at 2 a.m. We saw the occasional prostitute on the Strip. These were more of the upscale group, and Ollie loved to mess with them, with the window rolled down, talking to them as we cruised.

We got to Ollie and Robert's apartment at around 2:30 and I dropped them off. Ollie'd prearranged for me to meet Marilyn at the Bonaventure Hotel. She called and gave me the room number.

I didn't like going to the front desk. I preferred valet parking in the basement, where I could jump on the elevator, and two or three minutes later, I'd be in a room, and absolutely nobody knew where we were.

I lived that way once the cops got all over my heels. That night, in the room, a bath was already waiting for me, ready to go. My girl Marilyn knew how to take care of me. As soon as I got out and started to dry off, my pager beeped. It was Alan Fenster's number. *What the hell could he possibly want at three in the morning?*

I called him. He told me the police had picked up Ollie and Robert. Sure enough, the cops were on us again, just as Danilo had hinted at.

"That's impossible," I said to Alan. "I just dropped them off at home not more than thirty or forty minutes ago."

I told him I'd take care of whatever it cost; I knew it would be sky high. Then I called Jocelyn, another homegirl who helped out, and asked her to have the bondsman find out what the bail was going to be and get them out quickly.

Police must have had the apartment under surveillance, watching when I dropped them off. The thing that probably saved me was that my car had tinted windows and they didn't recognize it or me. Also, I'd dropped them off in the underground parking lot.

Man, these cops were getting close. Too close.

It was no wonder that around the same time, I developed stomach problems. Even though we were still making tons of money and doing minimum work to earn it, it felt like things were starting to crumble.

I got Ollie and Robert out of jail, but then a couple days later, two DEA agents showed up at my mother's house, one from Los Angeles and the other from St. Louis, to personally hand me an indictment out of St. Louis. I wasn't there, so they left their business cards and the indictment.

My mom called to tell me that St. Louis wanted me in connection with the four keys they'd found inside Mike's house. She took the indictment to Alan Fenster's law office.

After Alan read it, he called to tell me there was now an outstanding arrest warrant out on me. He asked what I wanted to do. I didn't feel like going to jail just yet, so I asked if he could see about getting me bail.

Alan talked with the two DEA agents and told them that the LAPD and the Los Angeles County Sheriff's Department had been tailing me for two years and hadn't been able to find anything tangible against me. He advised them that if they gave me a $50,000 bail, I'd surrender at the federal courthouse in two weeks. They agreed.

I was on pins and needles. I didn't want to go to jail, and certainly not for an extended period. I didn't expect to stay long, but the thought still gave me the creeps. I kept busy working.

Danilo kept asking me to buy, and we saw him daily. One day when Danilo stopped by one of houses, we kicked back and Ollie showed off his new 22-caliber pistol. The next day, Danilo dropped by with an Uzi submachine gun in its original box and gave it to Ollie. Then he gave me a .22 equipped with a silencer. If Danilo wanted to impress us, it was working.

I was so optimistic about my own case and not going to jail that I arranged to pick up 50 keys from Danilo on the same day I was to turn myself in to authorities. I was planning on it being a short trip to the federal courthouse and a quick release on bail.

On the designated surrender day, I showed up in the courtroom with Marilyn, my mom, and Alan Fenster. Also with us was the bail bondsman, who had the $50,000 bail money in hand, per part of our agreement with the DEA. At the end of the hearing, the judge approved the arrangement.

I figured I'd be walking straight out of the courtroom with everybody else. I was wrong.

Marshals, one on each arm, escorted me out of the courtroom, down to booking, fingerprinted and strip-searched me, took photographs, and placed me in a holding cell.

Sitting in that cell on those iron benches wore on my spirit. It was cold, uncomfortable, and stale. I'm sure the conditions contribute to defendants' states of mind, causing them to take plea deals rather than sit it out in jail awaiting their trials.

I sat down on a bench in the cell at 10 that morning. Finally, at around seven that evening, a big black marshal opened the holding-cell door. He acted as if he knew me, like he was my long-lost friend. I knew without a doubt I'd never seen him before. I walked down the hallway and they told me that my girlfriend was waiting for me in the lobby. Seeing Marilyn was a beautiful sight. As it turned out, I later learned that Mike Wingo wouldn't testify against me, so the case was dismissed for lack of evidence. I was off the hook.

As soon as I was released, I went into work mode. I had business to take care of. Marilyn drove a few blocks, and pulled over at a phone booth so I could call Danilo.

"You ready?" I asked him.

"Yeah, I'm ready. What took you so long? I'm waiting for you."

"I'll be there in forty-five minutes."

This was going to be a trip without my homies coming along. Marilyn and I had to pick up the 50 kilos on our own. It had been a long time since I'd driven with dope in my car. A lot of the homies were getting scared, so I figured I'd do it myself.

We rode out to Rialto. When I got there, Danilo was in the office, taking a few blows. He and a couple of his cronies were having some fun.

"Here, Freeway, have some," one of Danilo's boys said.

"No, no. I'll pass, thanks. Just want to get back to L.A."

"Do you have the money?" Danilo asked.

"Yeah, but you'll need to go and pick it up," I told him, asking him to follow me to the stash house. I hadn't brought the cash with me, because I didn't want to be stopped and have that sum of money in my possession.

Danilo gave me the 50 keys.

"That's cool for right now," I told him, anticipating I'd get even more coke later.

Danilo tossed me the car keys to a brown Honda parked on the street for the car switch. I walked out to the parking lot with Danilo, near where Marilyn was waiting in her car, and told her to follow us, but to keep her distance. We made the cash pickup and then Danilo drove his Honda back to his place. The deal was done, no problem.

That night Marilyn and I stayed at the Stouffer's Hotel out by LAX. By the time we checked in, it was late. I probably could have rounded up the fellas, but that would have meant going to every club and tittie bar in L.A. to find them. The crew had become quite the partiers. And my cousins from Texas had no problems joining in, tearing up clubs with them. Lately, it seemed like the homies would riot in the Hobart Club every night of the week. The owners regularly shook me down to pay for something the fellas had torn up the night before.

I was up early the next day. *Nothing like a little work to turn things around,* I thought. The fellas had been down since my arrest.

Who wouldn't be, what with the cops raiding or arresting us on a regular basis?

I got the word out to the fellas to meet me at one of our favorite breakfast spots, Twin Sisters. It probably held only 20 people, but the food was good, and we were treated well. Also, one of the owner's daughters was fine as hell and she gave us just enough action to keep us coming back for more. To my knowledge, none of the homies ever hit on her, which was a rare thing, but they enjoyed her at the restaurant. So, for many reasons, that place was cool.

I informed the homies that I'd picked up 50 chickens (our code for kilos). They were kind of surprised, thinking I was going to tone down the buying and selling since there was so much heat surrounding me and I'd been off doing my own thing, pretty much letting them handle the day-to-day business. I could tell they were glad that I was still around and got out on bail. When I explained that I was back and I'd be hands-on again with the day-to-day operations, it brought smiles to everyone's faces.

I also explained that we no longer needed rock houses, which brought too much heat and traffic. Our biggest tasks were to cook up the chickens, stash the rocks, and collect the cash. Everyone was telling war stories about the cops. We needed to avoid them.

Robert and Ollie, however, couldn't avoid the cops, because they went to their homes.

Ollie arrived home, locked the front door behind him, and made it to his bedroom when he heard an explosion at the front of the house. Instinctively, he reached for his pistol under a pillow on his bed. Then he realized it wasn't a burglar, a thief, or gang activity. It was the cops' battering ram against his front door. He put his gun back and waited. Right on cue, the cavalry burst into his room and cuffed his hands behind his back.

Then they started going crazy.

"Where's the money?" they yelled at him, inches from his face. "Where's the fuckin' money?"

He didn't answer.

He thought they'd look for drugs first, but not these cops. They wanted cold, hard cash, and they thought they'd hit the jackpot when they opened Ollie's closet and saw the two-ton safe sitting on the floor. Ollie's safe was a temporary cash spot. We used it for holding $200,000, $300,000, and even $600,000, instead of keeping it in stash cars. As soon as we could, we transported it to the safe houses, which I'd already done.

That night, however, the cops were in for a surprise.

Ollie refused to open the safe. The cops tried persuading him by putting a garbage bag over his head and smothering him almost to the point of unconsciousness.

Unfortunately for them, I'd emptied out the safe a few hours before and taken it to a stash house. Ollie didn't tell them it was empty; he let them push the issue and find out for themselves.

The cops weren't pleased to find it empty, so they pushed Ollie, who was roommates with Robert, on the floor, next his safe, then they put $40,000 inside the safe, along with half a key of crack, then they took photos for evidence. The $40,000 was a piece of the $140,000 they'd taken from Robert's bedroom when they raided Ollie and Robert's apartment earlier that day when they'd been to the apartment. They'd found Ollie's safe but couldn't open it, so they staked out the apartment, waiting for Ollie to return, so he could open it for them, but I'd beat them to it. Angry that it was empty, they planted the drugs and cash in the safe.

It was a down-and-dirty frame-up. We never kept crack and money together; that wasn't our M.O. But the cops didn't know that.

To be honest, I didn't know how I was going to get Ollie and Robert out of this jam. Both of them were nervous as hell about it. It didn't look good for either of them.

As always, we reacted and adjusted to the new circumstances.

Since we were now selling only large quantities, we started making one or two drops a day. The rest of the time, we counted money. Enough people were buying 10 to 15 keys for us to make a few hundred thousand a day. I'd also found some high-powered walkie-talkies, called repeaters, which included private lines. It cost $20,000 to set up, but it was worth it. This gave us instant communication within a 100-mile radius.

We arranged to move out of L.A. to Westwood. It was near the University of California at Los Angeles campus where it was common to see people wearing backpacks. We had Steve, June, and Nigh deliver the drugs on bicycles, and we picked out four locations where for the homies to meet up with them. The only major problem was finding cookhouses. Cooking was when we were most vulnerable, because it was time-consuming. It typically took four to six hours to cook up 100 keys. Thus, after getting things running smoothly again, my assignment was to find safer ways to cook.

I'd heard about guys I'd sold cocaine to reselling it as "cocaine hard," or "ready made," which was cheaper than what I was selling powder for. The word on the street was that the quality was good—super, even. Soon enough, I learned it was called "blow-up." Naturally, I was curious as to how they were doing it.

The rumors about blow-up were coming out of Watts. My boy Chubbs ran Watts. I made the trip to Jordan Downs, the Watts' housing projects bounded by Grape Street to the west, 97th Street to the north, Alameda Street on the east, and 103rd Street to the south.

When I pulled into the parking lot, it was rockin' and rollin'. I got out of my car and everyone eyeballed me. It was intense. I don't know how they knew I didn't belong, but they knew it instantly. It looked like some of our tracks where we sold drugs, but a few notches worse. Everyone was wearing purple, representing the Grape Street Watts Crips. Craps games were going on, and smoking and drinking was wide open. It seemed like the entire project was involved. This wasn't my first trip to the Jordan Downs, but the other times I hadn't gone all the way in to the 700-unit complex.

They relaxed, a little, once I asked to speak with Chubbs. Originally, I thought Chubbs was just a gangbanger and that because he knew Honcho, and later met me, he'd made himself some money. He didn't know exactly how many keys I was buying at a time, but he had a rough idea. He'd also introduced me to a couple of big guys, like Dennis Tortin and Cookie.

After a few minutes, Chubbs walked outside. By the looks of things, he was definitely the Don of the Jordan projects. Honcho had the biggest reputation, but as Chubbs used to say, the Baby Locs, a set of Grape Street, rode with him, not Honcho. Chubbs had cred.

We talked about the blow-up game. I knew from the smile on his face that he knew I was asking about making crack. He walked me back to my car.

"I'll come by your place tonight for a demonstration," he told me. "Have your guys bring over a key."

After that, every time I went to the Jordan Downs, I was treated like a celebrity. If you're a friend of Chubbs, then you're a friend of the Jordan Downs.

Chubbs and I hooked up that evening at my apartment on 79th and Avalon. I had the place barred up like Fort Knox. The one time police did raid it, they said it took an hour and a half to get inside.

The cops told my guys that they were going to beat some ass once they got inside, and they did.

JJ and Zo brought over the key and my top guys were there so they could see first-hand how it was done. Since I'd been gone, the fellas had been slipping. Stuff was going on in the 'hood I hadn't known about, including a new way to cook. I should have known about that. Now, I wanted to fine tune things.

True to form, he didn't give me a price for the demonstration. "I'll cook up what you have and you can pay me whatever you think is fair." It was easy doing business with him.

He'd brought two of his helpers with him. They broke the first key in half and cooked it up. I saw the stuff they put in, but I had no clue what it was. When they finished, there were 16 more ounces than when he started. And the stuff looked just as good as it had when it was raw.

I still wasn't totally convinced. We needed to do a smoke test. I sent JJ and Zo out to get us a smoker. This crack stuff passed the test.

Man, it was unbelievable: an extra 16 ounces on every key. It was like getting a pound for free. It felt like cheating.

The only problem was that Chubbs didn't want to give up the recipe, and I couldn't blame him. After he cooked for us, Chubbs told me that if we wanted him to cook for us again, it would be $20,000 at a time. I thought the price was reasonable for his knowledge and labor. The profit returned on one key would pay for the work on 50, so it was a win-win deal. I also knew it was only a matter of time before I, or one of my guys, learned the recipe.

So Chubbs took on the job of being our cook. That lasted for four days. Then, JJ radioed and said he'd figured it out. I went right over and, sure enough, he had.

This put me in a tricky position, though, because Chubbs was my boy and I didn't want to beat him out of anything. I called him up and explained. We agreed to meet at Fat Momma's for lunch.

He was a player to the bone. He said he respected the game and that it was all good.

"How much can I pay you for teaching us to cook?" I asked him.

"Whatever you want."

"How 'bout seventy thousand?"

Chubbs lit up like a Christmas tree.

We left the restaurant and rolled over to the quarter-pound house. They had around $35,000 there. I gave him that and assured him he'd have the rest later on that night. After that, business was like a run on fresh powder with newly waxed skis. All the police activity appeared to have had ceased and there was love in the 'hood for everybody. For the next nine months, business was at an all-time peak and it felt like we could do no wrong.

With things running smoothly and my guys taking care of business, I was bored again. I dove into real estate, buying and fixing up old houses. But I needed something more. I needed some excitement.

My guys were starting to get into fast cars and faster motorcycles. I hadn't gone to the street races for a while. Those usually spelled trouble, especially at a place where everybody goes to show off: Who has the nicest car, the best paint job, and who had the prettiest girl. Then it turned into whose car or whose bike could go the fastest.

Little Tommy and Black Tommy, both members of my crew, raced one of the Browning Brothers from Pasadena. Black Tommy was known as the best drag racer in the city and, man, could he ride a bike. Eventually, he was ranked nationally on the NORA circuit. He might have been in the top three in the world.

215

After I saw Little Tommy ride, I had Black Tommy give me lessons.

Black Tommy was Little Tommy's cocaine customer when we first hooked up, but as Black Tommy and I spent more time together, that inevitably changed. I didn't like cutting out people from the middle of their deals, so Black Tommy came up with a good solution. He said he'd still work Little Tommy's stuff, but he wanted to buy some for himself. I didn't see anything wrong with that. I thought everyone should take their money and invest.

We went out to a shop and bought a couple of bikes, for $6,000 each, with electronic shifters. They were fast, so I could get the feel of it. Then, Black Tommy told me if I really wanted to go fast, I'd have to get a Vance and Hines bike, so we made a trip to their shop in the city of Industry.

These guys held the world record. They had a motorcycle with a tire that was too big for most cars and a jet engine. We met with Bryant Hines, whose brother is one of the top racers in the country. We talked about them building me a bike, something I could ride. While we were talking, the president of the company walked in and told me about a bike he'd just built. Bryant had done the work, but the president had done the specs. They expected it to break the world record. They wanted me take a look at it the next weekend at a race.

Bryant thought that bike would be my best bet and I'd probably save a lot of money with one already built instead of having them build one for me. They told me the price would be about $40,000.

We went to the races that weekend and, just like they said, the bike broke the world record. Bryant sold me the bike.

With a fast bike, I also figured I had the capability to be the fastest in the pro comp category. I started building myself a pro-stock racecar. I was looking for thrills.

Time would prove that I was spending too much time on fun.

CHAPTER 17
POLICE RAIDS

As Ollie and I rolled out one day to go to the pool hall, we checked all the usual spots, looking for the fellas. We rolled through Manchester Park, then down 87th and past my mom's house, just to make sure everything was cool there. This was something I did two or three times a day. Mom still living in the 'hood was one of my weak spots. I couldn't get her to leave. Plenty of times, I rode down the street and saw my kids on their bicycles.

By this time, I had three kids with two different mothers. I worried about somebody trying to hurt them. It had become a common thing in South Central Los Angeles to kidnap children. It never occurred to me that it was my lifestyle, and not the neighborhood, that was putting my family in danger. I was usually a peace-loving guy, but having one of my kids in harm's way would surely drive me to hurt someone.

That day everything was fine as I passed my mom's street. To think we used to strip cars on that same block, and Richard's crew had shot up my mother's car. A few of the homies had other shootouts right there on the street. Now, those same homeboys were smoking hundred dollar joints.

Rolling down Main Street, as we got closer to the pool hall, we could see a commotion. We slowly cruised by without stopping. It looked like a police raid. We drove a few blocks to park, where we could watch. We observed the cops, wearing their green jackets, going in and out. Ollie and I were concerned for the homies inside, but not too much; we knew there was no dope inside, because that's not how the guys operated, to protect themselves from this very situation. At first, we sat in the car and had a good laugh. At the same time, we knew the cops might whoop some ass, so we were serious as we waited. When we saw them take homie Cruz Dog out, that puzzled us, because Cruz wasn't a dealer. He'd been smoking dope for about five years, but he wasn't selling. *How could they confuse him with a worker?* I asked myself.

After about 30 minutes, the cops left. We sat back and watched to make sure they were gone before we moved in to check on everybody. Just as we approached the front door, an ambulance pulled up.

We walked in to find the place a total shambles with some of the homies injured. It looked like something you'd see on a TV cop show. Guys complained about their arms, and some had large knots on their heads. It was hard to believe that the cops had dropped pool tables on these guys' backs while they were handcuffed and hit them over the heads with pool balls and sticks. The Cruz situation was still puzzling. We definitely had a problem on our hands. Ollie and I didn't hang around long.

I tried to figure out just who these cops were who used those tactics. I wondered if they did any advance investigating, because it looked like they'd simply found a spot we hung out at and, even if we weren't selling dope there, they raided it.

Later that night, Cruz Dog finally came back.

"Can you believe they thought I was Rick?" he asked the homies.

"So that was it!" I said. "We couldn't figure out why they grabbed you. They thought you were me!" We all laughed about it.

Cruz and I were close in height, although he may have been an inch or two taller. But Cruz's skin was jet black. The only thing we had in common was we both wore waves in our hair and had beards. It gave me an inside look at what the cops knew about me. Not very much, from what I observed.

I started using disguises in public places, like Manchester Park, and whenever I was out to discuss business. The park had become pretty much a ghost town. A few people got killed and parents no longer wanted their kids going there. But we considered it our park; we took control and turned it around. We had the power, so we used that power to help make Manchester Park a safer place. It became a neutral ground, a place where Bloods could openly wear red in the heart of a Crips 'hood and no one battled. Occasionally a few skirmishes erupted where guys drew guns. Homies like Lil' Rod, Rolaid, and a few others would say, "Man, we don't want these mutherfuckas in our 'hood." Then I had to step in. This was during the time I developed a love for basketball. I spent my days going from gym to gym, looking for pick-up games. Mr. King, the park director, had given us keys to the Manchester Park gym, so we could play whenever we liked. We always brought Mr. King lunch. I also paid to have fiberglass backboards with breakaway rims installed, and he was grateful.

I remember the day as if it were yesterday when the city gave him a plaque for the great job he'd done with the park and the gym. It felt good, because I'd helped some.

The gym became a favorite meeting place. All the dope boys from the area started sponsoring teams. Man, during the playoffs with the league I sponsored, the gym was jumpin'.

On one of those days, we had a really close call. We were always heavily armed, no matter where we went—even at the gym. Handling the kind of money we took daily, we had to stay prepared and on alert.

I got to the gym one day and Tony T, an original customer, ran up on me. He showed me the kind of love that you rarely got. Whenever he knew I was in the park, he patrolled it from one end to the other. He and I got in the habit of talking in code and riddles to each other. He never called me Rick. It was always "J.R." after the character J.R. Ross Ewing in the TV show *Dallas*.

Tony saw police surrounding the area and put out an alert that the cops were preparing to raid the park. It was a heads-up to the homies to put their straps up and away. We ran into Mr. King's office, where the guys put their straps in his closet—and not a minute too soon.

Narcotics agents, plainclothes detectives, and black-and-white patrol units surrounded the park. People scrambled past the police barricades to get out. I joined right in, unnoticed. My low-key persona had paid off and gotten me out of the park and away from the raid without being seen.

The cops grabbed just about everyone else in the crew. It was no big deal, because no one took dope into the park. And very few had convictions; most were still juveniles.

I calmly walked down the street, went to my mom's house, and got her car. I had a hearty laugh about it. Those cops were so confused.

I'd heard rumors that people thought were urban legends that I had built catacombs under the streets, like I was some kind of superpower. The truth was simpler. I'd bought a house across the street from a couple of our dope houses. So we cut a door into one of the closets so the workers could quickly run from one house to the other. That way, if police raided us, my crew could exit the house, cut across the yard, and look like a neighbor checking outside to see what all the commotion was about.

My confidence was growing, or maybe it was just my ego. I was determined to expand the business. I still wanted to be the biggest and the best.

The cops were just as determined to bring us down. They began using new tactics—at least they were new to us. They hardly ever found dope on us, so they started attacking our customers.

The first was Cliff on 107th and Vermont. Cliff was coming along and just starting to get his paper right. He'd recently made his first $100,000. But he forgot one of the cardinal rules: Never mix money with dope. The cops found the drugs *and* the money. They gave Cliff a good ass whoopin' as well, but they let him go. The cops couldn't pin the dope on him, because the house wasn't in his name. We always used smoker's houses or apartments. They told Cliff they knew he was getting dope from me and to be sure to pass on the word to me that I was going to go down hard.

Next, the cops got J.C. Chapman from 93rd and Normandie, where they found him with a small amount of drugs. They roughed up J.C., too, but unlike Cliff, they charged him with possession. J.C.'s spot was rollin' so hard he opened back up that night, after he was released on bond, hardly skipping a beat. Within two days, though, he was back in jail. He was eventually convicted and got a life sentence for two prior convictions after he caught a case in Oklahoma.

Then there was "Stupid," whose real name was Bret. Man, did he live up to his nickname. Bret was a Swaun Blood. I knew him from my low-riding days. He bought his first three grams from me. He made a joke out of everything and it was hard to believe he was serious about being in the dope game. But he got good at it, despite tripping all over himself. Stupid regularly bought between five and 15 keys.

When the cops hit Bret's place, it was the first time I'd heard about simultaneous raids going down at multiple locations. It was a new police strategy. The cops recovered quite a bit of dope from Bret, somewhere around nine keys of hard ounces. His mom and dad posted a $100,000 bond, and Ollie and I picked him up; we wanted to know more about what had happened. We went to his mom's house just before dawn. We thought it would be safe. We got to the house and went into the back room, with the pool table. We shot pool and talked over what had just gone down. Bret's older brother Ken was a welder and loved building stuff. Ken said the way we barred up our houses was done wrong. The cops' new battering ram made it easier work for them to enter should they hit our houses. But the way Ken barred up Bret's place, it brought in a whole new way to barricade houses. It slowed down the cops so that by the time they made it in, Bret had already flushed the drugs. By that time, he was sitting on his couch watching a video.

Bret told us about a law enforcement mobile trailer. He overheard officers, after they grabbed him, talking about it as some kind of headquarters for what the cops called the Freeway Ricky Task Force, though at the time we didn't know what the name was. Among the photos Bret saw at the trailer when the cops questioned him, he said, were a few of my guys, but not even one of me. I'd heard stories about this police trailer, but I did not intend to see it up close. I steered clear because I didn't want them to get that first photo.

The cops also had photos of duffel bags of money, drugs, and ballers from all different areas, which sounded like detectives had gone undercover. I knew some of the ballers, like Tootie Reese, Cadillac Will, Whitey from Whitey Enterprise. Others I didn't know. The way Bret described it, it seemed the task force hung pictures on the walls like they were trophies.

True to form, Bret laughed and played like nothing had happened. He even busted up when he showed us the knots on his head from being hit by the cops.

Not me. I took the matter very seriously. Bret's latest experience gave us details about raids we hadn't known before.

Like every other time, these latest episodes died down, at least for a little while. Life in the game continued.

CHAPTER 18
COUNTING MONEY

The years 1985 and '86 were my best ever. Things were almost too good. I sold all the dope I could get my hands on and at good prices. I had bumped my way up the food chain and, by this time, I had four solid connects. What's more, I regularly bid them against one another. All these guys used to be friends and I played that up to get the prices I wanted, while on the other hand being acutely aware of how easy it is for money to come between friendships. Of course, I wasn't the only one playing this game. It worked both ways. Remember the old saying? It's always the people closest to you who get you. I learned that the hard way.

I now had a count house in South Central, and we knew everybody on the block. There was no way anybody would snitch us out, especially since it was just a count house. No drugs were ever there. The only money dropped was $100,000 or better, and most workers dropped their money and left. I stayed there the majority of the time. Our big customers started spending time there too, to chat and negotiate prices.

With people coming in and out and the cops watching our every move, I put security measures in place. We had the walkie-talkie system locked onto a private channel to synchronize our movements and keep our conversations secure. I also had a crew close to me— in business they would have been my administrative team in the executive branch—who were paid $1,000 a week to serve as crack cookers, money counters, bodyguards, lookouts, and drivers. I even had people who did nothing but dispose of potentially incriminating evidence.

Even with all that in place, it had become common for my guys, our street dealers, to be $5,000 to $10,000 short. Seriously, I was surprised when they weren't.

Big Mike and Chinese Dave were hands down my biggest workers. And I gave them a price to reflect that as a way of rewarding them for their hard work.

Then I noticed that Big Mike started calling Mary more often, bringing her gifts each time he and Chinese Dave dropped off money. I wondered briefly about it, but it was months later before I figured out what was really behind it.

Mary sat at her desk, counting money as usual. I heard the money machine clapping as it rolled off the bills. I was pulling money to buy my first 100 keys, but first I was trying to get them to go from $37,000 a key to 35K or even 34K. I needed 100 to 200 keys daily to push through and keep my guys going. They were now out in most major cities west of the Mississippi River selling my coke.

We were buying from 50 to 75 keys daily and I knew that once I started buying a hundred, it was only a matter of time before I'd need that many on a daily basis. I was about to buy my first hundred and I was just 26 years old. Listening to the *clap, clap, clap* of the bills in the counting machine, I thought, *Man, I really have arrived.*

I was awakened from my daydream by loud hammering on the door. Sometimes, just to scare me, the homies pounded on the doors like they were cops. I looked out of the window and saw JJ, Renzo, Tootie, and Kenny. They'd been making their rounds collecting money and brought in several Nike gym bags full of cash. I asked about Big Mike. He was one of the big homies and typically slow with his money. I needed cash for the 100 deal to go off.

No sooner had I asked about Big Mike than there was another bang at the door. It was Big Mike and Chinese Dave dragging a duffel bag. Before Chinese Dave made it all the way up the stairs, he said, "All the money's here."

I wasn't taking any chances. I paid Mary good money to count. And that's what she was going to do.

Watching money being counted sometimes made me hungry, so my homeboys and I took off for M&Ms. As we rode down Florence on the way back, Lil' Steve, who came with us, pointed out a group of narc cars on the road. My radar went on alert, my blood pressure rose, and my heart beat faster by the second, even though we were clean. When you're in the game, you can never be too safe.

We were definitely low-key, nothing like the usual dope-dealer flash. I drove a '77 four-door Impala. Even though we were four deep, we looked like everyday guys. The other fellas were in a '74 Continental Lincoln, four-door stock.

As we approached Van Ness, cop cars moved up fast. *Maybe they're on us*, I thought. Then, at the last minute, they swerved around us and made a right turn onto Van Ness. It was evident they were hitting someone in our area. Half of me wanted to follow them so I could see what was going on. The other half had 100 keys in mind.

When we got back to the counting house, a few of our customers were there, along with Big Mike and Chinese Dave. It quieted down when we walked into the room, which was odd. Mary, as she stacked money and wrapped the bills in rubber bands with one hand, waved me over.

I bent down and she whispered, "Chinese Dave and Big Mike are twenty-eight thousand short."

Had the money not been counted, I would have eaten that. My biggest and best workers were cheating me.

This is how their little scheme went down: Because of their time and grade, as they say in the military, I was giving the dope to them for about five or six thousand dollars cheaper than everyone else.

Then Chinese Dave turned around and offered my customers a cheaper price, taking my customers away from me with my own dope. On top of that, he was shorting me on the cash, counting on the fact that it often wasn't counted right away.

We needed several million for the next deal. It was the first time we'd bought a hundred keys at one time. They were going to drop $2,000 off the price of each key. We'd been paying 37 for each one for some time. My plan was to save the two thousand a few times and then pass the new price onto the homies. Two thousand on each one may not seem like a lot, but when you're buying hundreds of keys a week, it adds up.

We were moving nearly a million dollars in dope every day, sometimes up to 3 million dollars. The scale of the operation was crazy. One day I picked up the newspaper in Inglewood and read "Earvin (Magic) Johnson has signed a 25-year contract for $1 million a year." I thought, *He's only getting a million a year.* I had that amount sitting on the bed in the other room. It felt like I was on top of the world.

I'd gotten clued in about being shorted one evening when I got a call from of the lil' cats who'd been at the stash house earlier in the day.

"I'm ready for four, maybe five," he said. He tried to negotiate with me on the phone.

I stopped him mid-conversation. "I'm not far from your house," I said. "I'll be right over."

The kid was young, maybe 17 or 18. He quoted me the price Chinese Dave had offered him and wanted me to match it.

"It's just business, man," he told me, trying to make his argument. "It's not personal. I need the best price I can get." If I couldn't offer it to him for less, he said he'd be forced to move on.

It was understandable. But I didn't need his business—or Big Mike's, or Chinese Dave's, for that matter; I could sell all the dope I had in a few hours. So Ollie and I came up with a plan: When we copped the 100 kilos, we'd cut Chinese Dave and Big Mike out for a few days, just to make 'em sweat.

And, boy, did they sweat.

When I hooked up the kid the next day, he apologized and said he'd stay loyal. He did just that.

For Big Mike and Chinese Dave, that was just the beginning of what was to come. I brought them back into the fold. They each were seasoned vets. Big Mike knew everyone and everything going on. It was typical to pull up at one of his liquor stores and see him talking to three or four cars full of police. Also, this old Jewish cat, Red, was lacing him up and was probably the real owner of the liquor stores. You know the drill: Get a black to front a ghetto business as if they own it.

I admit that I adopted some of my low-key persona from observing Big Mike. Taking him at face value, you wouldn't think he owned a thing. I figured he was filthy rich, and if he wasn't, he should have been. But you couldn't tell by looking at him. I never saw him with a new pair of high-end tennis shoes or clothes. It was a long time before I saw any signs of wealth.

That only happened the first time I went to his house and Mike's wealth was finally visible to me. He lived in Ladera Heights, where uppity blacks lived. It's been said that the group of hills comprising the upscale area was one of the richest black communities in the world. He had two Benzes in the driveway—his and hers.

By this time, well into 1986, my tracks were making so much money, it was astounding. Most were averaging around $100,000 a day. And that was just the guys who sold rocks to cars pulling up. We were easily moving 100 to 200 keys a day. Best of all, except for a few of the homies I dealt with personally, I was entirely off the streets.

As an example of how hard it was rolling, Norman Tillman, known as Shitty Slim, got busted at the track on Denver Street. I happened to be at my mom's house when the raid went down. Tony T came to get me.

I rolled over to Denver to get the details. I took special interest because it was Norm, my old tennis partner and one of the original Freeway Boys.

The cops had a new tactic. Instead of driving up to the house, they walked up to it—and surprised everybody. About 20 guys who were selling on the street took off. It was total chaos with guys scattering in all directions. Norman, inexperienced at that point, tossed the drugs in the bushes as he ran. The cops caught him—and found the bag of dope. My homegirls said it was a large Ziploc bag full of small chunks of crack cocaine—ready rock. I didn't learn the amount of dope in the bag until I bailed out Norman from jail; it was a half-kilo!

His was a challenging case, what with nabbing him and the bag. But Norm beat the charges because, as is often the case, of excellent work by the defense attorney.

CHAPTER 19
HOMIES AND JAIL

Jocelyn was one of my earlier customers, and she'd gotten hooked. I helped her get off the stuff. She needed work as she tried to say clean, so I hired her to do just that: clean houses. She got paid well, but she was always asking for better work. She'd been sweating me for months about letting her earn some real money. She wanted to play a bigger role, and she learned I'd been sending people out of town to drop off dope, paying a fee of anywhere from $1,000 to $2,000 a key to pick up. That role in the dope game is called a mule. We referred to them as transporters. An opportunity arose, so I let Jocelyn transport some dope.

I'd gotten a call from Indian Tommy and Frank. Tommy had Cincinnati going good even though he was only getting one or two keys at a time. He bought one and I fronted him the other. This time, though, he didn't have money for even the first key.

"I'll send you one," I told him.

I made plenty of money off the out-of-town dealers, so it was a good investment to front him a key. I was hitting Tommy for about 52K a bird.

At the same time, I knew it was going to be tough to get one of the homies to make a trip all the way to Cincinnati to deliver just one key. The homies were off the charts, blowing money every night at clubs and craps tables. I saw them blow $5,000 in one night. And that went on several nights a week. Not one of them gave a damn about making $2,000 to transport. That was nothing to them.

I told Ollie I needed to get cocaine to Tommy. "He's waiting for me to call him back. He wants to know what time we're gonna be there. We need to send someone to Cincinnati tonight."

Jocelyn was in the room, cleaning the house, listening to my conversation with Ollie. She waited as Ollie and I came up with exactly nothing. She finally volunteered to be a courier to Cincinnati, and I didn't hesitate in saying yes. She knew Tommy. Hell, they'd gotten high together.

I told her how it would go down.

"Call the airport and make a reservation for a red-eye flight," I said. "Get a round-trip so you return a few hours after you get there."

I gave her Tommy's address and told her no one would be meeting her at the airport. "You need to catch a cab from there." We didn't want homies from Cincinnati bringing heat with them to the airport.

It was going to be a restless night. Sending dope on long trips always gave me a stomachache. I kept a bottle of Mylanta in my back pocket for anxious moments like that.

Ollie and I took her to LAX. Jocelyn was inexperienced in the dope game. She had several kids I adopted as my nieces and nephews, so she had a lot at stake.

After we dropped her off at the airport, we headed home. For me, evenings were always a toss up as to who I'd be staying the night with. A lot of it had to do with who I'd seen last and who I'd seen the least. That night, Marilyn was my girl. Ollie dropped me off at her place. When I woke up the next morning, I went straight to Mary's for the word from Jocelyn.

No one had heard from her.

It had already been close to eight hours; she should have already been there *and* on her way back home by now.

I called Tommy.

"I haven't heard from her," he said. He was panicking.

Something was definitely wrong, but I was still hoping for the best. Maybe she'd just lost the address and couldn't find the place. I tried to think of anything I could—anything other than she'd gotten busted.

At 6 o'clock that evening, the phone rang. It was Tommy. "The DEA just hit my house," he said in a somber voice.

Tommy explained what happened to Jocelyn. At the Cincinnati airport, in Florence, Kentucky, just across the state line, she had lagged down a cabby. As she started to get in the cab, the DEA approached her and took her into custody. All I could figure was that somebody in Tommy's crew tipped off the federal narcs. It wasn't like drug-sniffing dogs had found the goods. That wasn't a large airport. On top of that, agents had searched her without a warrant.

I hired Alan Fenster to represent her. It took 30 days and a $30,000 bond to bail her out. She flew back and forth from L.A. to Cincinnati for about two years for court appearances. Eventually, the charges were dropped due to the illegal search and seizure. Jocelyn continued working for me, maintaining and cleaning my houses.

———◆———

In late 1986, the cops caught up with me in a big way, specifically the same Los Angeles County Sheriff's deputies who'd been after me for years. It went down one night when Ollie, Cornell, and I were coming out of the Big Palace of Wheels. We walked to my Ford LTD station wagon, which I'd parked in the back alley, knowing the cops were always looking for me.

As I drove down 74th Street, I noticed a car coming up behind me, speeding, with its lights off. I knew the cop car was going fast, because I was speeding too.

"I'm gonna lose 'em," I told Ollie and Cornell. But I got caught at the red light.

A car pulled up beside us. The driver rolled down the window and we could see his green-and-white sheriff's badge.

"Amigo," Ollie yelled. "That's Tomar! He told me if he saw you, he was gonna kill you."

I punched out and stepped on the gas as fast as I could. I busted a left to lose him. But another car was ahead with its lights out too. Then I saw another. I thought, *No way am I gonna get past these cars.*

"Ollie, grab the wheel and put your foot on the accelerator!" Then I opened the door, rolled, and jumped while the car was moving. I hit the ground running.

As I ran toward a yard, at least one deputy fired shots at me. I heard the bullets whizzing past my head. There were no hollers of, "Freeze," "Police," or "Put up your hands." Just gunfire. I jumped over a fence, stopped, then backtracked, heading to the front of the yard as they went around the back, where they thought I'd be running. I lost them.

I walked to Western, where a city bus was coming. I took the bus to Gaines, got out, went to a pay phone, and called Marilyn. She picked me up and we went to my condo on Sepulveda and Ventura Boulevard—a great location in a rich neighborhood where the houses were going for a million apiece. I hid out there.

The next morning, my heart was still racing from the night before. I'd slept very little. It was another close call. I knew that Ollie and

Cornell had to have been arrested because they'd stayed in the car and hadn't run. I called Jocelyn first thing and asked her to bail them out. It was just a matter of a few hours before they'd be released.

If it hadn't been for my street savvy and a lot of luck, I'd be sitting in County with Ollie and Cornell. Or worse, I'd be dead from gunshot wounds. It didn't feel right with Ol' in jail, like a part of me was in there too; we'd been friends since we were boys and he was the one I got into the drug game with.

I chilled out in the bedroom, waiting to hear from both Jocelyn and Marilyn when my beeper went off. It was Jocelyn. I jumped up, ran outside to a nearby phone booth, and dialed her number. She practically squealed telling me the news, she was so excited: Both bails were posted. Even though the bond cost me $70,000, I was relieved they were getting out.

"David and I are driving downtown so we're there when they walk out of County," Jocelyn said.

I laid down in the bedroom, and my head was still swimming, trying to make sense of what had happened the night before, when I heard a knock at the door. *Who could it be?* Only a few people knew about this place. I'd sent Marilyn out to take care of the paperwork for Ollie and Cornell, so I was alone. I wasn't expecting her back this soon.

I tiptoed to the door, holding my breath, and peered out. It was June and Steve, two young cats, around 18 and 19. They'd probably been looking for me. They'd been in the habit of staying where I stayed ever since they were 15 years old. It was like having six eyes; these two kids were tough and would defend me with their lives.

I opened the door and let them in. They gave me the usual hug. "What up, Loco? What time we goin' to work?"

They hadn't heard, so I filled them in about the night before. They asked what we were going to do. I knew what was on their minds; they were ready to do what needed doing.

I paused, then said, "Nah, we just gonna chill. Matter of fact, let's walk down to Denny's and get something to eat." I was starving. We took the elevator to the parking lot garage so we wouldn't be seen.

As we walked down the street, I saw a police car was stopped at the red light. I'd worn my disguise. I'd cut my beard off and was wearing shades.

We walked directly in front of their car, close enough to touch. The two cops looked right at us. *Did they recognize me?* I thought. *Or were they just looking at us because we were black in a rich, white neighborhood?* We tried to look like we didn't notice them.

We knew they were watching, so we walked past Denny's to the Ventura Mall in case they followed us. They went ahead, and we turned around and walked back to Denny's.

I guess I was just being paranoid. Being on the run, you get like that. Or maybe that's just being black in America. Shit, now that I think back, I can remember when my Uncle George and Uncle Elmer C trained us to look out for the cops. This was going to be a long day.

At Denny's, one thing was going through my head: *Is this all worth it?* The game had caused a lot of tension—but not with the homies. It seemed like nothing would ever break up the team. We were homies 'til the end. Henry, JJ, and Eric were now my main three, besides Ollie, who was more of an equal partner.

Back at the apartment, it was about 2 o'clock by the time I hooked up with Ollie and Cornell and they filled me in on what happened after I ran. He told me how, when I jumped out the driver's side of the car while it was moving, he had to slide over and stop it from running into a house.

"When that cop shot at you," Ollie said, "the cops thought he'd hit you, so he stopped shooting."

Then he said, "They dragged me out the car, then they dragged Cornell and put us on the ground and kicked us."

While on the ground near the deputies' cars, Cornell said, "I watched a deputy take a key of cocaine from the trunk of his police car and drop it right by your station wagon, next to the door you jumped out of."

"What?" I asked.

Now, they were trying to plant cocaine on me too, just like they'd done a few times before with my homeboys.

Had I gotten caught with their dope, I thought, *what would've happened to me?*

Then I got a page from Kenny. I called and he said my mom needed to talk to me. I called home and she explained that the cops had been by her house all night and that they'd been airing on the news that I had shot at the cops, I was wanted, and I was armed and dangerous.

It was crazy.

It was a Saturday, but Alan Fenster worked all day on the cases. Ollie and Cornell were scheduled to be arraigned that Monday. Alan met them there. They were greeted with good news when they got to court: No charges would be filed against them and they were free to go.

The bad news was they'd filed charges against me, not only for that night, but also for previous supposed crimes I'd committed. My bond was set for a million dollars. I could make bail, no problem. But to post that, I had to have $1.2 million worth of property and $100,000 in cash. While I had property and cash, an amendment to a law—called the 1251—had passed that stated it you put up property, it couldn't have been obtained through drug proceeds. Bail approval had to go through a judge, who would have the property and cash investigated. So now I needed $1.2 million in equity and $100,000 check from someone who could show that it was earned legally. This was not an easy task. Most of my homies didn't own their own homes.

I was pleasantly surprised when the neighbors on my mom's street stepped up and said they'd put their houses up for me. After we tallied it up, we had only $700,000 and some change.

Alan called a meeting with me in his office. He had me go through the back so I wouldn't be seen, just in case it was under surveillance. He called the D.A.'s office while I was there and asked that bail be reduced to $100,000, but they wouldn't do it. So we went to Plan B, which was to go before the black judge whose courtroom the case had been assigned and ask for a reduced bail of $500,000.

Right before our meeting adjourned, Alan made a statement that made me think he didn't believe that the cops had planted the drugs and had lied about me firing a gun at them. He said, "Rick, I want you to go and take a lie detector test."

"Lie detector. That shit don't work," I told him.

"If you're telling the truth, it can help your case. It's not admissible in court, but the judge can review it for the bail hearing," he explained.

"What the hell. I don't have anything to lose. Line it up."

The test was scheduled for three days later. I was totally consumed with the case. The cops had been by my mom's house on a daily basis.

I made it to Alan's office at 8 o'clock that morning for the lie detector test. Before they even strapped the wires to me, I was nervous as hell. The tester was a middle-aged white guy, balding badly on the top. He explained to me that the test was only 95 percent accurate. All I wanted him to say was that I was innocent and it was the cops who were lying.

When Alan gave me the results the next day, I was shocked when he asked me, "Did you have cocaine on you the night of the chase, because that question came back positive?" I swore to him I didn't. The good news was that when I was asked if I shot at the police, the test showed that I was not deceptive when I answered, "No." But it didn't stop the case from moving forward.

After conversations with my attorney, Alan Fenster, I decided to turn myself in. Alan warned me about the cops trying to arrest me in front of the courthouse before I was to surrender. My lawyer contacted the district attorney's office and arranged for me to surrender to avoid a public spectacle where detectives do what they call "perp walks," parading defendants in front of the media as they walk them into court or to booking. I didn't plan on that happening, so I tried to disguise myself by trimming my beard and wearing a baseball cap.

Just as my luck would have it, as Alan, my mom, my homie Lil Stevie, and I sat in the seats lining the hallway outside the courtroom, two narcotics officers were 10 feet away looking directly at me. I could see them out the corner of my eye, hoping that my disguise worked.

Lil Stevie moved closer to them so he could hear their conversation.

When I stood up to walk to the men's bathroom, the cops relaxed. Lil Steve followed me to relay the conversation he'd overheard.

"One isn't sure it's you," Lil Stevie told me. "The other one is convinced it isn't you because you're a wanted man and there's no way you'd casually show up and sit outside the courtroom." Stevie walked back to the hallway so he could keep an eye on the detectives.

But as soon as I walked out of the bathroom, the bailiff opened the doors to the courtroom. It was packed from an earlier session. Municipal court was always like that on Monday mornings, and there were just three rows of seats in that courtroom. The cops were on the prosecution's side of the courtroom, like a line had been drawn.

We sat in the courtroom about 30 minutes when Alan walked up to the bailiff and handed him paperwork. Then the bailiff called my name. I stood up and looked directly at the two narc cops who'd been sitting outside, waiting for me to show up. They both had looks of shock on their faces as I walked to the front of the courtroom.

Alan argued the motion for lowering my bail, but the judge denied it. I was then admitted into the county jail in downtown Los Angeles, in block 4800, as it was called, in the gang module, even though I wasn't a gangbanger. The D.A. charged me with all kinds of bogus crimes: firing at an officer, fleeing the scene of a crime—they had bunches of charges.

A couple days later, sheriff's deputies went to the county jail to interview me without my lawyer's permission or knowledge. They recorded it, as they always do.

They told me they had me now. I told them they didn't have me because, "You know I didn't have any drugs with me."

"Oh, we always get our man," one of the cops said.

They told me not to tell my lawyer they'd been to the jail to see me. They also talked to my lawyer and told him he couldn't help me because I was going down.

At the preliminary hearing a deputy got on the stand to testify and my lawyer asked him, "Didn't you go to the county jail the other day?"

The deputy answered, "Yes." He couldn't lie and say he wasn't there, because everyone, including cops, has to sign in when they go to the jail.

"Did you go see my client?" Fenster asked.

"Yeah. I interviewed him," he said.

"Don't you record conversations?" my lawyer asked him.

"Yes, we recorded it."

Alan Fenster then asked the court for a copy of the recording, and the judge granted the request. Alan was given the tape almost immediately. Alan hired an expert to analyze the tape. The report came back a week later and my attorney sprung it on the court during the continuing preliminary hearing: The expert determined that the tape of my interview had been cut and spliced. In other words, it had been tampered with. He also informed the court of the negative comments the deputies had said to me about my lawyer.

For those reasons, my attorney told the judge during the prelim, "Your Honor, I ask that these charges against my client be dropped."

The court, in turn, dismissed all charges against me for police misconduct based on the police disparaging my attorney to me and because the tape presented to the court turned out to have a substantial portion edited out.

I not only beat the charge, because of the altered tape introduced in court and the fact that they'd planted drugs in my car, but the evidence Alan and I gathered helped launch a federal corruption investigation into the sheriff's deputies' actions. It took about a year for Frenchy, the private eye we hired, to get confirmation of the planted evidence. Frenchy gave Alan his reports, and Alan turned over everything, including the tampered-with tape, to the FBI.

Even though I was released and freed, I wanted a change. I decided to move to Cincinnati, Ohio, with Marilyn and our baby daughter. Marilyn needed to get off drugs. And I needed to chill. We settled in a quiet suburb on the east side of Cincinnati.

I'd been out of the cocaine business while living in Cincinnati for about a year when Danilo Blandón again contacted me. He offered me a cut from 130 kilos he needed to distribute. Having been in Cincinnati a while, I knew the lay of the land. I got back in the game, and eventually monopolized Cincinnati's crack market with Danilo as my supplier. I flew back and forth to L.A., reopening and overseeing my operation there as well as in Cincinnati.

The homies were now in charge, including JJ, a cousin originally from Texas. I remember JJ's first day in Cali. He'd been living in a trailer house in rural Texas with no lights and, when walking through it, you had to be careful not to fall through the floor. He was living what we called dirt-ball bad, so I gave him a shot.

He'd worked hard all of his life. As kids, I'd visit in the summer and help him work. He'd do everything from hauling hay, digging fence poles, chucking wood, and feeding hogs, to branding cows. The work was gruesome in that Texas heat. Sometimes the mosquitoes practically ate him alive. He'd have to be up from sunup to sundown. Hard work was nothing new to JJ. When he came to Cali, he jumped right in.

I started him out like everyone else, giving him an ounce of dope and a little instruction, then pointed him to the track. JJ showed signs that none of the other homies did. When he ran out of his product, he helped Ollie and me. For a brief period, he even stopped drinking. He was on the fast track.

In a matter of a couple of months, he became the guy I called on the most. He was dependable.

Of course, I still considered Ollie as my equal. We bought our first sack together and I'd never forgotten that.

Then, something went terribly wrong with JJ, right at the time when every day was critical to my ultimate plan: the exit strategy.

I'd already explained to my crew that we were close to finishing the game. I had one completed motel and two more under construction. As soon as I finished the other two, the motels would bring in more than a hundred grand a month, and I promised all my closest guys I'd put them to work.

We'd use the same formula from the dope game for running the motels I owned. The first three dope deals were going to pay for more motels. We also had a couple apartment rehabs going on, as well as a 32-unit apartment. I'd been burning up money, but it was all for investments. We'd be straight again once I finished with the projects.

But back to JJ. He'd gone off the deep end. One morning I was looking all over for him, but he was nowhere to be found. I went from house to house looking for him. None of the fellas had seen him. I figured JJ's honey must have been treating him real good.

I had business to attend to, as usual, and didn't have time to continue looking for him. I rounded up Paul, Zo, and Tootie for a 100-kilo buy. When we bought dope, we did it with an entourage. If something went down, we had a better chance of getting away. And we always had the location scoped and planned out, so we were sure no one would jack us.

Paul was the key driver back then. He'd drive with a ride full of dope right next to a police car and wouldn't blink an eye.

I called Ollie, now out on bail, to make sure he had the money together. That was pretty much all he and my brother David did by then. Every time the money houses got up to a couple hundred thousand, they'd pick it up and take it to the stash house. We'd been taking orders all day from the major players. We didn't miss any customers. Zo pretty much knew all the people that JJ knew.

At around 7 o'clock, with the sun going down, JJ finally showed up.

I was back at the Big Palace of Wheels when I heard the sound of screeching tires. I ran out the door to see who was getting their clown on. I saw that JJ had traffic blocked off as he did donuts in the middle of Western. When he finally stopped, he zipped up in the driveway with his tires still smoking, jammed on the brakes, and jumped out the car with a look on his face that could kill. He was steaming mad about something.

I asked him, "What's up, man?"

"I'm tired of this shit!" he practically spat. Then he got back in his car and sped away.

I never did find out what was bothering JJ, but clearly, trouble was brewing.

A short time later, as I shot hoops at Manchester Park, I overheard some youngsters saying that JJ had turned Hoover Crip and was going around 81st and Hoover throwing out wads of cash.

I called the guys and told them what I'd heard. Everyone agreed that JJ had been acting funny the last few days. And Lil' Steve informed me that $80,000 was missing from the stash can that JJ had access to. This was a tough one for me. JJ was my man. But I could not allow anyone to take my money and throw it away, family or not.

Then it got worse. I pulled into the driveway of the shop when Kenny and Tootie ran up and told me that JJ, Eric, and Jeta had just whooped on our youngsters Steve and NY, trying to find out where the money car was so he could steal more. I was hot. These were grown men ganging up on teenagers. My little homies wouldn't sing, and they took a beating for it.

Then I heard that Tootie and Kenny had witnessed the altercation and didn't do anything to stop it. Boy, did I go off on them. I expected them to have my back at all times.

It never crossed my mind that my main fellas were plotting a coup while the rest were choosing sides.

When it finally dawned on me, I couldn't believe it. I mean, I'd brought all of these guys in when most of them didn't have a dime and were begging me for help.

I'd always been a team player. That was part of my strategy, to get everything set up for the whole team, so that we'd all be set for the rest of our lives. I knew what they were all going through—the greed, petty jealousies, jockeying for position, dirty cops, clean cops, and legal troubles. I knew how hard it was for them to see millions going through their hands and making only workers' wages. It was all coming to a head and now, apparently, I'd have to deal with internal rip-offs, backstabbing, and power plays.

I was considered the leader who got all the credit and love, but by no means did I deserve it. All the businesses I owned, I considered to also belong to the entire crew.

We cooked as usual that night, even though a lot was going on. We'd only been cooking at 62nd Street a couple of weeks. It was an all-brick building and I'd spent $40,000 barring it up so it was safe. We stayed up all night cooking the latest batch. When I looked up, it was close to five in the morning. I couldn't wait to get to bed. But I couldn't get to sleep that night. When you cook up that much dope in a closed environment, you end up getting high. Plus, I had so much on my mind; I didn't know where to start to unravel it.

In the morning, I called a meeting for the next day to discuss things with the fellas. I was kind of pissed off and wanted to get it out of the way.

I got a call from Carolyn, one of my girls, who wanted to get a good price on some wheels from the Big Palace for her car. I met her there and was talking to her through her car window when I felt someone yank me back hard, by my shoulder. I turned around just in time for JJ to slap me like a bitch. Just as fast, I hit him with a three-piece.

JJ wasn't one I wanted to fight with. He'd hauled puck wood and hay all his life. His hands looked like they were permanently swoll. We'd fought many times as kids, but only for play. This time was for real.

Then, seemingly out of nowhere, Ollie and Compton Bobby grabbed JJ from behind. Once they had him, I stopped punching him.

Ollie yelled at JJ, "Nigga, I'm gonna kill you."

Then Bobby asked, "Do you want us to?" Bobby had just gotten out the pen and he was in even better shape than JJ. He was grateful to me because I had him on a fast track and he was making big money.

"I want mine!" JJ yelled at me. "You owe me money." JJ was practically foaming at the mouth when Ollie and Bobby dragged him inside the shop.

When I turned back, Carolyn, whose aunt was in the car with her, had pulled into the alley, watching from a distance. I was embarrassed. I took a lot of pride in the business and had close to a million dollars invested in it. Now, not only were Carolyn and her aunt looking, but all the people at the car shop could see and hear what was happening.

I walked back over to Carolyn's car and she told me she was leaving.

Man, that changed my relationship with JJ forever. Like I've said, he was the most trustworthy and hardworking member of the team. Not to mention, he'd been my favorite cousin since childhood. Now he was trying to injure me. It not only interfered with a valued family relationship, but I'd been planning an out from the game for the entire crew, and this threw off the entire plan.

When I walked back into the shop, JJ was gone, but not before he'd busted out every windshield on the cars in the place. Ollie was still talking about killing JJ, but I told him that was out of the question. He was still my cousin.

We held the meeting with the crew at the baseball diamond at Manchester Park. Everybody, about 30 of us, showed up, except for JJ. I wasn't surprised.

I started the meeting. "Man, I'm *this* close to having everything the way I want it, where we can all get out of this game," I told them. "Y'all know it's been hot."

Then I asked who had complaints.

The first to speak up was Bear. He was a heavy drinker and, as early in the day as it was, he appeared to already be liquored up. He let it all out, rattled off all the things I owned—the houses, the motels, the cars—plus the houses and cars I'd given my girlfriends.

Rolaid stood up and stared Bear as if he could kill him for talking to me that way. "You niggas just got out here. The homies started this shit by they selves and brought all of us in. You niggas didn't have nothin'. Now you fools driving Vettes, Z28s, trucks, Blazers." Then he said, "Fuck y'all. Y'all ain't the homies, no way."

Then Rolaid and Bear started fighting and had to be pulled apart.

Then my diehard homies stuck up for me. I appreciated the loyalty that Lil' Steve, June, NY, and Rolaid showed at the meeting.

I sat back and took it all in. At that moment, I made up my mind what to do; I'd cash out the disgruntled guys and slow way down. I knew that we could get the job done without the rest of them. When I added up all the money, we still had nearly two million to pay off about a dozen guys and cut them loose. It would only take a few days to get all that money back. I was ready for the drama to end so we could focus once again on business. Lord, I was close to walking away from the dope game.

When it was my turn to speak again, I offered what I thought was a fair price for everyone to go their separate ways. After a short discussion, we settled on $50,000 apiece and agreed to meet up that night so I could distribute the cash.

Ollie didn't say a word during the meeting. Afterward, on our way to the parking lot, he expressed his displeasure about the deal I'd just cut. I understood his feelings. "We been carrying these guys on our backs for years. We buy the food. We pay for the housing. We fund the parties. Ain't our fault they're broke and whining."

I understood his feelings. But could I go to war with my own flesh and blood over money? Kissing them off with 50 g's each would ease my conscience and then we'd all be free. I knew we'd make duffle bags full of money the next day, just as surely as the sun would shine.

After the meeting, no sooner had Ollie and I pulled into the Big Palace of Wheels than my homeboys Mobile Mike and Alfonso "Big Al" Jeffries came running up through the alley. They were out of breath and looked exhausted.

"Man, we were at 84th and Normandie," Mobile Mike explained, "and in the process of cooking up about seven keys. We'd broken down one and started cooking it in the beaker. It had just started bubbling when we saw the cops coming to raid the house. We hit the latch to the burglar bars and went out the side window, over the next-door neighbor's fence, then from yard to yard. We barely got away."

If it's not one thing, it's another, I thought. I'd been giving Mobile Mike his dope on credit. I knew this lick was going to cost me. On the bright side, I didn't have to bail them out of jail.

That night, I paid all the homies their money, and I was feeling broke. When it was time to re-up, we barely scraped together $700,000. We still had money on the street, but typically, it was no problem raising a million and a half or two and still have money on the street. The pressure was mounting.

I had five major real estate projects going on at the same time. The police had been arresting my people right and left; they weren't only attacking my personal crew, but also my customers. Lawyer fees and bails were eating me up. And the press was even starting to get wind of it.

It was embarrassing to have to tell my source, Danilo, that I had only $700,000 and not a million; I knew he'd go up on the price because of it.

Just as I expected, when I told Danilo how much money we had, he wanted to go up to 15,000 a kilo when we'd been getting them from him for about 12 to 12.5 g's at that time. I explained to Danilo that we'd been having problems. He already knew the cops had been on us. He wanted to talk about it further, so we planned to meet up in Van Nuys at seven that evening.

On the way, Ollie and I swung by the house in Inglewood. When we pulled into the driveway, we saw a note hanging on Ollie's boat. The note was from the city and said it was too big to be on the driveway. It was a 40-foot cigarette boat with dual 454 engines that I'd given Ollie for his birthday. I paid a $150,000 for it. It was one more headache to deal with.

This place had become our clubhouse and the homies. They were acting like they were on vacation, because we'd shut down the rock houses with all the heat around us. This night, a pool party was going on, barbecue and all. Pretty women were everywhere. Ol' and I went outside for a few minutes.

Then we took off to meet Danilo at a Mexican restaurant. It didn't look like much from the outside, but we figured if Danilo picked it, it must have been connected, and we'd be safe. When we walked in, it was practically empty.

As usual, Danilo was late, but that was okay, especially that day. I wasn't looking forward to facing him with so little cash. I'd probably have to stay in the game a little longer than I'd planned. It felt like we were going backwards.

I'd developed a real taste for Spanish rice, beans, chicken fajitas, and plantains, and they had everything on the menu I liked. As soon as we were ready to order, four guys, including Danilo and Henry, got out of an older model Mercedes 450. They swaggered into the restaurant like they owned the world. I couldn't wait to be in that position. You know what they say: The grass always looks greener on the other side.

Danilo told the owner we were his friends and to put our order on his bill. Two of the guys with him sat at a separate table. Danilo and Henry sat with us. I repeated to him that my money was low because I had to pay the homies. From my impression, I think they thought I made more money than I did. Danilo said, "Either that, or you smokin' the shit now."

We all got a chuckle out of that and, after 30 minutes or so, we agreed on $14,000—not as good as $12,500, but a little better than $15,000.

Ol' and I headed back to the 'hood. We thought we'd play some ball to get our minds off everything going on. I'd fallen in love with basketball. Other than being quick, I wasn't too good at it. When we pulled up in the park, Tootie and Kenny were already there and the gym was open.

Tootie stopped in the middle of his game so he and Kenny could talk to me. They told me JJ got busted for reckless driving. I thought, *What a blessing, getting that fool outta my hair.*

But, then, I went to my car and called Jocelyn to ask her to check it out. When she got back to me, she surprised me by saying that JJ was being held on charges of possessing dope that Mobile Mike and Big Al had purchased. Now JJ wouldn't be held for just reckless driving, but also for possession of more than seven keys. That threw me for a curve.

I had some decisions to make.

Part of the problem was that all the money was going into real estate on two apartment buildings, and digging a foundation for the third motel, with a fourth one on the way. I'd paid $500,000 for the building, and it needed about $150,000 worth of repairs and improvements. The plans alone cost $5,000. But the place would eventually be worth close to $2 million, so it was worth it. I hired a lawyer out of Beverly Hills to represent me at the Planning Commission meeting when I applied for permits. The previous owner's permits had been revoked for letting the place get run down and drug-infested. I knew I could turn the place around. Man, were my hands full. But it felt good to keep busy doing something other than distributing drugs. Plus, my exit from the game was in sight. After finishing all the projects, I'd be worth another $10 million to $15 million, and it would be legitimate money. I wanted to leave the drug business on my own terms.

Now, however, JJ and the other guys had put my plans in serious jeopardy. Just to finish these projects alone, I needed a couple more million dollars in cash. Being in the drug business, I lacked a credit history that could have gotten me business loans. So every business venture I entered was a cash deal.

Later that night, we hooked up for a game of Ping Pong with Waterhead Bo, a new kid rockin' on the streets of L.A. I was ready to learn more about his dope game. I wanted to know how many keys he was getting, what was he paying, and how was he selling it so cheap when he was relatively new to the game. Back then, very few people selling drugs spent the kind of money he was throwing around.

I kicked back with Bo and played Ping Pong on a $2,500 bet. We talked during the game and I agreed to stop by his spot the next day to see about setting up a deal for some work. I'd come up with another plan that meant paying Bo a little more, but at the same time, it was meant to make my Nicaraguan connection sweat, wondering who my new contact was.

The next day, Bo put in a call to get me 50 birds at $17,000 a key.

"I don't have all the bread for you right now," I told him.

"With my people, it doesn't matter," he said. "We'll give it to you on credit."

Little did I know that I was sitting with the future of the dope game.

Bo ran his operation a lot different than mine. He had a two-man operation: just Bo and his driver.

When we pulled up to Bo's house, it was still daylight. Two Latin guys in a car got out, went to the trunk, and carried two boxes to us. Bo opened the door to the house and we all went in. I was nervous as shit because it was done out in the open during the day. Bo had a barred screen on his front door, but none of the heavy-duty stuff I used. I could have gotten in with a crowbar in about five seconds. They sat the boxes on the floor and started counting birds. While they counted, I got on the phone to my crew. I wanted those birds out of the house as fast as possible. They were selling powder out in the open like it was legal. I didn't have my gun with me that day, so I asked Bo if he had one. He pulled out a .357 Magnum.

After he had made the count, Paul and the guys came and picked up the dope. Then we met Ollie to pick up as much money as we could gather. I wanted to get these guys their money and send them on their way.

Finally, I got a call from my cousin Joan, JJ's sister. She'd been down to the county jail to see him and said that he was doing a lot better and not acting as crazy as before. Still, he'd been there two weeks already and it was bothering me. I never liked leaving my people in jail. If there was any way to get them out, I did it. But things were hot with JJ and he needed to chill.

I finally broke down and made a call to Jocelyn to post his bond, which was hella high at $150,000. Almost immediately, just like that, JJ was back on the streets.

Then, Bo and I hooked up again. I respected him, and vice versa. He asked if I wanted to take over his connection. It caught me off guard. My money was building up at a rapid pace and I had set a goal to get out of the game and not take on new business. We'd moved our operation to West Los Angeles, Brentwood, Westwood, UCLA, and Sherman Oaks, trying to remove ourselves from the heat. I told Bo I'd think about it.

We worked predominantly white areas with lots of college kids who had apartments off campus. Two of my young guys, 16 and 17, fit in perfectly carrying backpacks and riding bikes. The young homies rode up on the dealers in their cars, handed them the bag of coke through the car window, and received a bag full of money in return. Then they bicycled the money to one of our apartments. It was easy sailing.

The apartments ran us up to $2,200 a month. We used one as a meeting spot for Danilo and his new sidekick Jose. Sometimes Danilo and Jose spent the night, snorted cocaine and got drunk. I didn't know if they ever had women up there, and I didn't care. I didn't socialize with Danilo. It was always about the business.

Ollie and I rolled to the apartment. He and Jose showed up minutes later.

"Where you been?" Danilo asked.

"I been around," I told him.

"You found a better price? From who? My big friends?"

"No, Danilo, you know that's not true."

He never believed me when I said, "No." But it was true; I hadn't found a better price. I was paying more. When he asked what price I wanted, I knew my plan to keep him guessing for a while had worked.

I didn't say anything. I just laughed. Danilo pulled me into the kitchen with his arm around my neck. "What is wrong with my friend?" he asked. "What is the problem? C'mon, man, talk to me." I still laughed and said everything was okay. I thought he was majorly hooked on the money. *Man, everybody got hooked on the game.* Before the meeting ended, Danilo agreed to give us keys for $10,000 a piece. Danilo mentioned to me once that a war was going on in his country; they'd lost their land, and were trying to get it back. That was all I knew about him. I thought he was just another drug supplier. I didn't learn until much later what his real connections were.

Ollie and I did our best to restrain ourselves so Danilo wouldn't notice how happy we were about the price. If somebody had told me a few months earlier that we'd be getting a key for as low as $10,000, I would've said they were lying. He told us he was moving to Miami and that he only wanted to be contacted in case of an emergency. Jose, his worker, would be taking over, he said.

We bought a hundred keys from Danilo and rolled out of the parking lot. Ollie and I high-fived each other. Our crew had thinned down because of all the arrests, and our clientele wasn't as large as it once was, but we knew it would catch up again—especially with high-quality Colombian product supplied via my Nicaraguan connections.

We were going strong and staying away from the 'hood because of the cops following us around. The police steadily turned up the heat anyway and they raided the Big Palace of Wheels. Witnesses said it was brutal, with tons of cops on the scene. We were on the other side of town from them; it seemed the cops didn't have a clue where we were. We didn't keep drugs or money at the Palace, so their raid turned up nothing.

After about two months of steady rolling, we hit a dry spot when Danilo couldn't supply us. We had a lot of cash from the last buy, so we kicked back for a few days and hit the basketball courts at Manchester Park, just like old times.

We had come a long ways. Man, it felt good to be up on it.

Outside the gym, from this small hill, you could see the skyline of downtown Los Angeles. As I looked out at the lights, I thought to myself, *How wonderful it is to live here in America. A man can start from the bottom and wind up on top.* In a few short months, I'd be able to walk away from the game. I'd always wanted to do what Ron O'Neal did in *Super Fly*: Get out of the game. That was my plan from the start.

During one of my trips to L.A., I bought another load of cocaine through Bo's connection, because it was cheaper in L.A., to hold us over in Cincinnati until I got more from Danilo. To transport the cocaine, I put a homie—a friend of a friend—on a bus in L.A., then I flew back to Cincinnati to meet him. We didn't know until afterward that a drug-sniffing dog at a New Mexico bus station during one of the stops along the route detected the cocaine. The courier walked away and wasn't arrested. I drove to the Cincinnati bus depot with Big Al, who walked into the depot and asked what time the bus from Los Angeles was supposed to arrive, and they arrested him just for showing up. Big Al did 20 years. DEA agents then linked the cocaine to me, based on witness statements, not on any physical evidence. Based on those statements, in 1989, I was indicted for drug trafficking.

I took a plea deal to trafficking cocaine and got a mandatory 10-year prison sentence, which I served in a jail in Boone County, Kentucky, across the Ohio River from Cincinnati, where federal prisoners were held along with state inmates.

Then, in November 1993 while still in custody in Cincinnati, a warrant for my arrest was issued from Smith County, Texas, because of an interception of a telephone call four years earlier, in 1988, where police said I'd agreed to supply my cousin in Tyler, Texas, with two keys of cocaine. Thus, they connected the case to me. I pleaded no contest to conspiracy to possess cocaine, and served a short sentence to run concurrently with my federal time in Ohio.

In the meantime, while incarcerated in Ohio, the federal corruption case my attorney and I had launched by hiring a private eye named Frenchy to infiltrate the narc units of the L.A. County Sheriff's Department finally lit up.

The FBI's anti-corruption case, Operation Big Spender, investigated the Freeway Rick Task Force's actions and led to more than two dozen L.A. cops, who'd been suspended from duty and were now facing a 34-count federal indictment in a case that became part of the worst corruption scandal in local law-enforcement history. At the same time, it put me in the unexpected position of being able to bargain. Federal prosecutors in Los Angeles wanted my help.

They needed more witnesses against the detectives who'd once been members of the task force, so they offered me a deal: Help them convict the elite narcotics squad—including the cops who shot at me and the one who planted drugs in my car. In turn, they'd get my prison time in Ohio reduced. They wanted me to talk about searches the task force had made on crack houses, how much money they'd seized, and who they'd beaten in the course of their operations.

I agreed to help. In fact, I could hardly wait to testify. I never would have turned on my guys in court. But these weren't my homies; they were bad cops. To think, a few years earlier, even Alan Fenster, my defense attorney, didn't believe that law-enforcement officers sworn to uphold the law had planted drugs on my homies and me. Now, I was a witness for the prosecution that would help roughly 100 black men in prison who had been framed and falsely accused by the same rogue cops.

The feds flew me out to Los Angeles to testify. It was a good day in L.A. Superior Court. I'd taken the stand to testify against the officers who for years had stalked me and victimized my workers. The *Los Angeles Times* called me a "key witness."

I told the truth when I testified against once-respected and seasoned narcotics detectives. I felt vindicated. I was guilty of selling drugs, sure, but I wasn't guilty of possessing the cocaine that the cops planted in my car that night. In exchange for my testimony, the court reduced my 10-year sentence to 51 months, to be followed by three years of supervised release. The government also agreed to not seize my remaining drug profits.

When I got out of prison in Cincinnati, corrections officers from Texas weren't there to pick me up and take me to Texas, so I could serve out that sentence. And Ohio could no longer hold me, because my time was up there. So, for the next several weeks, I stayed in Ohio, waiting for Texas authorities to come and get me. I didn't dare leave the state, so I let officials in Texas know where I was, and when they were ready, they extradited me to Texas to begin serving nine months in the Smith County jail.

After I was paroled from Texas in September 1994, I returned to South Central. I still had the Big Palace of Wheels plus some money in the bank. Cincinnati was the last place I sold drugs. I called the prison time my cooling-off period, my chance to back out of the game.

I didn't return to selling cocaine. I continued to run the Big Palace of Wheels, plus I had cash on hand. I was turning my life around.

I didn't know where Danilo Blandón was, and I didn't care. I was out of the game.

CHAPTER 20
REVERSE STING OPERATION

Just out of prison for a few months, I kept busy with my properties and a theater renovation. I made good money off of the motels and invested it in even more properties. I was also in the process of buying the old Adams Street Theatre and turning it into a youth center. I'd been hitting up community leaders for financial backing. And I was breaking into the record-producing business, trying to sign rappers.

I was forming my own rap label, I'd discovered the Alkoholiks, we were in negotiations, and I was about to sign them. Dick Griffey and Otis Smith, heavy hitters in the music industry at the time, had years earlier talked me into funding R&B singer Anita Baker. They told me, "This rap stuff is a fad. If you give us six hundred grand, we'll cut her first album." So, I shot them a duffle bag with $600,000 in it and it funded Anita's debut album, *The Songstress*. Little did I know at the time how bad an investment it turned out to be; I never saw a dime. Griffey, grateful that I'd backed Anita, was about to help me sign artists. I had successfully pulled out of the game and was ready to go legit.

Then, a call came in that I didn't want and I didn't expect: Danilo Blandón reached out to me about supplying me again with cocaine. He'd been my main supplier for years, but I later found out he'd been arrested and charged with conspiracy to possess cocaine with the intent to distribute, so I'd lost him for at least two years as my source. I thought Danilo was in prison, given the high-level of drug-dealing charges against him after his arrest in May 1992 with his wife, Chepita, and five others for buying and reselling wholesale quantities of cocaine. The indictment, charging him with conspiring to distribute, said he'd been trafficking for 10 years and had provided between two to four metric tons of cocaine to Los Angeles-area drug dealers. In reality, it was probably several times that amount. He was so high on the food chain that the judge ordered him and his wife be held without bail because, he said, they posed "a threat to the health and moral fiber of the community."

I later learned that Blandón's attorney, Brad Brunon, claimed in open court that the charges against his client were "politically motivated because of Mr. Blandón's activities with the Contras in the 1980s." It was a startling admission, made by his own attorney: Danilo, a known drug lord, was personally involved with the CIA-run Contras.

Even more startling, I also later learned, was when the prosecutor, Assistant U.S. Attorney L.J. O'Neale, filed a letter telling the court that the defendant was needed to continue his work as a full-time paid informant for the government.

The charges against Danilo's wife were subsequently dropped. Those arrested with Danilo pleaded out and received light sentences. Danilo himself pleaded guilty to the lesser crime of conspiracy and was sentenced to 48 months, which was reduced to just 28 months.

Once in Los Angeles again, Danilo, back in the game after the prison stint, pursued me to buy from him again. He sweated me for six months. At that point, I still believed that it was the money that motivated Danilo. Boy, was I wrong.

Walking out of Griffey's office on Wilshire after discussing signing artists, it felt good negotiating a legitimate business deal.

Then I took the call from Danilo. He wanted me to meet him at a downtown L.A. restaurant. I arranged to meet him just as I would any of my guys. I was out of the game and had no plans to get back in.

But as soon as I arrived, Danilo got down to business. "The Colombians are on my back," he said. "I owe them money for a shipment. I need to sell a hundred keys." Then, he added, "Why go around begging all these people for money for your theater when you can make it all at once?"

He had a point. If I found a buyer for the shipment, Danilo said he'd give me a $300,000 finder's fee. I wouldn't be the buyer, just the go-between.

Still, even though the quick cash was tempting, I didn't want to even arrange the buy. I'd seen what I could do legitimately on the streets. I was relieved of all the pressure of being in an illegal business. Danilo had given me good prices over the years and he was now in trouble; it was the least I could do. So, I broke down as a favor to Danilo and agreed to introduce him to a friend. It was a one-time thing and I'd still be out of the game.

I found a buyer, my homie Chico Brown, who, while I was in prison, had built up his own game. I knew he'd want coke from Danilo. I also hoped that if I gave him Chico as a contact, Danilo would let up and not press me into buying from him again.

So, on March 2, 1995, the deal went down in a shopping-center parking lot in Chula Vista, a suburb of San Diego. In two cars, my crew and I pulled into a Denny's parking lot. Danilo walked over to one of the cars and asked Chico, "Where's the money?"

"Where's the stuff?" Chico responded.

"It's around the corner," Danilo said, indicating the parking lot in front of a Montgomery Ward store. Danilo seemed jumpy and the deal was getting complicated. It was supposed to be a simple car switch.

"Is this guy gonna steal my money?" Chico asked me, leaning out of his car.

"Nah, nah, he's cool. It'll be fine." I told him.

We gave him the money. Mike McLoren and I were in one car and Chico and his homie Curtis were in another. We pulled into the Montgomery Ward parking lot. We met Danilo and he gave Chico the keys to the switch car.

Mike and I got out of his truck, opened the back of the switch car, and grabbed the bag of drugs. Later, Curtis told me that was when he saw heads of men popping up inside parked cars.

The second the transaction was complete, the DEA and local authorities swarmed all over us.

Without thinking, I jumped back in Mike's truck and took off.

A car pulled out in front of me, forcing me to swerve to avoid it. I thought, *What's that crazy motha doing?* It turned out to be an unmarked police car, but I didn't recognize it. Then I saw two marked police cars blocking the street.

Two helicopters were overhead, following me. As I peeled away, I saw Danilo standing with a DEA agent, both of them laughing as if to say, "They're going to get you."

I'd been set up.

I knew I couldn't get away in the truck. I drove into a hedgerow, jumped out of the driver's door, and took off like lightning on foot.

I ran for my life.

I ran and ran until I ran out of breath.

An army of men in suits and uniforms surrounded me in a back yard. But I couldn't feel any pain, even when a cop put his foot on the back of my neck. I had run so hard, I had nothing left. It was like

I was back at the chop shop running from the cops in what felt like a lifetime earlier.

Once in jail, people told me, "Forget about it, Ricky. You're going to get life. It's over."

———————◆◆◆———————

While awaiting trial, Alan Fenster, my attorney, telephoned me. "There's a reporter in San Jose who's investigating your drug source. He says your source was a major player."

I said, "Well, hell, I already know he's a major player. How else could he be selling me a hundred kilos at a time?" It was only when the reporter, Gary Webb with the *San Jose Mercury News*, interviewed me in prison, and Gary dropped the bombshell, that I learned just how big of a player Danilo was.

After his visit and many telephone conversations, Gary asked me, "What would you say if I told you he was working for the CIA and Contras, selling cocaine to help them buy weapons and supplies?"

I was shocked. First of all, I'd never even heard of the Contras, who I soon learned were a coalition of rebels who helped overthrow the Somoza dictatorship in Nicaragua, then felt betrayed and subsequently opposed the ruling Sandinistas. But more importantly, Danilo had been selling all this coke and *I* was the one sitting in jail. I was shocked. I told Gary, "I'd say that's some fucked-up shit. They say I sold dope all over, but, man, I know he sold ten times more than me." Then I asked Gary, "Man, are you being straight with me?" I couldn't believe what I was hearing.

"I have the documents to prove it," Gary answered.

I shook my head in disbelief. "He's been working for the government the whole damn time."

Even then, it took me a while to digest that Danilo Blandón, who I considered a friend and almost a godfather to me, had been working for the CIA in an attempt to take me down.

Later, in his book, *Dark Alliance*, in which Gary Webb broke news about the scandal, Gary wrote, "I spent hours with Ross at the Metropolitan Correctional Center. He knew nothing of Blandón's past, I discovered. He had no idea who the Contras were or on whose side they were.

"To Rick," Gary continued, "Danilo was just a nice guy with a lot of cheap dope."

In a nutshell, CIA undercover operatives like Danilo, acting on behalf of the U.S. government, were selling tons of cocaine, then laundering the profits to help fund the Nicaraguan Contras (money from the proceeds of secret arms sales to Iran were also funneled to the Nicaraguans, which became a huge political affair known as the Iran-Contra scandal, or Irangate, that nearly toppled the Ronald Reagan administration, because Reagan had been a supporter of the Contra cause). Gary provided his documentation to my attorney to help my case in court. Gary knew far more than Alan about the CIA's involvement and about Danilo and his drug partner, Norwin Meneses, who operated out of San Francisco, while Blandón operated from L.A. I'd heard the name Meneses over the years when Danilo mentioned him in passing.

Throughout my trial, which began in 1996, Gary sat in the front row of the courtroom, behind the defense table. Alan Fenster, as my defense attorney, relied heavily on Gary. At times, Alan asked him for suggestions about what questions he should ask of the witnesses. The prosecution put some serious heat on Gary for being there; they wanted him anywhere but in that courtroom. Gary didn't care; he showed up every day. He was in the middle of writing his book *Dark Alliance* and some of the material for his book came from my trial.

In addition to the admission of the Contra connection during Danilo's court hearings, the CIA admitted in court during my trial that they knew the Nicaraguans were selling drugs in the United States. We thought the information we'd gathered, that the CIA had set up and trapped me for their own illicit purposes, was enough to acquit me and free me from prison.

Wrong again.

Despite Gary's help, an all-white jury found me guilty and convicted me of conspiracy to distribute illegal drugs. We realized then that I had probably been lured to San Diego County for the reverse sting operation, because a drug arrest in L.A. would have meant a downtown Los Angeles jury, in which case a few of the jurors were more likely than not to be black.

Now here I was, on November 19, 1996, about 20 months after the government sting operation that sent me to jail, sitting in U.S. District Court in the heavily guarded, crowded courtroom, at the defense table next to Alan Fenster. When he rose to speak, Alan argued persuasively that Danilo Blandón had been working for the CIA in an illegal enterprise, as their operative and my source for cocaine, and that I was "a victim of the most outrageous government misconduct known to man."

Judge Marilyn Huff responded that my conduct was "not excused by any tenuous ties to the CIA." She not only denied the defense motion that my conviction be set aside, she went on to sentence me to life in prison without the possibility of parole. With that, she handed down a sentence that the prosecutor called my "third felony strike."

I knew that the three strikes the prosecutor referred to were wrong and didn't apply to my case. In fact, I'd been sentenced twice for the same crime and I passed that on to Fenster. At that point, because the sentence had already been rendered, for me to challenge the sentence, it had to be appealed.

I stood up, my hands and feet shackled and wearing a khaki prison jumpsuit, as Judge Huff ordered me to do my time in the Lompoc Federal Penitentiary. Even though I wasn't a violent offender, she remanded me to the maximum-security facility in central California that was originally a World War II disciplinary barracks. Back then, the criminal-justice system considered all drug dealers to be violent offenders, even if they'd never been charged with a violent crime.

I was led away from the courthouse on Broadway by U.S. marshals, and transported by van from the basement parking lot to the San Diego Metropolitan Correctional Center around the corner and two blocks away. At that time, I had no way of knowing how long I'd remain at MCC. I was considered a three-striker with no chance of parole, serving hard time.

On the ninth floor, where I was housed, were mostly gang members with the Mexican Mafia were on that floor. Those guys didn't typically get along with brothers, but they showed me nothing but love.

Inmates typically run out of commissary money each month, so they have to go without cigarettes and snacks, until their accounts are refreshed. Because I had plenty of money and connections, I ran my own commissary. I wasn't the only inmate running an illegal commissary in the prison compound; probably 50 or 60 prisoners at MCC ran unofficial stores for inmates while I was there. The difference was, the Mexican Mafia honchos allowed their homies to buy from me.

My hustle never stopped; it changed from crack cocaine to smokes and candy.

I stayed on the ninth floor of MCC for six years before I was transferred to the Lompoc federal pen, which was nicknamed The New Rock, because a boulder from Alcatraz now sits outside the prison.

At Lompoc, I wore a red wristband, which meant I had to be watched 24 hours a day and, while on work duty, had to check in every hour with a guard. I was assigned to a janitorial crew in the hallway within view of the lieutenant and captain's offices. Thirty of us wearing red wristbands were assigned to that hallway, where we cleaned a strip 50 feet long by four feet wide.

The only time I got in trouble in the pen was for what prison officials called "doing business." It was when I was on the phone, which was monitored by guards. Even though I just talked about cutting records and shooting videos with rappers, any kind of outside business conversations were against the rules. As punishment, I was sent to solitary confinement, also known as the hole, a few times for anywhere from two weeks to 45 days. In the hole, I read and did a lot of push-ups. I also caught up on years of sleep deprivation. Prisoners in solitary learn how to sleep a lot.

Back in my cell at MCC after court, I vowed to right the wrong and get my sentence straight. Here I was, behind bars and illiterate. To fight the sentence, I had to know how to read, so I could research my own case in the prison law library. As I've said, the teachers in elementary school, junior high, senior high, and junior college never taught me to read; some of them didn't even know I was unable to.

Ironically, a cellmate helped teach me. He got me to understand that when you read, you have to sound out words, and he made cue cards to drill me. I read and re-read words and sentences, over and over, until I started to recognize the common words and could sound out the words I hadn't seen before.

The first books I read cover to cover were *The Malcolm X Autobiography* and Anthony Robbins' *Awake the Giant Within*. Then I read Napoleon Hill's *Think and Grow Rich* and *The Richest Man in Babylon* by George Clayson, in my opinion two of the best self-help books ever published.

My entire horizon changed. I started looking at the world differently. Reading those books saved my life.

Then came my appeal on the double jeopardy, being sentenced twice for the same crime. Inmates helped me with my case. I was respected in prison because of where I came from. Besides the Mexican Mafia, the Hoover Crips were one of the biggest prison gangs at MCC when I was there. They protected me, and not because I asked them to. They'd say things like, "You think we'd let anything happen to you? You the big homie."

My court-appointed public defender was successful in getting my time reduced. A panel of three appellate-court judges in September 1998 overturned the life sentence, saying that Judge Huff erred when she counted my previous convictions in Ohio and Texas as separate crimes rather than as a single conspiracy. The panel of judges overturned Huff's sentence.

I was re-sentenced and given 20 years, with about half left to serve. Even though that was still a long time, knowing I was no longer in for life gave me something to look forward to.

I was paroled in March 2009 and went straight to a halfway house in the Lincoln Heights community of San Diego, where I lived with about 200 other federal and state inmates. Two months before my post-prison time was up, I was transferred to an El Monte, California, halfway house. In September 2009, I was released from custody and returned to Los Angeles under the supervision of the parole office. My parole was for seven years; it ends in late 2016.

———◆—◆—◆———

On a side note, newspaper reporter Gary Webb made history with his August 1996 series titled "Dark Alliance," in which the *San Jose Mercury News* reported that crack cocaine was being peddled into L.A.'s black ghettos to fund the CIA-backed war carried out by Contra rebels in Nicaragua and that my chief supplier, Nicaraguan exile Oscar Danilo Blandón Reyes, was a major backer of the Contras. Danilo's drug profits, earned from selling to me—his top buyer—as well as to others, were used to arm the rebels.

Gary explained that his research led him to an anti-communist guerrilla army, formed by the U.S. Central Intelligence Agency, that was called the Fuerza Democratica Nicaraguense, or FDN, which eventually became known as the Contras. Paying for the guerrilla army's weapons was money from cocaine trafficked to wholesalers like me, to the streets. I also learned that the money I gave Danilo for the tons of cocaine he provided to me for several years funded arms for the Contras, which was overseen by the CIA.

It was news to me.

After the stories appeared in the *Mercury News*, editors at the *Los Angeles Times* were rumored to have been appalled that a distant San Jose daily paper had beat them to a story about America's most powerful spy agency and its role in allowing drug dealers to flood South Central L.A. with crack cocaine. In response, *Times* editors assigned a platoon of reporters—17 in all—to find fault with Gary's reporting. The newspaper's articles in response to the "Dark Alliance" newspaper series were loaded with anonymous CIA sources denying, of course, that the CIA was connected to Contra-backing cocaine dealers in the ghettos.

One of those reporters on the story was Jesse Katz, who came after me. I'd met Jesse a couple years earlier when he wrote feature stories about me. This was different. The *L.A. Times* flew Katz in from Houston, where he worked as a correspondent for the paper, and assigned him to cover the Gary Webb story. Katz, in an article in the *Times*, wrote, "If there was an eye to the storm, if there was a criminal mastermind behind crack's decade-long reign, if there was one outlaw capitalist most responsible for flooding Los Angeles' streets with mass-marketed cocaine, his name was Freeway Rick."

There was more. "He didn't make the drug and he didn't smuggle it across the border," Katz wrote, "but Ricky Donnell Ross did more than anyone else to democratize it, boosting volume, slashing prices and spreading disease on a scale never before conceived. He was a favorite son of the Colombian cartels, South-Central's first millionaire crack lord, an illiterate high school dropout whose single-minded obsession was to become the biggest dope dealer in history."

Katz came to San Diego where I was housed at the downtown federal prison to interview me. In an article Katz later wrote for the *Texas Monthly*, he claimed that Danilo "Blandón's tenuous ties to the Contras already were severed by the time he met Rick," and that "Rick already was a big player by the time he met Blandón." Furthermore, Jesse Katz surmised, "no evidence could be found to link either Rick or Blandón to the CIA . . . ."

Boy, was Jesse off track. It appeared to me he was pressured to peddle the story to fit what others wanted to be told in a campaign to discredit Gary's "Dark Alliance" articles.

The three-day series that appeared in the *Times* didn't hurt my reputation, but it did irreparably injure Gary Webb's. The paper attacked his reporting about the Contra affair. In the beginning, the *Mercury News* backed Gary. But then, in the midst of the media frenzy, the paper backed down. Gary's career as a journalist was ruined.

After I read the stories Jesse Katz wrote about Gary, I was angry and called Jesse from prison and told him what I thought of it. In the end, Gary Webb was vindicated by a 1998 CIA Inspector General report, which revealed that for more than a decade, the CIA had covered up a business relationship it had with Nicaraguan drug dealers, namely Danilo Blandón and others. For Gary, it was too little, too late. His marriage had ended and his career as a national reporter had been destroyed.

The *Los Angeles Times* didn't acknowledge the Inspector General report's release for months, and the *Times* actually continued running negative pieces about Webb and his stories, discrediting him even after his death in 2004, when Webb died from two shotgun blasts to his head. His death in a suburb of Sacramento in December 2004 was ruled a suicide.

Jesse Katz did later publicly admit, "It was a really kind of tawdry exercise . . . . And it ruined that reporter's career."

I take my hat off to Gary for what he did. All of the media ganged up on him. I don't know how many people would put their lives on the line for the truth like he did.

As for Danilo Blandón, at one point, he was facing up to four life sentences. Instead, he took a deal: Help nab Freeway Rick and do less time.

After Danilo testified for the prosecution during my San Diego trial, he was granted a green card that gave him the right to stay in the country. He'd been in the United States illegally, a convicted felon for drug trafficking, which meant an automatic deportation with no waivers—at least for everyone else. When it came to Blandón, the government granted him a coveted green card. My understanding is that only two people can make that happen: the Attorney General or the President of the United States. Danilo, now with permanent residence status, was out of prison after 28 months.

━━━━◆◆◆━━━━

Meanwhile, I started serving out a life sentence, which was later overturned on a technicality.

My attorney, Alan Fenster, described the case against me as a "trial by ambush." The feds put cocaine in my hands, figuratively and literally. They financed it. I didn't go to Nicaragua to get cocaine; planes brought it to me. Their guy, Oscar Danilo Blandón, set up the market. They picked me to sell it.

Do I feel remorse for the role I played in the cocaine game? I do. I can't change my role.

At the time, I saw no alternative work prospects in South Central for an illiterate high-school and junior-college dropout with a broken-down car and a mother who worked two jobs just to put food on the table. Hemmed in by my circumstances, including losing a prospective sports scholarship the second the coach learned I couldn't read and write, I felt trapped. So, I did what I thought I had to do to get by.

I ended up a teenager in an illegal business running around South Central with duffel bags of cash. Though it was not the best career choice, I looked at drug dealing as a full-time job, just as I would have had it been a legitimate enterprise.

Needless to say, I no longer am in the drug business. I'm an entrepreneur, representing performers in the music and sports industries, and a speaker who talks to kids across the country. I visit schools in the ghetto, where I let students and young people know that they have alternatives to a life of crime. I talk to them about staying straight and working hard to become successful in life.

I will forever be reminded of that winter day in 1996 standing before a judge at the defense table, next to my lawyer, in a packed federal courtroom with my distraught mother, brother, cousins, and homies looking on, surrounded by the media as well as federal agents and police who were there to witness my downfall. At 36 years old, I was sent to prison for life, which meant I would literally die behind bars. I felt helpless to change what had just happened.

I relay that feeling of hopelessness to kids in the 'hood. Today, I teach economics to kids in a continuation high school in the Watts community of Los Angeles, as well as speak at other schools across the country. I am a reformed drug kingpin who paid my debt to society. I will continue giving back to my community. I also go out and help feed the homeless in downtown Los Angeles.

Across the country, I share with high school and college kids the story of my life as Freeway Rick Ross, that books and knowledge reformed me, changed my life for the better, and helped me challenge the harsh sentence I received for a non-violent crime. Books can change their lives as well, regardless of the adversities they face; knowledge is power.

I cannot change the negative impact that crack cocaine had on my community, the people in it, and the role I played. When I started dealing, I didn't sell drugs because I wanted to cause devastation in my community; I sold cocaine because I was running away from poverty.

Today, I lead by example. I haven't sold drugs in more than 20 years. I tell kids in inner cities that they need to make informed choices, stay in school, stay clean, and stay positive. They cannot do that by gangbanging or dealing. That is my message and my legacy.

ADDENDUM

Business Principles To Live By

These are business concepts I've learned from the books I've read and from first-hand experience. Follow these keys to success, and you can't help but improve your business.

- Make work your best friend.
- Choose wisely the people you get your information from.
- Be sure and set aside twenty percent of everything you earn, so that it's yours to keep.
- Instead of buying unnecessary things (watches and cars, for example), put that money back into your business.
- Let your money work for you; don't work for your money (then you'll find that your money works harder than you do).
- Guard your money.
- Try to buy your residence instead of renting, to help you reach your money goals.

ACKNOWLEDGMENTS

This book has been 15 years in the making, and I have many to thank. My deepest appreciation to co-author Cathy Scott, who worked beside me on the manuscript, tied this book together, and made my words better.

For the undying support of my family and friends who understand where I've been and where I am today, I am grateful. I am especially thankful to my sons and daughters, Carrie, Bricen, Jordan, Jamal, Rikiya, Ricky, Ricardo, and my late infant son Landon. I thank my wife, Mychosia Nightingale, who helped me put my life back together. You are my rock.

To my brother David, I love you, man. You've been the best big brother a guy could have. Thanks also to the support of my sister Angie Richardson and my cousins, who are like brothers and sisters to me: The Mauldins (Ken, George Jr., and Tonya); and the Wilsons (Ted, Bennett, Rene, Evita, and Yvette).

To my uncles, aunts, and cousins in Texas and California: Jimmy, Johnny, and their sisters, Jimmy D, Wanda, Joyce Ann, and Joanne, Uncle James, and Uncle NT who taught me my work ethic; Aunt Luretha and Uncle Johnny Wilson for taking my mom and me in when we first moved to Cali; Uncle Joe, Auntie Debbie, Auntie Joyce, Uncle Cove, Uncle Beck, and Uncle Jessie Lee; thank you to my baby mamas, Myeisha Struggs and Sharon Shaw; I am grateful for my late Uncle George Mauldin, who was a father to me when I needed one the most; and to my late Aunt Bobbi Jo, who treated me as her own.

To my Freeway Studios team, Antonio Moore and Neil Harrington, who gave their continual and ready encouragement and advice to this book and continue to do so with our other projects, I appreciate you both more than you know.

Thanks as well to my homies Ollie Newell, Cornell Ward, Chico Brown, Mary Monroe, Karen Monroe, Saree Payne, Josh Clemens, Mama Tillman, Norman Tillman, Mama Youngblood and the entire Youngblood family, Robert Robertson, Larry Burnett, Larry Smith, Bruce Graham, Jack Brown, Wendy Day, and Ivan.

And to all my homies no longer here, including Chubbs, Cruz Dog, Leon, Mike McLoren, and Stephan Moore, I miss you guys.

For their support, I thank Floyd Mayweather, Nick Cannon, Cat Williams, Maurice Stoudmire, and Darin Davis; thank you to tennis Coach Richard Williams for taking the time to give a young tennis player some pointers; I am also indebted to Congresswoman Maxine Waters for launching a Congressional probe into the role U.S. government agencies played in the crack cocaine explosion of the 1980s; to my MDC cellmate "Harry-O" Harris for his friendship and advice; and my gratitude to Bishop Noel Jones for his spiritual guidance and all that he's done for the community.

A special acknowledgment as well to Mike Assefa, Eddie Booze, Patrick Brennan, Marc Cardwell, Charlene Castrejon, Eric Van Cleaf, Jose Flores, Walter Jaminson, Rob McVeigh, Jose Chava Morales, Joseph Raffone, Robert Salazar, Albert and Rebecca Sandoval, The Simmons family, John Solarczyk, Patrick Thomas, TFC, Jan Yoss, John Younesi, and Michael Zuniga.

My gratitude to defense attorneys Alan Fenster and Harlan Braun, and probation officer Jim Galipeau.

The authors thank Deke Castleman for his expert care and dedication to detail in editing the manuscript on deadline; and thanks to the journalists and writers at the *Los Angeles* magazine, *Hollywood Reporter*, *Huffington Post*, and *Esquire* magazine for sorting through the politics and understanding the story. Transcribed by Nancy Padron: Thank you for your assistance.

I am forever indebted to two men no longer with us: To journalist and author Gary Webb, who had the courage to tell the truth when he broke the CIA-backed Contra scandal wide open in one of the worst official abuses in our nation's history; and to former LAPD narcotics investigator Michael Ruppert for standing up for justice and the truth. May they rest in peace.

—Rick Ross

ABOUT THE AUTHORS

Rick Ross is a high-school dropout who was an All-City tennis star. The ultimate pawn in the international drug trade, Ross is recognized as a pioneer in the crack-cocaine game in Los Angeles, as well as in other parts of the U.S., where he earned millions as an unknowing participant in CIA and U.S. Drug Enforcement Agency operations. His connections to the Iran-Contra scandal were first revealed in a series of articles in the *San José Mercury News*. Convicted of conspiracy to traffic drugs and sentenced to a federal penitentiary, while in prison, he taught himself to read and write. Today, he teaches an economics class at a Watts high school and regularly speaks to teens across the nation about making better choices in life. His legacy is as an inspirational mentor to people in need. He is currently writing a second book, *The Freeway Boys*. He lives in Long Beach, California, with his wife and children.

Cathy Scott is a veteran crime writer, award-winning investigative journalist, and *Los Angeles Times* bestselling author who has written 10 books. Best known for penning *The Killing of Tupac Shakur* and *The Murder of Biggie Smalls*, her work has appeared in *The New York Times Magazine, New York Post,*

San Diego Union-Tribune, George magazine, *The Christian Science Monitor, Las Vegas Sun,* and Reuters. Scott taught journalism at the University of Nevada Las Vegas and has covered the mob extensively, including murdered Mafia daughter Susan Berman and racketeer "Fat Herbie" Blitzstein. Her latest books are *The Millionaire's Wife* and *Murder in Beverly Hills.* Her recent TV appearances include Investigation Discovery, VH1 and A&E. Scott, who blogs about forensics and evidence for *Psychology Today*, is based in Las Vegas and San Diego County.